Engineering drawing
and construction

Engineering drawing and construction

SECOND EDITION

L. C. MOTT
M.Ed., M.I.E.D.

Principal Lecturer
School of Electrical and Mechanical Engineering
Bordon, Hampshire

OXFORD UNIVERSITY PRESS

Oxford University Press, Walton Street, Oxford OX2 6DP

OXFORD   NEW YORK   TORONTO
DELHI   BOMBAY   CALCUTTA   MADRAS   KARACHI
PETALING JAYA   SINGAPORE   HONG KONG   TOKYO
NAIROBI   DAR ES SALAAM   CAPE TOWN
MELBOURNE   AUCKLAND

and associated companies in
BEIRUT   BERLIN   IBADAN   NICOSIA

Oxford is a trade mark of Oxford University Press

ISBN 0 19 859114 4

FIRST EDITION 1965
SECOND EDITION 1976
REPRINTED (WITH CORRECTIONS) 1978, 1980, 1984 and 1987

PRINTED IN HONG KONG

Preface

This book is the ISO metric edition of two previous volumes having the same title. Its production was prompted by the success of the Imperial editions and in response to the establishment of ISO metric standards in engineering generally, and in engineering drawing practice in particular. In deciding to combine most of the work contained in two books into one volume, the opportunity was taken to completely redraw all the diagrams, revising where necessary, and adding new material where this was deemed essential to a clearer understanding of the subject.

The book is aimed, principally, at the wide range of existing and projected mechanical engineering technicians' courses, but it is hoped that it will also appeal to the young draughtsman and the interested layman.

There are 28 chapters in all, the first 10 of which deal with plane geometry, including the projection of points, lines, and planes and loci. Chapters 11 to 18 deal with pictorial projections, first- and third-angle projection, freehand sketching, auxiliary projection, developments of surfaces, solid geometry, and the intersections of solids. The remainder of the book is devoted to what might be called the more practical aspects of engineering drawing, and includes chapters on dimensioning and tolerancing, cams, involute gears, jigs and fixtures, and gauges.

There are numerous exercises of examination standard and, although some amalgamation has been found necessary to economize on space, most chapters have their own exercises placed conveniently to act as test questions on what has been learnt and also as classwork and homework.

It is with gratitude that the following acknowledgements are made:

British Standards Institution, for permission to reproduce items from the following standards

BS 308:1972, Engineering drawing practice

BS 4190:1967, ISO metric Black Hexagon Bolts, Screws and Nuts;

BS 4500:1969, Selected ISO Fits: Hole Basis;

BS 4620:1970, Rivets for General Engineering Purposes. (Copies of the complete specifications can be obtained from British Standards Institution, Sales Department, 101 Pentonville Road, London N1 9ND).

City & Guilds of London Institute, 76 Portland Place, London, W1N 4AA, for permission to reproduce a selection of questions from past examination papers. These questions are labelled (C.G.L.I.).

Southern Regional Examinations Board, for permission to reproduce questions set in past examination papers on Technical Drawing for the Certificate of Secondary Education, covering both syllabuses S and N. These questions are labelled (CSE).

Associated Examining Board, for permission to reproduce questions set in past examination papers on Geometrical Drawing (Engineering), Papers 1 and 2, for the General Certificate of Education, Ordinary level. These questions are labelled (AEB).

University of Cambridge Local Examinations Syndicate, for permission to reproduce questions set in past examination papers on Geometrical and Mechanical Drawing for the General Certificate of Education, Papers 1 and 2. These questions are labelled (Camb).

Each of these examining bodies has permitted modifications to their set questions, where appropriate: for example, the alteration of dimensions from Imperial to SI units. Many of the CSE questions reproduced were required to be completed on the examination papers. In these instances dimensions have been applied to the reproduced diagrams and students will be required to redraw the objects before completing the questions. This is additional work not called for in the examinations themselves.

Thanks are also due to members of the staff of Oxford University Press for their assistance and encouragement.

L.C.M.

Contents

1. INTRODUCTION   1
   Drawing equipment—Drawing paper—Set squares—
   Pencils—Compasses—Protractor—Scales—British
   Standards—Lines—Lettering
2. PERPENDICULARS, BISECTORS, AND
   PARALLEL LINES   5
   Plane geometry—Perpendiculars—Bisectors—
   Parallel lines—Dividing a line—Exercises
3. CONSTRUCTION OF TRIANGLES   9
   Triangles—Scale of chords—Pythagoras'
   theorem—Exercises
4. CONSTRUCTION OF QUADRILATERALS   15
   Quadrilaterals—Constructions
5. CONSTRUCTION OF REGULAR POLYGONS   17
   Polygons—Constructions—Exercises 4 and 5
6. THE CIRCLE   21
   Elements of a circle—Tangents—Concentric and
   eccentric circles—Escribed circle
7. THE ELLIPSE   25
   Elements of an ellipse—Constructions—Exercises 6 and
   7
8. AREAS AND SIMILAR FIGURES   33
   Constructions—Similitude—Similar figures—
   Exercises
9. LOCI   39
   Involute—Cycloid—Archimedean spiral—Parabola
   —Hyperbola—Helix—Points on link mechanisms—
   Exercises
10. POINTS, LINES, AND PLANES   49
    Principal planes—Projections of a point—Auxiliary
    planes—Oblique and inclined planes—Traces—True
    length
11. OBLIQUE PROJECTION   55
    Cabinet projection—Cavalier projection
12. ISOMETRIC PROJECTION   57
    Isometric scale—Constructions—Approximations—
    Exercises
13. FIRST AND THIRD ANGLE PROJECTION   65
    The four quadrants—First angle projection—Third
    angle projection—Exercises
14. FREEHAND SKETCHING   75
    Principles—Construction lines—Exercises
15. AUXILIARY PROJECTION   81
    True view—True length—First auxiliary—Exercises
16. PROJECTIONS AND SECTIONS OF SOLIDS   93
    Rotation—Cutting planes—Sections of solids—
    Exercises

17. DEVELOPMENTS   101
    Development of flat and curved surfaces—True
    lengths—Exercises
18. INTERSECTIONS   119
    Lines of intersection—Methods of projection—
    Exercises
19. SECTIONING AND CONVENTIONS   127
    Objects of sectioning—Cross-hatching—Section
    planes—Conventions—Examples—Exercises
20. DIMENSIONING   145
    Conventions—Rules—Functional and non-functional
    dimensions—Auxiliary dimensions—Screw
    threads—Chain dimensioning—Datum dimen-
    sioning—Ordinates—Tapers—Tolerances—
    MMC—Geometrical tolerances—Positional
    tolerances—Limits and fits—Surface
    roughness—Machining marks
21. FASTENERS AND FASTENINGS   165
    Screw threads—Screws—Nuts—Locking devices—
    ISO metric bolts and nuts—Conventions—
    Studs—Construction of square threads—
    Rivets—Riveted joints—Welding—Welding
    symbols
22. ROTATING SHAFTS   177
    Keys and keyways—Couplings—Universal joints—
    Constant velocity drives—Plain bearings—Ball and
    roller bearings—Lubrication
23. CAMS   187
    Followers—Displacement diagrams—Follower
    motions—Constructions—Cylindrical cam—
    Machine-tool cam
24. INVOLUTE GEARS   195
    Definitions—Calculations—Constructions—
    Machining—Materials—The involute—Bevel gears
25. JIGS AND FIXTURES   201
    Location—Locators—Clamping—Clamps—Jigs—
    Drill Bushes—Indexing jig—Fixtures—Setting
    blocks
26. PRESS TOOLS   213
    Blanking—Punches—Follow-on sets—Bending
    sets—Forming punches—Coining set—Exercises 25
    and 26
27. GAUGES AND GAUGE TOLERANCES   221
    Plug gauges—Ring and gap gauges—Dimensions and
    tolerances—Exercises

28. ASSEMBLY DRAWINGS   229
General arrangement—Balloon referencing—Parts
list—Drawing sheets—Single-part drawings—
exercises

MISCELLANEOUS EXERCISES   239

INDEX   243

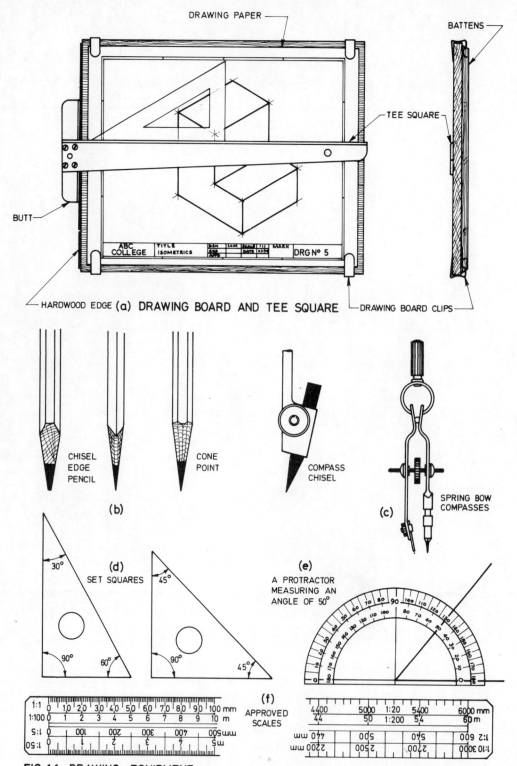

DRAWING PAPER

BATTENS

TEE SQUARE

BUTT

ABC COLLEGE   TITLE ISOMETRICS   DRG Nº 5

HARDWOOD EDGE (a) DRAWING BOARD AND TEE SQUARE   DRAWING BOARD CLIPS

CHISEL EDGE PENCIL   CONE POINT   COMPASS CHISEL

SPRING BOW COMPASSES

(b)   (c)

30°

(d) SET SQUARES   45°

(e) A PROTRACTOR MEASURING AN ANGLE OF 50°

90°   60°   90°   45°

(f) APPROVED SCALES

1:1   0 1.0 2.0 3.0 4.0 5.0 6.0 7.0 8.0 9.0 100 mm
1:100 0 1 2 3 4 5 6 7 8 9 10 m
1:5   0   100   200   300   400   500 mm
1:50

4400   5000   1:20   5400   6000 mm
44   50   1:200   54   60 m
440 mm   500   540   1:2 600
2200 mm   2500   2700   1:10 3000

FIG. 1.1 DRAWING EQUIPMENT

Drawing equipment

In most technical colleges the equipment provided for classwork consists of a drawing board and a matching tee-square (see **Fig. 1.1(a)**) or a drawing board fitted with a movable straight edge. The usual size of board is A2 (650 mm × 470 mm). The student is expected to purchase the remaining items, which will often be supplied by the college bookshop or a retail stationer. It is in the student's own interest to equip himself with a drawing board and tee-square similar to that provided by the college, so that homework and drawing practice may be carried out accurately and neatly. The following list of additional items should be considered as minimum requirements.

Drawing paper

Good-quality A2-size drawing paper (594 mm × 420 mm) should be used for classwork and homework, and may be attached to the drawing board by drawing-board clips or draughting tape. Table 1.1 shows the range of A size papers available.

Set squares

45° and 60° set squares will be required, but if the student feels that the extra expense is justified, an adjustable set square is strongly recommended. Set squares should be bevel-edged. (**Fig. 1.1(d)**).

Pencils

Good-quality pencils are essential and the grade should be chosen to suit the individual. H grades are hard, B grades are soft. As a guide, 2H is generally used for drawing and an H or HB for lettering and dimensioning. Straight lines may be drawn equally well with the pencil sharpened into a chisel point or cone point. However, the chisel point retains its edge longer, and is less likely to break when applied to the paper. The cone point should always be used for lettering (**Fig. 1.1(b)**).

Compasses

A pair of compasses to draw circles up to 250 mm diameter and a pair of spring bow compasses are essential. Compass leads should be of the same grade as the drawing pencil, and similarly sharpened to ensure uniformity of line (**Fig. 1.1(c)**). It does sometimes happen, however, that particular individuals find that they can produce improved work with a compass lead one grade softer than the drawing pencil.

Having placed a lead in the compasses, the correct position of the chisel edge relative to the compass point should be determined. When a shouldered point is used the edge of the lead should be level with the shoulder. When a conical point is used in the compasses, the lead should be positioned in such a way that the smallest possible hole is made in the paper before the chisel edge meets the drawing surface, the compasses being held in an upright position.

Protractor

When an adjustable set square is not available, a protractor is required to set out angles other than 30°, 45°, or 60°. This is usually a semicircular piece of transparent plastics material divided around its curved edge into 180 equal divisions. A typical example, divided only into 5° intervals, is shown measuring an angle of 50° in **Fig. 1.1(e)**.

Scales

Fig. 1.1(f) shows parts only of some standard scales on which the smallest unit of measurement is the millimetre. The scales should include full-size measurement, i.e. 1 : 1, and scale values of 1 : 2, 1 : 5, and 1 : 10. In addition, a good quality eraser and a small sandpaper block for sharpening pencil leads will be required.

British Standards

BS 308 is the standard work on drawing-office practice and the student should familiarize himself with its contents.

The Standard is published in three parts; *Part I: General principles of engineering drawing practice* being the most important from the student's point of view.

Table 1.1. ISO sizes of drawing paper

ISO code (A) sizes	Paper sizes (mm)	drawing board sizes (mm)
A0	841 × 1189	
A1	594 × 841	650 × 920
A2	420 × 594	470 × 650
A3	297 × 420	
A4	210 × 297	

ABCDEFGHIJKLMNOPQRSTUVWXYZ   1234567890 0.5

ABCDEFGHIJKLMNOPQRSTUVWXYZ 1234567890 0.5   ABCDEFGHIJKLMNOPQRSTUVWXYZ 123456

abcdefghijklmnopqrstuvwxyz   abcdefghijklmnopqrstuvwxyz   abcdefghijklmnopqrstuvwxyz

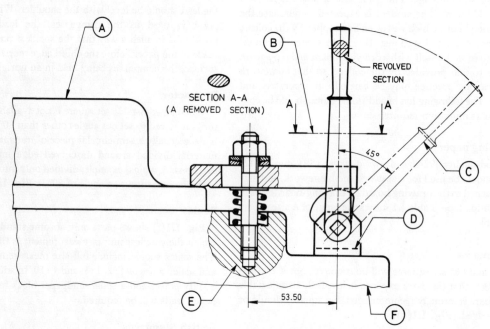

SECTION A-A
(A REMOVED SECTION)

REVOLVED
SECTION

45°

53.50

(A) Continuous thick line for visible outlines and edges

(B) Long chain thin line thick at the ends for cutting planes

(C) Thin chain line for centre lines and extreme position of movable parts

(D) Short dash medium line for hidden outlines and edges

(E) Continuous thin line for dimension and leader lines, hatching, outlines of adjacent parts and outlines of revolved sections

(F) Continuous irregular thin line for the limits of partial views or sections

FIG. 1.2   LINES AND LETTERING

1. Introduction

Lines

The thickness of all lines on a drawing should bear a relationship to the main finished outline and to the size and type of the drawing. In general it is recommended that thick lines should be from two to three times the thickness of thin lines. All views of an item on the same drawing, to the same scale, should have an outline of even thickness.

The importance of line thickness cannot be overstressed, because a variation in the thickness of lines of similar form will convey a different message to the trained eye.

For example, a long-chain thin line is used for centre lines and for path lines indicating movement of a part from one position to another. A long-chain thick line, however, is used to indicate surfaces which require additional treatment, such as plating.

The relationship between line thicknesses is shown in *BS 308* and **Fig. 1.2.** The only lines not mentioned in this publication are the very faint construction lines which are used as a 'scaffolding' into which the finished outline is fitted on completion of the drawing.

When commencing a drawing the main construction and outlines should be drawn very lightly so that, on completion, the darker outline can be drawn within these scaffold lines. There will be no need to erase the lighter lines because a boldly outlined drawing will tend to catch the eye and the scaffold lines will recede into the background.

Lettering

Well-formed, well-spaced lettering will enhance the appearance of a drawing. Most draughtsmen quickly attain speed at lettering, developing an individual style to suit that speed. For the student, it is recommended that all lettering should be either upright or sloping block capitals, although script letters are admissible. It is not possible to lay down rules governing the actual size of lettering to be used on a drawing; this must be 'sensed' by the student. Obviously, a tiny drawing with very large lettering would appear out of proportion. A balance must be struck to ensure that lettering suits the drawing size and is always clear and legible. An attempt has been made throughout this book to correlate drawing, lettering and dimension sizes, to act as examples.

The drawing in **Fig. 1.2** uses every type of line approved for engineering drawings. Each type is *balloon referenced* and an explanation of the use of the lines is given beneath the drawing.

Further points to note, which will be dealt with again later in this book, are the examples given of clear dimensioning, the treatment of sections, the portrayal of tapped holes and the recommended method of showing the travel, or movement, of the lever through a 45° arc, using line *C*.

A revolved section is a cross-sectional view of an object shown in place on the feature to which it refers. It is enclosed within a continuous thin line.

A removed section is a cross-sectional view of an object removed from it, with its position indicated by a long-chain thin line thick at the ends and with arrows indicating the direction of view. It is enclosed within a continuous thick line.

Leader lines are lines from notes or reference balloons which end in arrow heads (or in some cases large dots) pointing to particular features on a drawing.

3

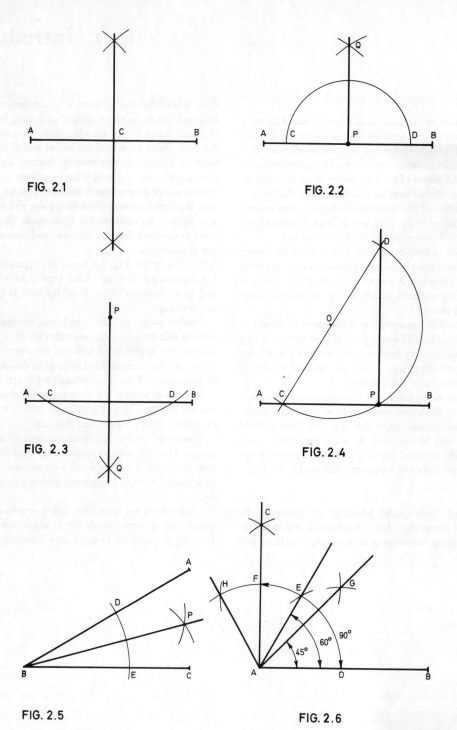

FIG. 2.1

FIG. 2.2

FIG. 2.3

FIG. 2.4

FIG. 2.5

FIG. 2.6

2. Perpendiculars, bisectors, and parallel lines

A *plane* is a flat surface. A *surface* has length and breadth but no thickness.

Plane geometry is the science of drawing figures on plane surfaces which, by definition, have no thickness. The figures will therefore be two-dimensional. An understanding of plane geometry is essential for the draughtsman. A close study of a complicated drawing will reveal that it is made up of a combination of relatively simple constructions, many of them exercises to be found in the following chapters. 'Marking out' a shape to be made from metal is another practical application of this science.

Fig. 2.1 To bisect a given straight line (i.e. divide into two equal parts)

Draw AB, the given straight line, any convenient length. With A and B as centres, and a radius greater than half AB, draw arcs to intersect above and below the line. A line drawn through these intersecting arcs will bisect AB at point C. It is also perpendicular to AB at this point.

Fig. 2.2 To erect a perpendicular from a given point in a given straight line

Draw AB, the given straight line, and mark the given point P. With centre P and any convenient radius, draw an arc to cut AB at C and D. With C and D as centres and any radius greater than CP, draw arcs to intersect above AB at Q. A line drawn through these intersections, terminating at P, is perpendicular to AB (i.e. angles QPC and QPD are right angles).

Fig. 2.3. To erect a perpendicular to a given straight line from a given point outside it

Draw AB, the given straight line, and mark P, the given point. With P as centre and any convenient radius, draw an arc to cut AB at C and D. With C and D as centres, any convenient radius, draw arcs below AB to intersect at Q. A line drawn through P and Q will be perpendicular to AB.

Fig. 2.4 To erect a perpendicular to a given line from a given point near the end of the line

Draw AB, the given straight line, and mark the given point P. Mark any point O outside the line. With centre O and radius OP, draw a wide arc to pass through P and cutting AB at C. Draw a line from C, passing through O to cut the arc at D. Join DP, the required perpendicular. By drawing AB at various angles and repeating this construction, it will be seen that *the angle contained in a semicircle is a right angle.*

Fig. 2.5 To bisect a given angle

Let ABC be the given acute angle, i.e. an angle less than a right angle. With B as centre and any convenient radius, draw an arch to cut the arms of the angle at D and E. With D and E as centres and any convenient radius, draw arcs to intersect at P. Join BP the required bisector.

Fig. 2.6 To bisect a constructed right angle and to construct an angle of 60°

Draw AB any convenient length. Using the method shown in Fig. 2.4, erect a perpendicular at A. CAB is the required right angle. With centre A and any convenient radius, draw an arc to cut AB at D and passing through AC at F. With the same radius and centre D, cut the arc at E. A line drawn through AE will make an angle of 60° with AB. Angle CAB may now be bisected at G, using points F and D as D and E in Fig. 2.5. By marking off radius AD from E along the arc, to produce point H, and by joining AH, an obtuse angle HAB of 120° will be formed.

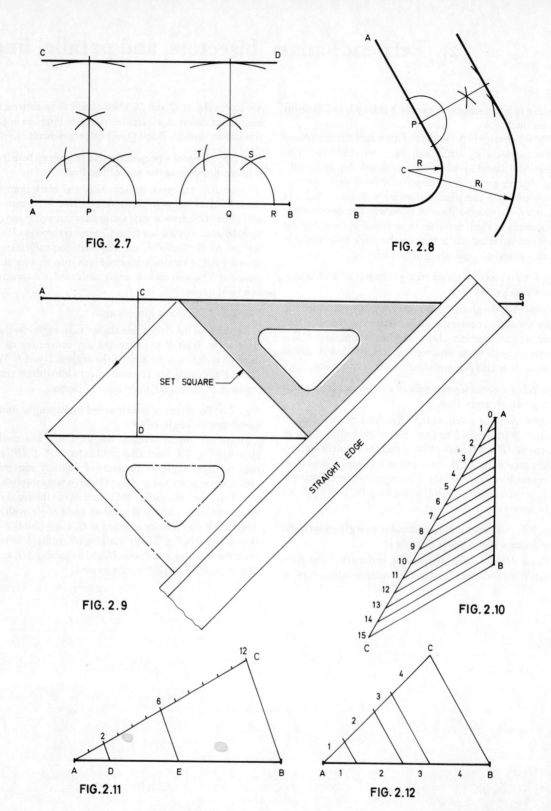

FIG. 2.7

FIG. 2.8

SET SQUARE

STRAIGHT EDGE

FIG. 2.9

FIG. 2.10

FIG. 2.11

FIG. 2.12

2. Perpendiculars, bisectors, and parallel lines

Fig. 2.7 To draw a straight line parallel to another straight line

Draw a straight line *AB* any convenient length and mark on it two points *P* and *Q*. Erect perpendiculars at these points. With *P* and *Q* as centres, radius equal to the distance required between the parallel lines, draw two arcs. A line *CD* drawn through the intersection of these arcs with the perpendiculars will be parallel to *AB*.

Fig. 2.8 To construct a radius and tangential arm parallel to a given line of similar form.

Let the given line be *AB* and the radius *R*. With R_1 as radius, centre *C*, draw an arc. From any point *P* on the tangential arm erect a perpendicular whose length is R_1 minus *R*. Construct a tangent to the end of this line which will be parallel to the given line. Join this tangent and its radius.

Fig. 2.9 To draw a straight line parallel to another straight line using a straight edge and set square

Draw a straight line *AB* any convenient length. With a set square pressed firmly against a ruler or another set square, align one edge of the set square with *AB*. Holding the straight edge firmly in place, move the set square until the required distance between the lines is achieved. Drawing along the free edge of the set square will produce the parallel line.

The required distance between the lines can be preset by erecting a perpendicular and marking off the distance. This is shown by the line *CD*.

Fig. 2.10 To divide a straight line into a number of equal divisions

Draw the straight line *AB* any convenient length. Draw *AC* any length at any convenient angle and on it mark the number of equal divisions required (in this case seven). Number them as shown. Join the last numbered point to the end of the line *AB*. Through each succeeding division draw a line parallel to the first by the method described in **Fig. 2.9**. The line *AB* will be divided into the required number of equal parts.

Fig. 2.11 To divide a line in the same proportion as the numbers 2, 4 and 6

Draw the line *AB* any convenient length. Draw *AC* at any suitable angle and divide it into 12 equal parts (2 + 4 + 6). Join *C* to *B* and draw lines through points 6 and 2 parallel to *CB*. *AB* is now divided in the same proportion as the numbers 2, 4, and 6; that is, *AD* : *DE* : *EB* : : *2* : *4* : *6*.

Fig. 2.12 To divide a line in the same proportion as another given line

Let *AC* be the given line in proportion and *AB* the line to be divided. *Draw AB* and, at any suitable angle, draw *AC*. Divide *AC* into the same proportional lengths as shown by the figures 1, 2, 3, and 4. Join *CB* and draw parallel lines through the other division on *AC*. *AB* is divided in the same proportion as *AC*.

Exercises for Chapter 2

1. Draw a straight line *AB* 80 mm long at an angle of 30° to the horizontal. Bisect the line at *C* and construct a perpendicular to it at point *C*.
2. Draw a straight horizontal line *AB* 80 mm long and erect a perpendicular at a point *C* 25 mm distant from *A*.
3. Draw a straight, horizontal line *AB* 80 mm long. Locate a point *P* anywhere below the line and 45 mm distance from it. Erect a perpendicular through *P*.
4. Construct three straight, parallel lines 90 mm long and 30 mm apart.
5. Draw a series of straight, parallel lines using only a straight edge and a set square, or two set squares.
6. Draw a straight line *AB* 87 mm long. Divide *AB* into seven equal parts.
7. Draw a straight line *AB* 80 mm long and divide it in the same proportion as the numbers 1, 3, and 7.
8. A line *AB* is 55 mm long and, starting from *A*, it is marked off into the following parts, all measured from *A* : 15 mm, 27 mm and 43 mm. Draw a line *CD* 90 mm long and divide it in the same proportion as *AB*.
9. Draw a straight, vertical line 63 mm long and divide it into four equal parts using compasses.
10. Draw a straight line 70 mm long, bisect it and erect another straight line perpendicular to it.
11. A line *AB* is 72 mm long and has a point *P* situated 17 mm from *A*. Erect a perpendicular at *P*.
12. Draw a horizontal line *AB* 57 mm long and position a point *P* approximately 30 mm below it. Erect a perpendicular to *AB* passing through the point *P*.
13. Draw two straight lines, 75 mm long, parallel to one another and 36 mm apart.
14. Using two set squares only, draw three straight lines parallel to one another and 15 mm apart.
15. Draw a straight line 83 mm long and divide it into nine equal parts.

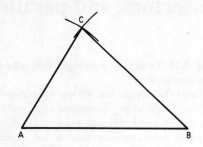

FIG. 3.1

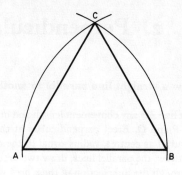

FIG. 3.2

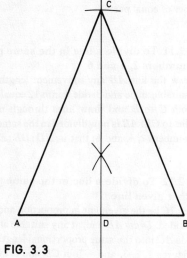

FIG. 3.3

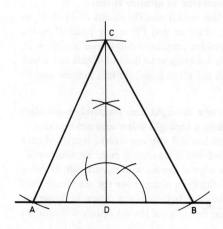

FIG. 3.4

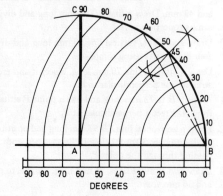

FIG. 3.5 SCALE OF CHORDS

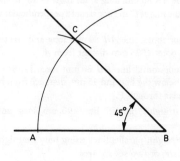

FIG. 3.6

8

3. Construction of triangles

A *triangle* is a plane figure bounded by three straight lines. The characteristics of triangles are denoted by the lengths of the sides and contained angles.

Some of the names given to angles are as follows.

1. *Right angle*. An angle of 90°.
2. *Acute angle*. An angle less than a right angle.
3. *Obtuse angle*. An angle greater than a right angle but less than two right angles.

Some of the names given to triangles are as follows

1. *Scalene triangle*. Has all sides and all angles unequal (**Fig. 3.1**).
2. *Equilateral triangle*. Has all sides and all angles equal (**Fig. 3.2**).
3. *Isosceles triangle*. Has two sides and the two angles opposite these sides equal (**Fig. 3.3**).
4. *Right-angled triangle*. Has one angle that is a right angle (*CDB* or *CDA* in **Fig. 3.3**).

All internal angles of any triangle total 180°.

It is possible to construct a triangle *when* the length of the three sides are known, or *when* the lengths of two sides and the angle between those two sides, are known, or *when* one side is known and the angles at each end of this side are known.

Fig. 3.1 To construct a triangle, given the lengths of the sides

Draw *AB* to represent one side. With *A* and *B* as centres and radii equal to the other sides, draw arcs to intersect at *C*. Join *AC* and *CB*.

Fig. 3.2 To construct an equilateral triangle given the lengths of one side

Draw the given length *AB*. With *A* and *B* as centres, radius *AB*, draw arcs to intersect at *C*. Join *AC* and *BC*.

Fig. 3.3. To construct an isosceles triangle, given the length of the base and the perpendicular height

Draw the given base *AB*. Bisect the base at *D*. With *D* as centre and given height as radius draw an arc above *AB*.

Erect a perpendicular at *D* to cut the arc at *C*. Join *AC* and *BC*.

Fig. 3.4 To construct a triangle, given the length of two sides and the perpendicular height

Draw a base line of any convenient length. Erect a perpendicular at *D*. Mark off the height *CD*. With *C* as centre and the two given lengths as radii, mark off *CA* and *CB* respectively. Join *AC* and *BC*.

Fig. 3.5 To construct a scale of chords, which is a geometrical method of angle construction

Draw the base line *AB* of any convenient length. Erect a perpendicular at *A*. With *A* as centre and *AB* as radius, draw an arc to intersect the perpendicular at *C*. With *B* as centre and *BC* as radius, draw an arc to cut *BA* produced. Divide the arc *BC* into nine equal parts, using compasses or dividers, and, with *B* as centre, drop arcs (chordal lengths) from these points on to *BA* extended. Number the divisions from 0 to 90 as shown, to obtain intermediate divisions. Bisect as required. (Note that for 60° the length of the chord BA_1 is equal to the radius of the arch *BA*.)

Fig. 3.6 To construct an angle of 45° by using the scale of chords

Draw a base line of any convenient length. With centre *B*, radius *BA* (or 0–60) on the scale, draw an arc cutting the base line at *A*. With *A* as centre, and 0–45 as radius, cut the arc at *C*. Then *CBA* is an angle of 45°.

To construct an angle of 55° using a scale of chords.

Draw *AB* of any convenient length. With *B* as centre, radius equal to the chord *B* to 60 (or 0 to 60) on the scale, draw an arc to cut the base line at *A*. With *A* as centre, radius equal to the chord *B* to 55 on the scale, draw an arc to cut the first one at *C*. Join *BC* to give the required angle of 55°.

To construct an angle of 40° using a scale of chords.

Draw *AB* of any suitable length. With *B* as centre, radius 0 to 60 on the scale, draw an arc to cut the base line at *A*. With *A* as centre, radius equal to the chord *B* to 40, draw an arc to cut the first one at *C*. Join *CB* to give the required angle of 40°.

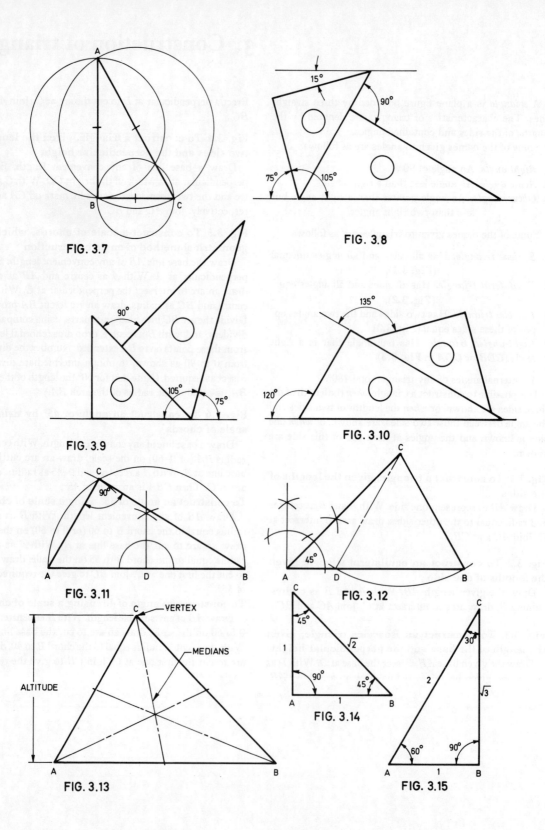

FIG. 3.7

FIG. 3.8

FIG. 3.9

FIG. 3.10

FIG. 3.11

FIG. 3.12

FIG. 3.13

FIG. 3.14

FIG. 3.15

Fig. 3.7 To apply the theorem of Pythagoras to the areas of circles

Construct a right-angled triangle and bisect the sides. With the points of bisection as centres draw three circles whose diameters are equal to the lengths of the sides. The area of the circle on the hypotenuse is equal to the sum of the areas of the circles on the other two sides.

Fig. 3.8, 3.9, and 3.10 show the angles that can be obtained using the 60° and 45° degree set squares in combination.

Fig. 3.11 To construct a right-angled triangle, given the length of the hypotenuse and one other side.

Draw AB equal in length to the hypotenuse and bisect it at O. With O as centre draw a semicircle of diameter AB. With either A or B as centre, radius equal to the length of the other side, draw an arc to cut the semicircle at C. Join AC and BC, to give the required right-angled triangle. (The angle of a triangle contained in a semicircle is always a right angle.)

Fig. 3.12 To construct a triangle, given the lengths of two sides and one opposite angle

Draw AB of any suitable length and construct the given angle at A (45° in this example). Along this angled line mark off AC, the length of one given side. With C as centre, radius equal to the length of the other given side, draw an arc to cut AB at B (or D). Join CB (or CD), the required triangle.

Fig. 3.13 indicates some features of a triangle. The vertical height is called the *altitude* and the topmost point C is called the *vertex*.

Lines drawn from the mid-length of the sides of a triangle to the angles opposite those sides are called *medians*. Medians intersect at the centre of area of a triangle.

Fig. 3.14 shows the relationship between the length of the sides of a triangle containing an angle of 90° and two angles of 45°. When the length of the base AB is 1 and the length of the side AC is 1, then the hypotenuse BC will have a length of $\sqrt{2}$. These proportions will always be the same whatever the base length may be. Thus, when AB is 3 units long and AC is 3 units long, then BC will be $3\sqrt{2}$ units long, i.e. 4·242 units. It will be noted that this triangle is one-half of a square of unit side.

Fig. 3.15 shows the relationship between the length of the sides of a triangle containing an angle of 90°, one of 60°, and one of 30°. When the length of the base AB is 1, the hypotenuse AC will be 2 units in length and the vertical side BC will be $\sqrt{3}$. These proportions will always be the same whatever the base length may be. Thus, when AB is 3 units long, AC will be 6 units long and BC will be $3\sqrt{3}$ units long, i.e. 5·196 units.

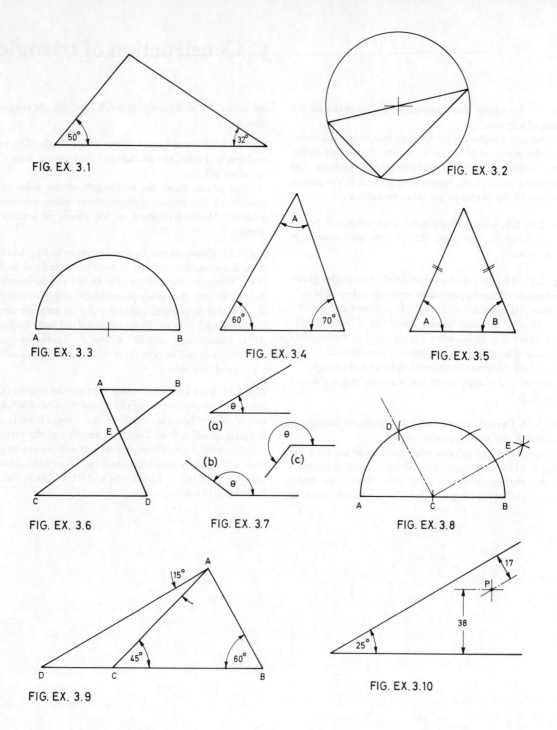

FIG. EX. 3.1

FIG. EX. 3.2

FIG. EX. 3.3

FIG. EX. 3.4

FIG. EX. 3.5

FIG. EX. 3.6

FIG. EX. 3.7

FIG. EX. 3.8

FIG. EX. 3.9

FIG. EX. 3.10

Exercises for Chapter 3

1. Construct, on a base line of 65 mm, the angles 22·5°, 45°, 60°, 75°, and 90°.
2. Construct an equilateral triangle whose sides are 53 mm long. Measure the internal angles and verify that they are all 60°.
3. Construct a triangle having a perimeter of 125 mm and whose sides are in the proportion 3 : 5 : 7.
4. Construct a triangle whose sides are in the proportion 3 : 4 : 5 when the length of the longest side is 65 mm. Measure the lengths of the other sides and the contained angles.
5. On a base of 42 mm construct a triangle having one base angle of 60° when the length of the side opposite this angle is 84 mm.
6. Construct a right-angled triangle whose hypotenuse is 70 mm long.
7. On a base line 57 mm long, construct an acute-angled triangle containing base angles of 45° and 60°.
8. Construct a right-angled triangle on a base of 40 mm and having a vertical height of 50 mm. Construct squares on each of the sides and determine the areas of each. Show that the total areas of the squares on the shortest sides is equal to the area of the square on the longest side.
9. Two circular pipes are to be laid to replace a third. If the area of the third pipe is 250 mm², determine the diameters of the other two pipes so that the total area remains the same.
10. Name the triangle shown in **Fig. Ex. 3.1.** *(CSE)*
11. Name the triangle shown in **Fig. Ex. 3.2.** *(CSE)*
12. **Fig. Ex. 3.3** shows a semicircle drawn on a diameter *AB* 90 mm long. On *AB* draw a triangle *ABC* with *C* touching the semicircle. Determine the angle *ACB*. *(CSE)*
13. Name the triangle shown in **Fig. Ex. 3.4** and state the size of angle *A*. *(CSE)*
14. Name the triangle shown in **Fig. Ex. 3.5** and state the relationship between the angles *A* and *B*. *(CSE)*
15. In **Fig. Ex. 3.6** *AB* and *CD* are parallel to one another. List the angles that are equal in size to each other. *(CSE)*
16. The hot and cold water pipes feeding a shower mixer unit are 44 mm and 57 mm internal diameter. What internal diameter outlet pipe is required so that it is equal to the combined areas of the other two pipes?
(Answer to the nearest millimetre) *(CSE)*
17. Name the angles shown in **Fig. Ex. 3.7 (a), (b),** and **(c).** *(CSE)*
18. State the angles *BCD* and *BCE* in **Fig. Ex. 3.8.** *(CSE)*
19. On a new baseline *EF* 75 mm long re-draw a similar figure to the triangles *ABCD* shown in **Fig. Ex. 3.9.** All angles are to be constructed using compasses. *(CSE)*
20. **Fig. Ex. 3.10** shows an angle containing a point *P*. Draw a circle which touches both arms of the angle and passes through the point *P*. *(CSE)*

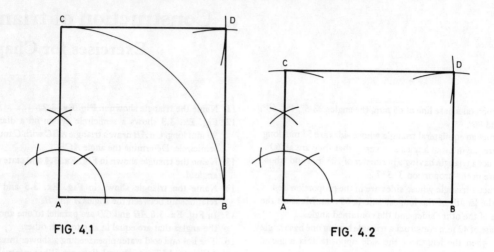

FIG. 4.1   FIG. 4.2

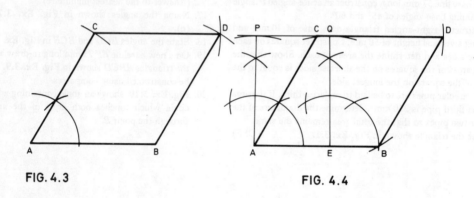

FIG. 4.3   FIG. 4.4

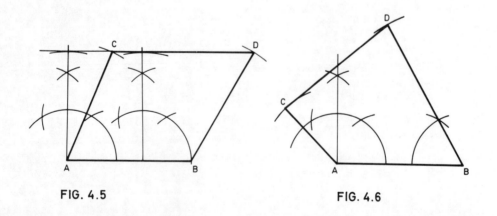

FIG. 4.5   FIG. 4.6

Quadrilaterals are plane figures bounded by four straight lines.

A *square* has all sides equal and all angles are right angles.

A *rectangle* has its opposite sides equal and all angles are right angles.

A *rhombus* has all its sides and opposite angles equal, but contains no right angles.

A *parallelogram* has its opposite pairs of sides and opposite angles equal, but contains no right angles.

A *trapezium* has two sides parallel.

A *trapezoid* has no two sides parallel.

Fig. 4.1 To construct a square given the length of the sides

Draw *AB* to the given length. At *A* erect a perpendicular and, with centre *A*, radius *AB*, draw an arc to cut the perpendicular at *C*. With centres *B* and *C* and radius *AB*, draw arcs to intersect at *D*. *ABCD* is the required square.

Fig. 4.2 To construct a rectangle given the length of the sides

Draw *AB* equal to one given length. Erect a perpendicular at *A*. With centre *A*, radius equal to the other given length, draw an arc to cut the perpendicular at *C*. With *C* as centre, radius *AB* and with *B* as centre, radius *AC*, draw arcs to intersect at *D*. *ABCD* is the required rectangle.

Fig. 4.3 To construct a rhombus given one angle and the length of the sides

Draw *AB* equal to the given length. Set off the given angle (in this case 60°) at *A*. With centre *A*, radius *AB*, draw an arc to cut the arm of the angle at *C*. With *C* and *B* as centres and the same radius, draw arcs to intersect at *D*. *ABDC* is the required rhombus.

Fig. 4.4 To construct a rhombus given the vertical height and offset distance

Draw a line any convenient length. Erect perpendiculars at *A* and any convenient point *E* along the line. With *A* and *E* as centres, radius equal to the vertical height, draw arcs to cut perpendiculars at *P* and *Q*. Draw a line through *P* and *Q* produced. From *P* mark off the offset distance *PC*. Join *AC*. With *C* as centre and *CA* as radius, draw an arc to cut *PQ* produced, at *D*. With *A* as centre, same radius, draw an arc to cut the base line at *B*. Join *AB* and *BD*. (Note the method of construction for drawing parallel lines.)

Fig. 4.5 To construct a trapezium given the vertical height and the lengths of three sides

Draw *AB*, the length of one side. Erect perpendiculars and mark off the vertical height as previously described. Draw a line parallel to *AB*. With *A* as centre, radius equal to one other given length, draw an arc to cut the parallel at *C*. Join *AC*. With *C* as centre, radius the third given length, draw an arc to cut the parallel at *D*. Join *CD*. Join *BD*.

Fig. 4.6 To construct a trapezoid given the lengths of four sides and two base angles

Draw *AB* the length of one given side. At *A* construct the given angle (135°). With centre *A* and radius equal to a given length, draw an arc to cut the arm of the angle at *C*. Join *AC*. Erect the second base angle (60°) at *B*. With *B* as centre, and radius equal to a given length, draw an arc to cut the arm of the angle at *D*. Join *BD*. Join *CD*.

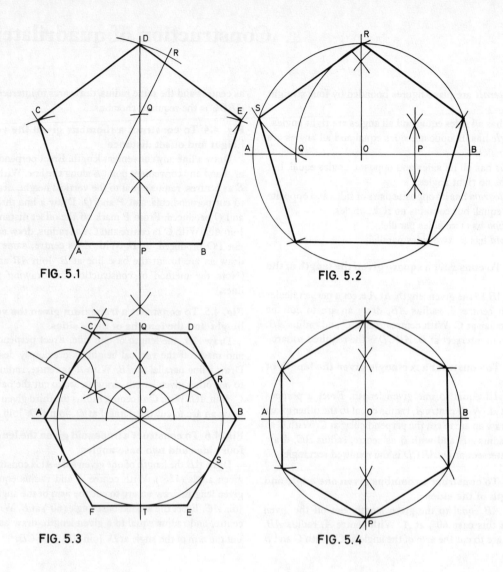

FIG. 5.1

FIG. 5.2

FIG. 5.3

FIG. 5.4

16

5. Construction of regular polygons

A regular *polygon* is a plane figure bounded by any number of equal sides, which contain equal angles. The figures are named according to the number of sides, as follows.

Pentagon: five sides.	*Nonagon:* nine sides
Hexagon: six sides.	*Decagon:* ten sides.
Heptagon: seven sides.	*Undecagon:* eleven sides
Octagon: eight sides.	*Duodecagon:* twelve sides.

The sum of the internal angles subtended at the centre equals the sum of the external angles, i.e. 360°.

The internal angle contained by any two sides may be calculated by subtracting the magnitude of the internal angle at the centre from 180°.

Thus, for a regular hexagon:

Internal angle at centre = 360° ÷ number of sides

$$= \frac{360°}{6} = 60°.$$

∴ Angle contained by sides = 180° − 60° = 120°.

This would be the angle set on an adjustable square or bevel, for checking the angle of a regular hexagon bar or hexagon bolt head.

Fig. 5.1 To construct a regular pentagon given the length of the sides

Draw AB equal to the given side. Bisect AB at P and erect a perpendicular. Mark off PQ equal to AB. Join AQ and produce to R, making QR equal to AP. With A as centre and AR as radius, draw an arc to cut the perpendicular bisector at D. With A and D as centres, AB as radius, draw arcs to intersect at C. Join AC and CD. With B and D as centres, same radius, draw arcs to intersect at E. Join BE and DE.

Fig. 5.2 To construct a regular pentagon within a given circle

Draw the given circle from centre O, on the diameter AB. Erect a perpendicular at O, to cut the circle at R. Bisect OB at P. With P as centre, radius PR, draw an arc to cut AB at Q. With R as centre, radius RQ, draw an arc to cut the circle at S. Join RS, the required length of side, which may now be stepped off inside the circle. (Note: this is an inscribed figure.)

Fig. 5.3 To construct a regular hexagon outside a given circle given the length of the sides

Draw the given circle from O. Draw AB any convenient length. Bisect and erect a perpendicular at O. Construct angles of 30° above and below AB to make diagonals OP, etc. Erect a perpendicular P on OP and produce to cut AB at A. With A as centre, radius equal to the given length, mark off AC. Repeat on diagonals OR, OS, and OV, to produce points B, D, E, and F. (Note: this is a circumscribed figure.) A study of the figure will show that, in practice, this hexagon may be produced by using the 30°–60° set square.

Fig. 5.4 To construct a regular hexagon inside a given circle

Draw the given circle from centre O. Draw AB, the diameter of the circle, and erect a perpendicular at O to cut the circle at P. With P as centre and radius equal to the radius of the circle, step off the required sides inside the circle.

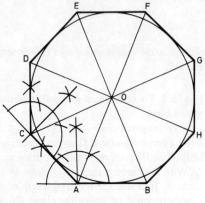

FIG. 5.5

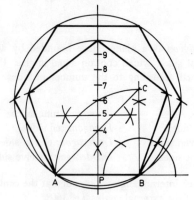

FIG. 5.6

5. Construction of regular polygons

Fig. 5.5 To construct a regular octagon given the length of the sides

Draw *AB* equal to the given length. Erect a perpendicular at *A* and bisect the angle. Step off *AB* along the bisector to give *C*. Erect a perpendicular at *C* and bisect the angle. Step off *AB* along bisector to give *D*. Repeat for the remaining sides.

It will be noted that a similar construction may be used when the diagonal lengths are given. When the diameter of the inscribed circle is given, a study of the figure will show that the construction may be completed with the aid of a 45° set square.

Fig. 5.6 To construct any regular polygon on a line of given length

Draw the given line *AB*. Bisect and erect a perpendicular at *P*. Erect a perpendicular at *B*. With *B* as centre, *AB* as radius, draw an arc to cut perpendicular on *B* at *C*, and perpendicular bisector at 6. Join *AC* to cut perpendicular at 4. Bisect 4 and 6 at 5. Step off unit distance from 6 to give points 7, 8, 9, etc. These points are the centres of circumscribing circles to contain the number of sides indicated by the centre number.

Exercises for Chapters 4 and 5

1. Using an accepted method of construction, draw a square of 70 mm side.
2. Construct a rectangle having sides of 70 mm and 55 mm.
3. Construct a rhombus of 70 mm side having an internal angle of 60°.
4. Construct a rhombus of 75 mm side which is offset by 15 mm.
5. The diagonal of a square is 85 mm long. Draw the diagonal and construct the square.
6. Construct a square within a circle of 80 mm diameter. What is the length of the sides of the square?
7. Construct a quadrilateral *ABCD*, given that the lengths of the four sides are: $a = 6.6$ cm, $b = 3.0$ cm, $c = 4.2$ cm, $d = 5.1$ cm, and the angle at *A* is 59°.
8. Draw a parallelogram *ABCD*, given that $AB = 55$ mm and the diagonals *AC* and *BD* are 80 mm and 60 mm respectively.
9. Construct a quadrilateral *ABCD*, in which *AB* is 2.6 cm, *AC* is 5 cm, angle *ABC* is 108°, angle *BAD* is 130° and angle *CDA* is 90°.
10. Construct a pentagon having sides of 50 mm.
11. Draw a circle of 9 cm diameter and construct a regular pentagon within it.
12. A pentagon has a side length of 5.5 cm. Draw the pentagon showing the method of construction.
13. Construct a hexagon having a side length of 53 mm.
14. Construct a hexagon within a circle of diameter 87 mm.
15. Draw a hexagon outside a circle of 8 cm diameter using a set square.
16. Draw a square of 80 mm side and construct an octagon within it.
17. On a line *AB* 4 cm long, construct figures having five, six, and eight sides.
18. Draw a regular hexagon having a side length of 4.3 cm using only compasses in the construction.
19. Draw two interlocking hexagons within a circle of 70 mm diameter, to produce a spanner head.
20. Construct polygons of 24 mm side having nine and twelve sides.
21. Draw a hexagon of 3.5 cm side and, using it to represent a nut, design a simple locking plate to prevent rotation.
22. Two lines *AB* and *BC* are both 3.8 cm long and join one another to form a vee shape. Draw these two lines. If they then form two sides of a regular polygon, complete the polygon and name it.
23. A line *AB* is 150 mm long and lies at an angle of 45°. If it is the diagonal of a square, complete the square and inscribe the largest regular octagon possible within the square.

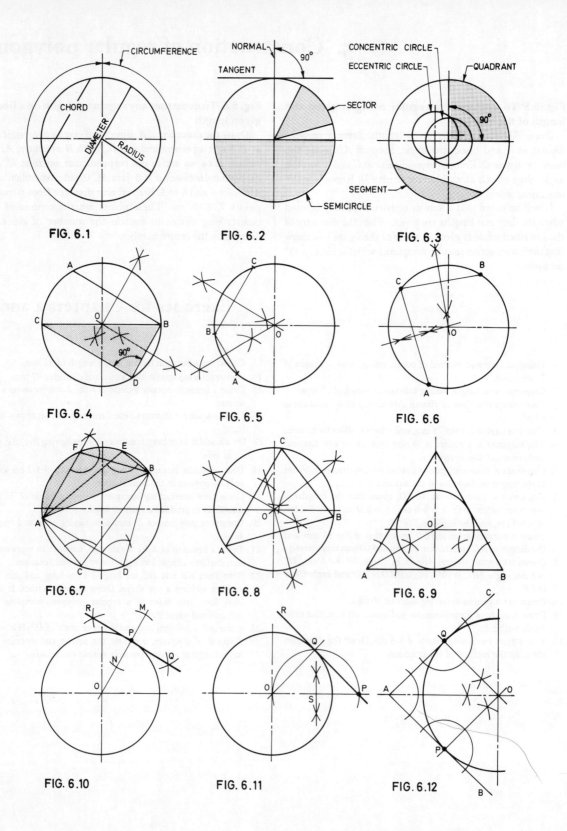

FIG. 6.1

FIG. 6.2

FIG. 6.3

FIG. 6.4

FIG. 6.5

FIG. 6.6

FIG. 6.7

FIG. 6.8

FIG. 6.9

FIG. 6.10

FIG. 6.11

FIG. 6.12

6. The circle

A *circle* is a plane figure bounded by one continuous curved line, which is always equidistant from a fixed point, the centre.

Figs **6.1, 6.2,** and **6.3** show some elements of the circle.

Fig. 6.4 shows a circle containing a chord *AB* and a triangle *BCD*. Any triangle contained in a semicircle makes a right angle at the point of contact with the circumference. Bisect the chord *AB*. Consider the side *BD* of the triangle as a chord and bisect it. The two bisectors meet at the centre of the circle; therefore the bisector of any chord will pass through the centre of the circle.

Fig. 6.5 To construct a circle that will pass through three given points in space

Let *A*, *B*, and *C* be the given points. Join *AB* and *BC* and bisect both, producing the bisectors until they meet at *O*, the centre of the required circle.

Fig. 6.6 To locate the centre of a given circle

Draw the given circle from centre *O*. Mark on its circumference the three points *A*, *B*, and *C*, and draw the chords *AC* and *BC*. Bisect the chords, producing the bisectors to meet at the centre.

Fig. 6.7 To show that the angle in a segment is constant

Draw a circle of a convenient diameter. Draw any chord *AB* and draw triangles in each segment. Measurement of the contained angles with a protractor will show that angle *AFB* = angle *AEB* and angle *ACB* = angle *ADB*. Also the angles in one segment are *supplementary* to the angles in the other segment, i.e. they total 180°.

Fig. 6.8 To draw the circumscribing circle of a given triangle

Draw the given triangle *ABC* and bisect the sides. The bisectors will intersect at *O*, the centre of the circumscribing circle, i.e. a circle whose diameter will touch the three points (or *vertices*) of the triangle.

Fig. 6.9 To construct an inscribed circle in a given triangle

Draw the given triangle *ABC*. Bisect any two angles and produce the bisectors to meet at a point *O*, the required centre of the inscribed circle.

An inscribed circle is a circle contained within a figure and touching all its sides at a point.

Fig. 6.10 To draw a tangent to a given circle at a given point of contact

Draw the given circle, centre *O*, and at any point on its circumference mark a point *P*. Draw a straight line from *O* passing through *P*. With *P* as centre, any suitable radius, draw two arcs on *OP* produced at *M* and *N*. With these points as centres, any suitable radius, draw arcs to intersect one another at *R* and *Q*. Join *RQ*, the required tangent.

Note that *OM* is a normal.

Fig. 6.11 To draw a tangent to a given circle from a given point outside the circle

Draw the circle, centre *O*. Mark the given point *P* outside it. Join *OP* and bisect at *S*. With *S* as centre, radius *SP*, draw a semicircle on *OP*, cutting the circle at *Q*. Join *OQ*. Draw the required tangent from *P*, passing through *Q*, to *R*.

Fig. 6.12 To draw a circle to touch two given points on the arms of a given angle

Let *BAC* be the given angle and *P* and *Q* be the two given points on the arms *AB* and *AC* respectively. Erect perpendiculars at *P* and *Q* to intersect at *O*, the centre of the required circle..

Note that the bisector of the angle can be used with one of the perpendiculars to locate the centre.

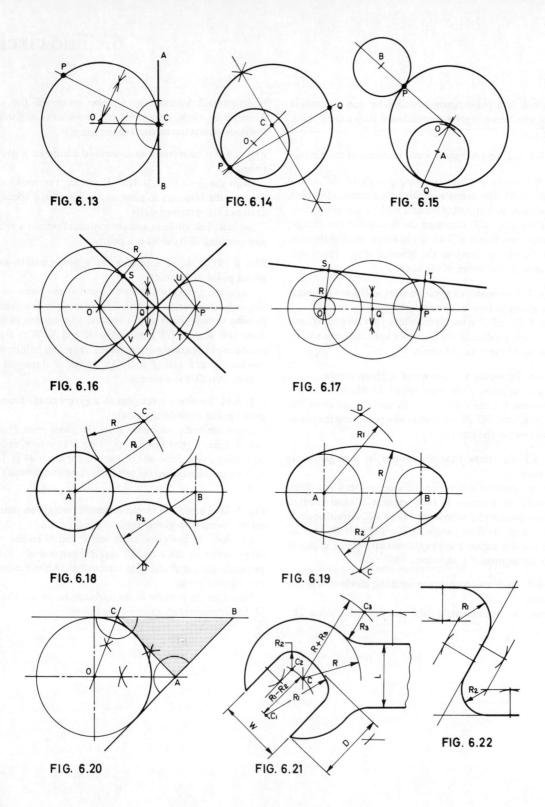

FIG. 6.13

FIG. 6.14

FIG. 6.15

FIG. 6.16

FIG. 6.17

FIG. 6.18

FIG. 6.19

FIG. 6.20

FIG. 6.21

FIG. 6.22

Fig. 6.13 To draw a circle to touch a given point and be tangential to a given point on a line

Draw the line AB, any convenient length, and mark on it a point C. Let P be the given point. Join CP and bisect. Erect a perpendicular C to intersect with the bisector of CP at O, the centre of the required circle.

Fig. 6.14 To draw a circle to pass through a given point and to touch a given circle internally at a given point

Draw the given circle, centre O, and mark on it a point P. Let Q be the given point. Join PQ and bisect. Draw a line from P passing through O and intersecting the bisector C, the centre of the required circle.

Fig. 6.15 To draw a circle of given radius to touch two given circles, one internally and one externally

Let OP be the given radius and A and B the centres of the given circles. With centre A, radius OP minus radius A, draw an arc. With centre B, radius OP plus radius B, draw an arc to cut the first arc at O, the centre of the required circle which touches the two given circles at P and Q.

Fig. 6.16 To draw internal tangents to two given circles of different radii

Let O and P be the centres of the given circles. Join the centres and bisect at Q. With Q as centre draw a circle passing through O and P. With O as centre, radius equal to the sum of the given radii, draw an arc to cut the circle on Q at R. Join OR to give point S on one given circle. From centre P, draw a line parallel to OR cutting the circle on P at T. A line drawn through S and T will be the one required tangent. The other tangent through U and V can be constructed in similar manner.

Fig. 6.17 To draw a tangent to two given circles of different radii

Let O and P be the centres of the given circles. Join OP and bisect at Q. With Q as centre draw a circle passing through O and P. With O as centre, radius equal to the difference between the radii of the two given circles, draw a circle cutting the circle on Q at R. Join RP. Draw a line from O through R to give S. Draw a line from P parallel to OS to give T. Join ST, the required tangent.

Fig. 6.18 To draw two circles of the same radius tangential to two given circles of different radii a given centre distance apart

Let A and B be the centres of the given unequal circles.

Join A and B. With A as centre, radius equal to the sum of the radii of the contacting circles A and C, draw an arc R_1. With B as centre, radius equal to the sum of the radii of the contacting circles B and D, draw an arc R_2. The intersection of these arcs will give the centres, C and D, of the required circles (or arcs in this case).

Fig. 6.19 To draw two arcs of the same radius tangential to two given circles of different radii a given centre distance apart

Let A and B be the centres of the given unequal circles and R the radius of the given arcs. Join AB. With A as centre, radius R minus the radius of circle A, draw an arc. With B as centre, radius R minus the radius of circle B, draw another arc to intersect the first at C. With C as centre, radius R, draw one of the required tangential arcs. Repeat the construction for centre D.

Fig. 6.20 To escribe a circle to a given triangle

Draw the given triangle ABC and produce the sides BA and BC. Bisect the exterior angles at A and C to intersect at O, the centre of the required escribed circle which touches one exterior side of the triangle.

Fig. 6.21 shows a practical application of blending radii in the construction of a spanner.

With centre C draw, faintly, a circle of radius R. From the centre draw a line at $45°$ to intersect the circle at C_1. About this line, mark the spanner width W for a depth D. With C_1 as centre, radius C_1D draw an arc. Draw lines parallel to the inside faces of spanner jaw and distance R_2. With C_1 as centre, radius R_1 minus R_2, draw an arc to cut the parallels at C_2. With C_2 as centre, radius R_2, draw the corner radii. Mark off width L, and draw parallel lines distance R_3 away. With C as centre, radius $R + R_3$, draw arcs to locate the centres of the blending radii.

Suitable dimensions are: $R = 35$ mm; $R_1 = 40$ mm; $R_2 = 10$ mm; $R_3 = 18$ mm; $W = 38$ mm; $D = 40$ mm; $L = 38$ mm.

Fig. 6.22 shows a method of using intersecting lines as a means of locating the centres of blending radii. The dark outline is representative of a portion of a casting which requires blending radii at positions where the contour changes direction. By drawing parallel lines a distance from the surface equal to the respective radii, centres are produced at their intersections from which the blending curves can be drawn.

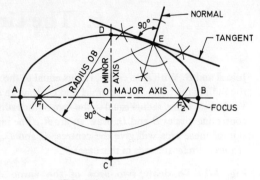

FIG. 7.1

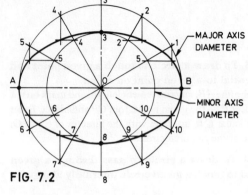

FIG. 7.2

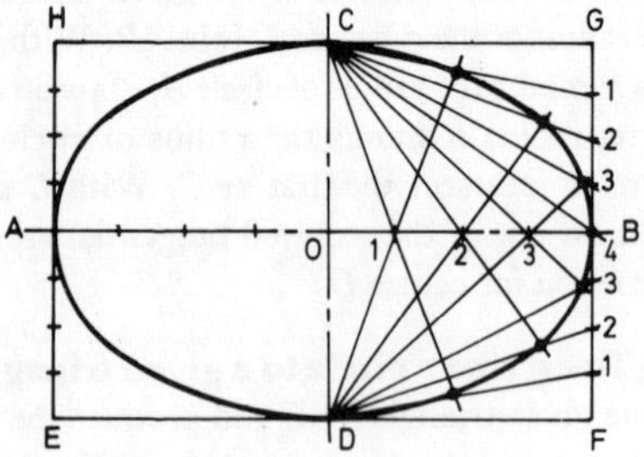

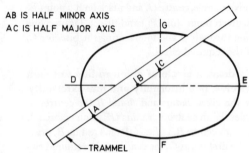

AB IS HALF MINOR AXIS
AC IS HALF MAJOR AXIS

FIG. 7.4

FIG. 7.3

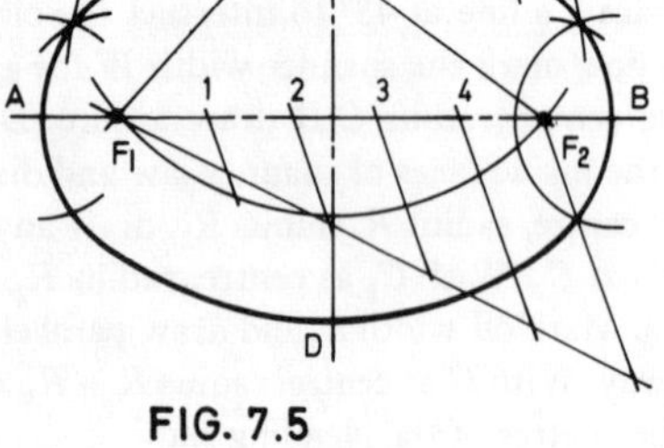

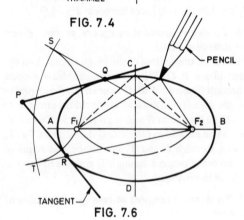

FIG. 7.5

FIG. 7.6

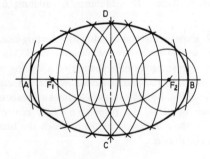

FIG. 7.7

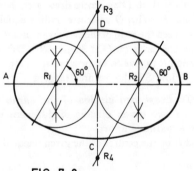

FIG. 7.8

7. The ellipse

Fig. 7.1 shows an ellipse. Distance AB is the major axis and CD is the minor axis. Half the major axis struck as a radius from D or C will give the foci F_1 and F_2.

From a vertex E draw lines to F_1 and F_2. Bisect the angle at E. This bisector is called a *normal*. A line at right angles to the normal, touching the circumference at E is called a *tangent*.

Fig. 7.2 To construct an ellipse given the lengths of the major and minor axes

From centre O draw two circles equal in diameter to the given axes. Divide both circles into twelve equal parts and number as shown. Drop vertical lines from the points on the major diameter to intersect with horizontal lines drawn from the points on the minor diameter. A smooth curve passing through these intersections and the points A, B, 3, and 8, will give the required ellipse. This is known as the *auxiliary circle method* of construction.

Fig. 7.3 To construct an ellipse within a given rectangle

Draw the given rectangle $EFGH$. Bisect EF and FG to give the minor and major axes DC and AB which meet at the centre O. Divide OB, FB, and BG into four equal parts, numbering as shown. From C, draw lines to pass through points 1 to 4 on OB and BG. From D, draw lines to pass through points 1 to 4 on OB and FB. The intersections of these lines will give points on the circumference of half the required ellipse.

Repeat the construction to the left of CD for the complete figure. This is know as the *rectangle method* of construction.

Fig. 7.4 To construct an ellipse using the trammel method given the major and minor axes

Draw major and minor axes DE and FG. On a strip of thin card (the *trammel*), mark AB equal to half the minor axis and AC equal to half the major axis. Move the trammel, keeping B always on the major axis and C always on the minor axis. Point A will trace out a path (called a *locus*) which will be an ellipse.

Note that a pencil lead could be fixed at A.

Fig. 7.5 To construct an ellipse by the intersecting-arc method given the major and minor axes.

Draw AB and CD, the given axes. With C as centre, radius half the major axis, draw an arc cutting AB at the foci F_1 and F_2. Divide the distance between F_1 and F_2 into a number of equal parts (five in this case), numbering as shown. With F_1 as centre, radii $A1$, $A2$, $A3$, etc., draw arcs above and below AB. With F_2 as centre, radius $B1$, $B2$, $B3$, etc., draw arcs to intersect those struck from F_1. Join these points of intersection with a smooth curve to obtain the required ellipse.

Fig. 7.6 To draw an ellipse by the foci method given the major and minor axes

Draw the axes AB and CD and mark the foci F_1 and F_2 as previously described. Insert pins at point C and the foci and around them stretch tightly a continuous thread. Remove the pin at C, replacing it with a well-sharpened pencil. Keeping the thread taut, move the pencil to trace out the required ellipse.

To construct tangents to an ellipse from an external point

Locate the external point P. With P as centre, radius PF_1 draw an arc. With F_2 as centre, radius AB, the major axis, draw an arc to intersect the former arc at points S and T. Join S and T to F_2. These lines intersect the ellipse at points Q and R. Lines from P though Q and R give the required tangents.

Fig. 7.7 To construct an ellipse from intersecting arcs given the major and minor axes

Draw the axes AB and CD and locate the foci F_1 and F_2 as before. With F_1 as centre, using any succession of radii extending across the major axis, draw a series of arcs. With F_2 as centre, and the same succession of radii, draw arcs to intersect the first ones. A smooth curve drawn through the points of intersection of the arcs will give the required ellipse.

Fig. 7.8 To draw an approximate ellipse given the major and minor axes

Draw the axes AB and CD. Divide each half of the major axis into two equal parts, marking R_1 and R_2. With R_1 and R_2 as centres, radius R_1A, draw circles. Through R_1 and R_2 draw lines inclined at 60° to AB, extending to intersect the minor axis CD produced at R_3 and R_4. With R_3 as centre, radius R_3C draw an arc and with R_4 as centre, same radius, draw an arc. These arcs will join with the two circles to form an approximate ellipse.

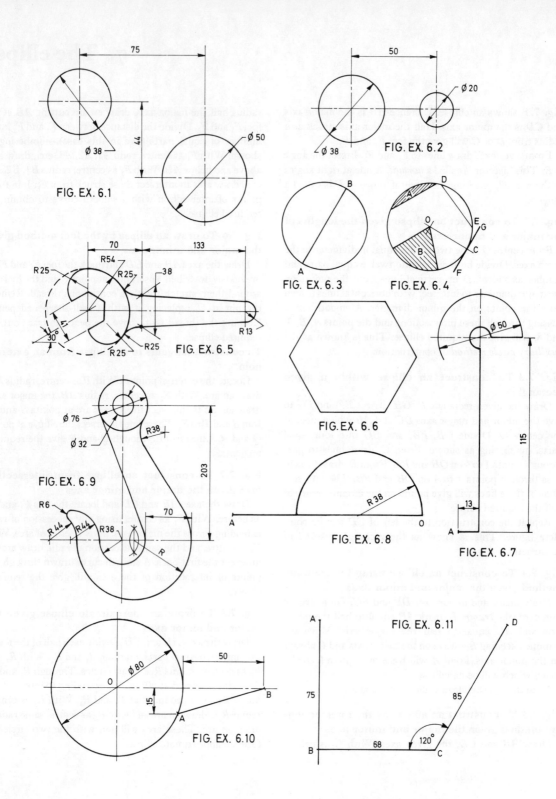

FIG. EX. 6.1

FIG. EX. 6.2

FIG. EX. 6.3

FIG. EX. 6.4

FIG. EX. 6.5

FIG. EX. 6.6

FIG. EX. 6.7

FIG. EX. 6.8

FIG. EX. 6.9

FIG. EX. 6.10

FIG. EX. 6.11

7. The ellipse

Exercises for Chapters 6 and 7

1. Find a point 25 mm away from both the circles shown in **Fig. Ex. 6.1**. From this point construct a tangent to the larger circle. *(CSE)*
2. Draw a circle of 25 mm diameter to touch the given circles in **Fig. Ex. 6.2**. Next draw a part of a circle of 50 mm radius which will touch and include the two larger circles. *(CSE)*
3. **Fig. Ex. 6.3** shows a circle of 50 mm diameter containing a line *AB* which is the diagonal of a square. Show a method of completing the square. *(CSE)*
4. Name the following parts of the circle shown in **Fig. Ex. 6.4**:
   (a) the shaded area *A*;
   (b) the shaded area *B*;
   (c) the line *ED*;
   (d) the line *OC*;
   (e) the line *FG* *(CSE)*
5. Draw the open-ended hexagonal spanner shown in **Fig. Ex. 6.5**. Show clearly the construction for all centres *(CSE)*
6. **Fig. Ex. 6.6** shows a hexagon 65 mm A/F. Inscribe three equal circles each touching one side of the hexagon and the other two circles. *(CSE)*
7. **Fig. Ex. 6.7** shows part of a gauge plate. Construct the tangent from *A* to the 50 mm diameter arc. Indicate the point of contact with an arrow. *(CSE)*
8. Draw a circle of 25 mm radius which touches both the semicircle and the line *AO* in **Fig. Ex. 6.8**.
9. **Fig. Ex. 6.9** shows a crane hook. Draw this full size showing clearly how tangents and tangential curves are constructed. *(CSE)*
10. In **Fig. Ex. 6.10**, draw a circle to pass through point *B* and touch the circle at point *A*. *(CSE)*
11. In **Fig. Ex. 6.11**, draw a circle to touch the lines *AB*, *BC*, and *CD*. *(CSE)*
12. Two lines join to form a vee. *AB* is 32 mm long and *BC* is 47 mm long. The internal angle between *AB* and *BC* is 120°. Construct a circle which will pass through the points *A*, *B*, and *C*.
13. Draw a line around the circumference of a circular washer or coin. Find its centre.
14. Draw a semicircle of 7·4 cm diameter. Using the diameter as a base line draw, within the semicircle, any triangle. Measure, record, and note the angles of the triangle. What important fact emerges?
15. A triangle *ABC* has *AB* and *AC* 65 mm long and *BC* 53 mm long. Construct a circle which will pass through the points *A*, *B*, and *C*.
16. Draw an equilateral triangle of 8 cm. Construct within it a circle tangential to the three sides.
17. Draw a circle of 7 cm diameter. Mark on its circumference two points *P* and *Q*. Construct tangents to these two points.
18. Draw a circle of 7 cm diameter and locate a point *P* some distance outside it. Construct a tangent to the circle which passes through the point *P*.
19. The corner of a room at floor level is required to be filled in with a radiused fillet. Assuming the corner to be square, construct a fillet of 6 cm radius neglecting the thickness of material.
20. Set out an angle of 80° from a point *A*, making the arms of the angle 9 cm long. Along each arm, from *A*, mark two points *P* and *Q* each 4·5 cm from *A*. Construct a circle to pass through these two points.

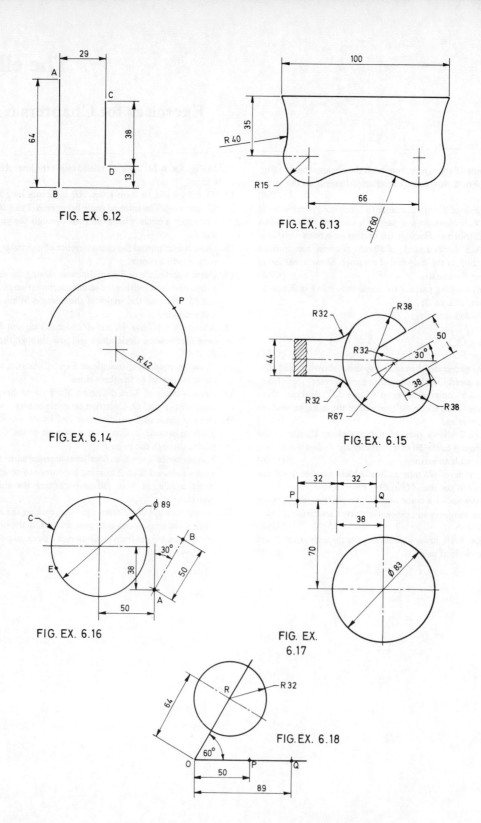

FIG. EX. 6.12

FIG. EX. 6.13

FIG. EX. 6.14

FIG. EX. 6.15

FIG. EX. 6.16

FIG. EX.
6.17

FIG. EX. 6.18

Exercises for Chapters 6 and 7

21. Draw a circle of 73 mm diameter. Draw any triangle ABC within the circle, all three points touching the circumference. Measure and record the angles of the triangle.

22. Locate three points in space any convenient distance apart. Construct a circle which passess through all three points.

23. In a circle 50 mm diameter draw a chord 38 mm long. Construct tangents at both ends of the chord.

24. Draw a straight line AB 6 cm long. 2 cm from A mark a point C. Mark a point D in space 6·5 cm from the line lying within the distance of the line AB. Construct a circle to pass through the points C and D.

25. **Fig. Ex. 6.12** shows two chords of a circle, AB and CD. Draw these two chords and, by a geometrical construction, draw the circle which passess through points A, B, C, and D. State clearly the diameter of this circle to within 3 mm.

26. Set out, full size, the figure shown in **Fig. Ex. 6.13.** (*CSE*)

27. At the point P in **Fig. Ex. 6.14**, geometrically construct both a normal and a tangent to the circular arc. (*CSE*)

28. (a) A parallelogram with one vertex angle of 60° has adjacent sides of 102 mm and 76 mm.
    Construct the parallelogram and inscribe an ellipse.
    (b) **Fig. Ex. 6.15** shows an elevation of the head of a spanner, in which the curves are tangential. Draw this elevation and show clearly the constructions employed to determine the positions of the various centres. (*Camb.*)

29. In **Fig. Ex. 6.16** the position of point E is approximate only. Draw a circle D which passes through points A and B and touches point E on circle C. State the diameter of circle D to the nearest millimetre. (*Camb.*)

30. Describe two circles to pass through both points P and Q and touch the given circle shown in **Fig. Ex. 6.17**. Measure and state the diameter of each circle to within 2 mm. (*AEB*)

31. **Fig. Ex. 6.18** shows the relative positions of two points P and Q on a straight line OA and a circle of 32 mm radius with its centre at R.
    Draw the circles which pass through the points P and Q and touch the given circle, and state their diameters. (*Camb.*)

32. The centres of two circles are 105 mm apart. One circle is 95 mm diameter and the other is 57 mm diameter.
    (a) Using geometrical constructions draw the internal tangents for the circles. Measure and state, to the nearest 2 mm, the lengths of the tangents between the points of contact with the circles.
    (b) Describe a circle, smaller than either of the circles in (a) above, to pass through the centre of the 57 mm diameter circle and touch the external tangents produced. Measure and state the diameter of this circle to within 2 mm. (*AEB*)

33. (a) Construct a triangle ABC so that AB is 152 mm, angle BAC equals 30° and the diameter of its inscribed circle is 50 mm. Measure and state the length of BC and the magnitude of the angle BCA.
    (b) Two parallel lines CD and EF each 44 mm long are 64 mm apart. (i) Describe a circle to pass through C and D and touch line EF. State its diameter. (ii) To the circle draw two tangents which contain an angle of 60°. (*Camb.*)

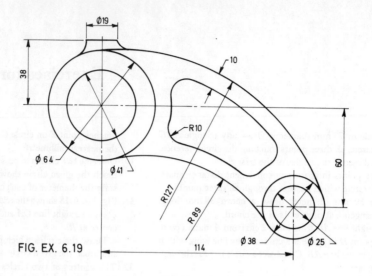

FIG. EX. 6.19

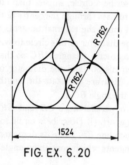

FIG. EX. 6.20

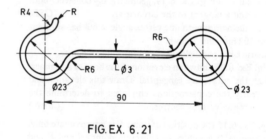

FIG. EX. 6.21

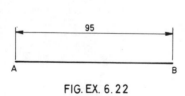

FIG. EX. 6.22

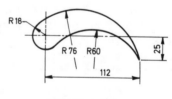

FIG. EX. 6.23

7. The ellipse

Exercises for Chapters 6 and 7

34. Draw the view given in **Fig. Ex. 6.19**, showing clearly all centres of radii and all points of tangency. *(AEB)*

35. **Fig. Ex. 6.20** shows the outline of a tracery window.

    Draw, to a scale of 1 mm to 1 cm, the window showing clearly the construction used for determining:

    (a) the centres used for the arcs, and

    (b) all points of contact. *(AEB)*

36. Draw, twice full size, the hook shown in **Fig. Ex. 6.21**, showing the constructions used to determine the centres of all radii.

37. **Fig. Ex. 6.22** shows a line *AB* 95 mm long. Points *A* and *B* are the centres of two circles with diameters of 50 mm and 76 mm respectively. Find the centre and draw another circle *C* of 64 mm radius such that *A* touches *C* but lies outside it, circle *B* lies inside and also touches circle *C*. *(CSE)*

38. **Fig. Ex. 6.23** shows the profile of a turbine blade. Draw the blade full size, showing the constructions used to obtain the centres of the radii.

39. Construct a regular pentagon within a circle of 114 mm diameter.

    Construct an internal semicircle on each side of the pentagon such that each semicircle has the same radius and touches the two adjacent semicircles.

    Measure and state the length of:

    (a) a side of the pentagon, and

    (b) the radius of a semicircle. *(AEB)*

40. Draw two lines at 60° to each other. Using a locus method to find the centre, describe a circle 76 mm diameter cutting the lines in chords of 38 mm and 64 mm respectively. Measure and state the distance from the centre of the circle to the meeting point of the two lines to within 3 mm. *(AEB)*

41. The three medians of a triangle are 64 mm, 83 mm, and 102 mm respectively.

    (a) Construct the triangle. Measure and state the length of each side to within 2 mm.

42. A point *P* is 114 mm from the centre *O* of a circle 70 mm diameter.

    (a) Construct two circles to touch the given circle.

    (b) Construct two circles to touch the given circle and both tangents. Measure and state clearly the diameter of each circle to within 2 mm. *(AEB)*

43. Construct a triangle *ABC* whose base length *AB* is 76 mm and whose angles are in the ratio 2:3:4. Measure and state the altitude of *C* above *AB*. Construct a circle which just touches the sides of the triangle and state its diameter. *(Camb.)*

44. Draw a rectangle 95 mm long and 65 mm high and construct an ellipse within its boundary.

45. Draw a line *AB* 132 mm long to represent the major axis of an ellipse. 22 mm from *A* mark a focal point. Construct half of the ellipse.

46. The major axis of an ellipse is 10 cm and the minor axis is 7 cm. Make a trammel from a piece of cardboard and draw the ellipse.

47 Draw two concentric circles of 10·5 cm and 7·3 cm and use them to draw an ellipse having these dimensions as major and minor axes.

48. The major and minor axes of an ellipse are the same as those in question 47. Draw an approximate ellipse and compare it with the projected drawing. (Transparent paper should be used for this question.)

49. Construct half of an ellipse having a major axis 86 mm long and a minor axis 66 mm long. Locate a point *P* 40 mm radius from the focus and lying on a line at 30° to the major axis. From the point *P* construct two tangents to the ellipse.

(b) Redraw the triangle and construct the circumscribing circle. *(AEB)*

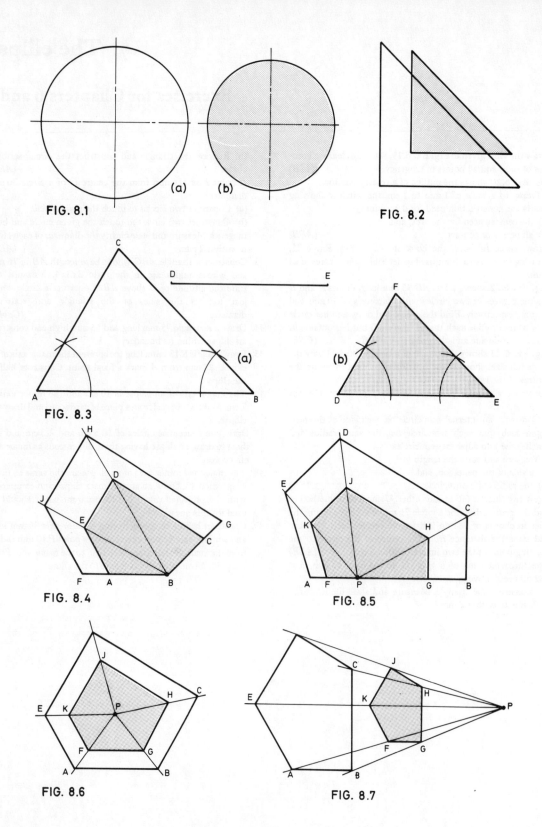

FIG. 8.1

FIG. 8.2

FIG. 8.3

FIG. 8.4

FIG. 8.5

FIG. 8.6

FIG. 8.7

32

8. Areas and similar figures

This chapter is concerned with plane figures which are equal in area to other figures though of different shape, or are proportional in area owing to a definite relationship between the lengths of corresponding sides. Similar figures, other than circles, have their angles equal and their sides proportional.

The areas of irregular plane figures bounded by straight lines can often be found by constructing a more simple regular figure of equal area, or by dividing the figure into rectangles and triangles.

Fig. 8.1 (a) and (b) show two circles, one of which is greater in diameter and area than the other. They are similar figures because there is a definite relationship between their areas. The areas vary as the square of the diameters.

Fig. 8.2 shows two similar triangles superimposed. Although the shaded triangle is smaller in its dimensions than the plain triangle, the contained angles are the same. Therefore the figures are similar.

Figs 8.3 (a) and (b) To construct a triangle similar to a given triangle on a given base

Let *ABC* be the given triangle and *DE* the given base. Draw *DE* the given base. At *D* and *E* construct angles of 60° and 45° to intersect at *F*. *DEF* is a triangle similar to triangle *ABC*.

Fig. 8.4 To construct an irregular polygon on a given base similar to a given polygon

Let *ABCDE* be the given polygon and *BF* the given base. Produce *BA* to *F*. From *B*, draw straight lines passing through *E*, *D* and *C*. From *F*, draw a line parallel to *AE* intersecting *BE* produced at *J*. From *J*, draw a line parallel to *ED* intersecting *BD* produced at *H*. From *H*, draw a line parallel to *DC* intersecting *BC* produced at *G*. Join *BGHJF* to give the required similar polygon.

Fig. 8.5 To construct an irregular polygon on a given base similar to a given polygon

Let *ABCDE* be the given polygon and *FG* the given base. Mark the given base *FG* anywhere between *A* and *B*. From any convenient point *P* within the given base, draw straight lines to intersect with points *C*, *D*, and *E*. From *F*, draw a line parallel to *AE* intersecting *PE* at *K*. From *K*, draw a line parallel to *ED* intersecting *PD* at *J*. From *J*, draw a line parallel to *DC* intersecting *PC* at *H*. From *H*, draw a line parallel to *CB* intersecting *PB* at *G*. Join *FGHJK* to give the required similar polygon.

Fig. 8.6 To construct an irregular polygon within a given polygon given the length of a diagonal

Let *ABCDE* be the given polygon and *PF* the given diagonal. From any point *P* close to the centre, draw the diagonals *PA*, *PB*, *PC*, *PD*, and *PE*. From *P*, mark off the given diagonal *PF*. From *F*, draw a line parallel to *AE* intersecting *PE* at *K*. From *K*, draw a line parallel to *ED* intersecting *PD* at *J*. From *J*, draw a line parallel to *CB* intersecting *PB* at *G*. Join *FGHJK* to give the required polygon.

Another method of drawing similar plane figures to scale is that known as *radical projection* or *similitude*. This employs a *focal* or *pole point*, through which all the projection lines pass, in much the same way as the three previous examples. The method produces projected areas which contain angles equal to those in the given figures and the lengths of the sides are proportional. It has the advantage of providing a quick and neat projection of an irregular or curved outline, and is used in architectural drawing for such things as moulded sections. After some practice it will be seen that the projection lines from the pole point can be dispensed with, projection of the required points taking place along imaginary radial lines.

Fig. 8.7 To draw a polygon the length of whose sides are one-half the length of the sides of a given polygon

Let *ABCDE* be the given polygon. Locate the pole point *P* conveniently outside the given figure. Join *AP*, *BP*, *CP*, *DP*, and *EP*. Bisect *BP* at *G*. From *G*, draw a line parallel to *BC* intersecting *PC* at *H*. Repeat this process for all the lines of the given figure to produce the polygon *FGHJK*, which will be the required half-scale figure.

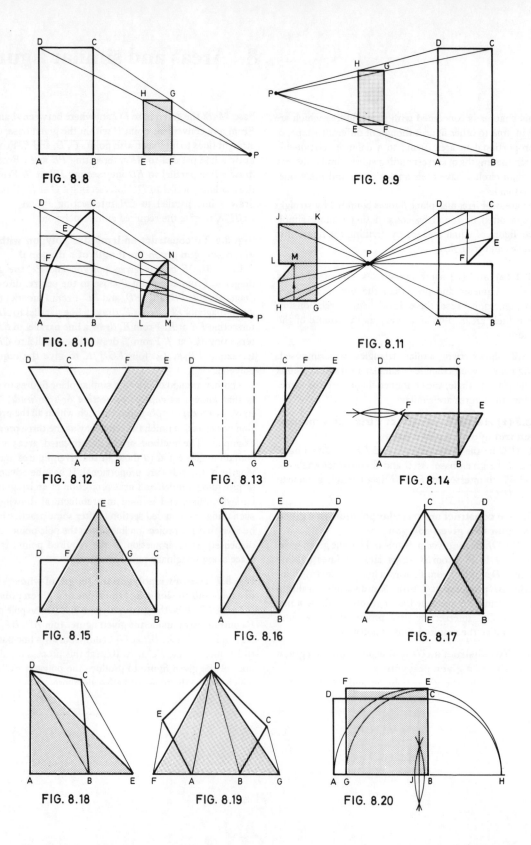

FIG. 8.8

FIG. 8.9

FIG. 8.10

FIG. 8.11

FIG. 8.12

FIG. 8.13

FIG. 8.14

FIG. 8.15

FIG. 8.16

FIG. 8.17

FIG. 8.18

FIG. 8.19

FIG. 8.20

8. Areas and similar figures

Figs 8.8 and 8.9 To draw a rectangle the length of whose sides are one-half the length of the sides of a given rectangle

Draw *ABCD* the given rectangle. Locate point *P* some distance outside the given rectangle and join *P* to the four corners. Bisect *AP* at *E* and construct the required half-scale figure in the manner previously described.

Fig. 8.10 To produce a half-scale drawing of a given section

Let *ABC* be the given curved section. Enclose it in a rectangle *ABCD* and, at any convenient points on the curve locate *E* and *F* (more points can be used where greater accuracy is required). Locate point *P* on the base *AB* produced. Bisect *BP* at *M*. Construct the half-scale rectangle *LMNO*. Draw radial lines from *P* through *E* and *F*. Produce horizontals through *E* and *F*. Project from *P* and locate the horizontals on the half-scale rectangle. The intersection of these horizontals and the radials from *P* to *E* and *F* will give the two points on the curve. Join *LMN*, the required half-scale section.

Fig. 8.11 shows a method of drawing a figure to scale and inverting it, by placing the pole point between the two figures. The scale effect is produced by drawing the radial projection lines from *P*, to left and right, in the proportions required. To locate *F* on the scale diagram it is necessary to project vertically upwards to meet the perimeter of the figure, project through *P* on to the base line of the smaller figure, then project vertically upwards to intersect, at *M*, a horizontal projector from *F*.

Fig. 8.12 To construct a parallelogram having the same area as a given parallelogram

Let *ABCD* be the given parallelogram. Extend *DC* and, on the same base *AB*, construct between the same parallels the parallelogram *ABEF* which will have an area equal to the given figure.

Fig. 8.13 To construct a parallelogram having an area one-third of a given rectangle

Draw the given rectangle *ABCD* and divide it into three equal parts. On a base of one of these equal divisions *GB*, construct the parallelogram *GBEF* which will be a third the area of the rectangle.

Fig. 8.14 To construct on the same base a parallelogram having half the area of a given rectangle

Draw the given rectangle *ABCD* and erect a perpendicular bisector on *AD*. Mark off *FE* equal to *AB*. *ANEF* is a parallelogram having half the area of the rectangle.

Fig. 8.15 To construct on the same base a triangle equal in area to a given rectangle

Draw the given rectangle *ABCD*. On *AB* erect a triangle whose altitude is twice that of the rectangle. Triangle *ABE* is the required figure. The sum of the areas of the triangles *AFD* and *BCG* is equal to the area of the triangle *EFG*.

Fig. 8.16 To construct on the same base a parallelogram having twice the area of a given triangle

Draw the given triangle *ABC*. Draw *CD* parallel to *AB*. Draw the diagonal line *AE* and draw *BD* parallel to it. *ABDE* is the required parallelogram.

Note that a rectangle *ABEC* would also contain twice the area of the given triangle.

Fig. 8.17 To construct between the same parallels a triangle having half the area of a given triangle

Draw the given triangle *ABC* and draw a line from *C* parallel to *AB*. Bisect *AB* at *E*. Erect a perpendicular at *B* to give *D*. *EBD* is the required triangle.

Fig. 8.18 To construct a triangle equal in area to a given quadrilateral

Draw the given quadrilateral *ABCD*. Draw the diagonal *BD*. From *C* draw a line parallel to *BD* to intersect *AB* produced at *E*. Join *DE* to give the required triangle *AED*.

Fig. 8.19 To construct a triangle equal in area to a given polygon

Draw the given polygon *ABCDE*. Join *DA* and *DB*. From *C* and *E* draw lines parallel to *DB* and *DA* respectively, to intersect *AB* produced at *G* and *F*. Triangle *FGD* is the required triangle, equal in area to the polygon.

Fig. 8.20 To construct a square equal in area to a given rectangle

Draw the given rectangle *ABCD*. With *B* as centre, radius *BC*, draw an arc to cut *AB* produced at *H*. Bisect *AH* at *J* and, with *J* as centre, radius *JH*, draw a semicircle, cutting *BC* produced at *E*. With *B* as centre, radius *BE*, draw an arc cutting *AB* at *G*. Erect a perpendicular at *G* to intersect at *F* a line from *E* drawn parallel to the base. Join *GBEF*, the required square.

8. Areas and similar figures

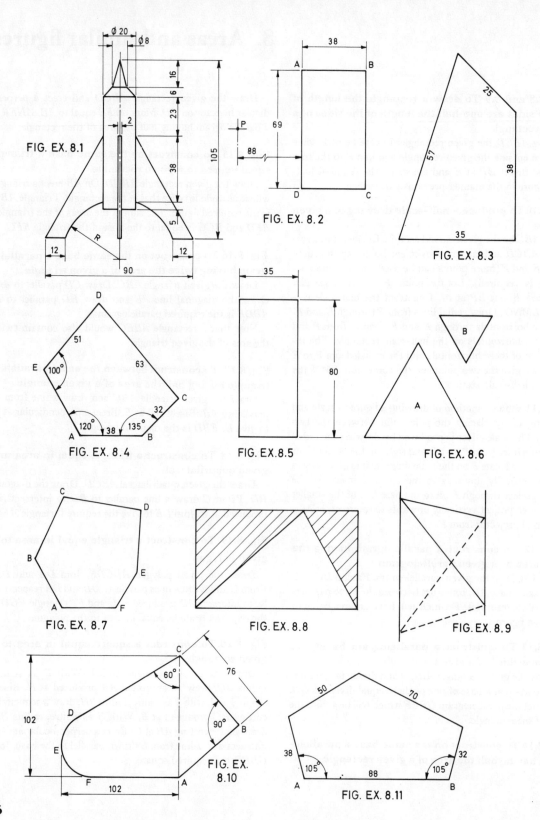

Ø 20

Ø 8

16

6

23

2

105

38

5

FIG. EX. 8.1

R

12   90   12

38

A   B

69

D   C

FIG. EX. 8.2

P

88

25

57

38

35

FIG. EX. 8.3

D

51

E 100°   63

C

120°   32

A   38   135°   B

FIG. EX. 8.4

35

80

FIG. EX. 8.5

B

A

FIG. EX. 8.6

C

B   D

E

A   F

FIG. EX. 8.7

FIG. EX. 8.8

FIG. EX. 8.9

C

60°   76

D   90°

102   B

E

F   102   A

FIG. EX. 8.10

50   70

38   32

105°   88   105°

A   B

FIG. EX. 8.11

8. Areas and similar figures

Exercises for Chapter 8

1. Draw a 60°–30° triangle ABC on a base AB of 12 cm. Construct a similar triangle DEF on a base DE of 9·5 cm.

2. Draw an irregular polygon $ABCDE$ in which AB is horizontal and measures 35 mm, BC is inclined at 135° to AB and measures 30 mm, CD is at 75° to BC and measures 65 mm and DE is at 90° to CD and measures 33 mm. On a new base line of 52 mm construct a similar polygon.

3. An irregular polygon $ABCD$ stands on a horizontal base AB which is 40 mm long. AD is at 90° to AB and is 35 mm long. BC is 25 mm in length and CD is 59 mm long. Draw the polygon and construct another figure having twice the area of the given polygon.

4. Draw a rectangle $ABCD$ having sides of length 70 mm and 38 mm. Place a point P in space 87 mm from one of the sides. Use this point to construct a similar figure whose sides are reduced in length in the ratio of 3 : 5.

5. A rectangle $ABCD$ has dimensions of 5 cm and 5·8 cm. Construct a rectangle having one-third the area of the given rectangle.

6. A rectangle has the dimensions 7 cm by 5 cm. Construct a parallelogram having the area of the rectangle.

7. An equilateral triangle has a side length of 70 mm. Draw the triangle and construct a rectangle on the same base having an equal areal.

8. Draw an equilateral triangle having a side length of 8 cm. Construct another triangle having half the area of the equilateral triangle.

9. An irregular polygon $ABCDE$ stands on a base AB 3 cm long. AE and BC are both inclined at 120° to AB and each measures 3·8 cm and 3·2 cm respectively. CD is 4·5 cm long and DE is 4 cm long. Draw the polygon and construct a triangle having the same area.

10. Draw a rectangle 60 mm by 40 mm and construct a square of equal area.

11. Draw any triangle ABC and construct a square of equal area.

12. Draw a regular pentagon of side 5·5 cm. Construct a similar pentagon having an area in the ratio of 7 : 4.

13. Draw any suitable triangle and construct, on the same base, another triangle which has five-ninths the area of the first one.

14. Draw a circle 60 mm in diameter and construct a square which has the same area.

15. Redraw the rocket shown in **Fig. Ex. 8.1**, making the overall height 140 mm and increasing all other dimensions proportionally. *(CSE)*

16. By the use of radial lines from the point 'P', draw a similar figure to that shown in **Fig. Ex. 8.2** with the sides reduced in the ratio of 3 : 5. *(CSE)*

17. Draw another figure having twice the area of the figure in **Fig. Ex. 8.3**. *(CSE)*

18. Convert the irregular pentagon in **Fig. Ex. 8.4** to a triangle of equal area. *(CSE)*

19. Change the rectangle in **Fig. Ex. 8.5** into a square of equal area. *(CSE)*

20. **Fig. Ex. 8.6** shows two equilateral triangles A and B. The side length of A being *64* mm and that of B 32 mm. Construct an equilateral triangle having an area equal to the difference in area between triangle A and B. *(CSE)*

21. Draw a similar polygon to that shown in **Fig. Ex. 8.7** but having an area of one-third of that shown in the figure. $AB = 32$ mm, $BC = 38$ mm, $CD = 51$ mm, $DE = 32$ mm, $EF = 25$ mm, $FA = 32$ mm (horizontal). $AC = 60$ mm, $AD = 73$ mm, $AE = 51$ mm. *(Camb.)*

22. What is the relationship between the area of the triangle and the shaded area of the rectangle in **Fig. Ex. 8.8**? *(CSE)*

23. **Fig. Ex. 8.9** shows two triangles lying between parallel lines. Is the area of the dotted triangle (a) less than, (b) equal to, (c) greater than the area of the other triangle? *(CSE)*

24. The plan of a lamina is shown in **Fig. Ex. 8.10**. Construct the view, then measure and state the radius of the circular arc.

    By a geometrical construction determine the length of that side corresponding to AB in a figure similar to, but having an area three-fifths of that of $ABCDEF$. *(Camb.)*

25. Draw the figure shown in **Fig. Ex. 8.11**. Using AB as a base line, reduce this figure to a similar figure with sides in the ratio of 5 : 3. *(CSE)*

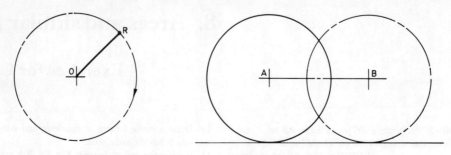

FIG. 9.1 LOCUS OF A POINT   FIG. 9.2 LOCUS OF A CENTRE

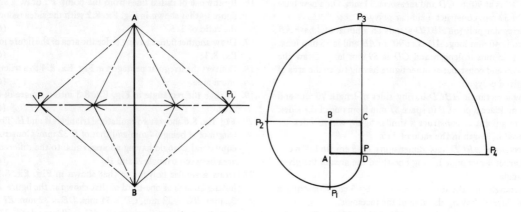

FIG. 9.3 LOCUS OF A POINT   FIG. 9.4 INVOLUTE OF A SQUARE

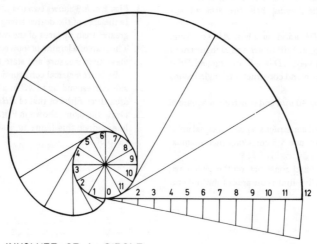

FIG. 9.5 INVOLUTE OF A CIRCLE

The *locus* of a point is the path traced by that point when moving in accordance with a given law.

In **Fig. 9.1** the arm *OR* is free to rotate about *O*, a fixed point, such that *R* is always the same distance from *O*. The locus of the point *R* is a circle.

Fig. 9.2 shows a circle resting on a horizontal line. The circle is free to move from position *A* to position *B* such that the centre is a constant distance from the horizontal line. The locus of the centre is the line *AB*.

Fig. 9.3 To draw the locus of a point *P* which moves such that it is always equisdistant from two given points *A* and *B*

Draw *AB* any convenient length. With alternate centres of *A* and *B* and radius more than half *AB*, draw arcs either side of *AB*. Joining the intersections of these arcs will give the locus of *P* required. It will be noted that the line PP_1 is the bisector of *AB*.

Fig. 9.4 To draw the locus of a point *P* lying on the perimeter of a given square which unwinds itself from the perimeter on the end of an imaginary taut line

Draw the square *ABCD*. With centre *A*, radius *AP*, draw an arc terminating at *BA* produced in P_1. With *B* as centre, radius BP_1, draw an arc terminating at *CB* produced in P_2.

With *C* as centre, radius CP_2, draw an arc terminating at *DC* produced in P_3. With *D* as centre, radius DP_3, draw an arc terminating at *AD* produced in P_4. The curve is an *involute* curve.

Fig. 9.5 To draw the locus of a point *P* lying on the circumference of a given circle which unwinds itself from the circumference on the end of an imaginary taut line

Draw the given circle and divide into any number of equal parts. Number as shown and from 0 draw a tangent equal in length to the circumference of the circle ($\pi \times D$). Divide this line into the same number of equal parts as the circle, and number.

Draw tangents from each point on the circle in the same direction as the first tangent. With station 1 on the circle as centre, radius 01 on the tangent, draw an arc to intersect the tangent from 1. With station 2 on the circle as centre, radius 02 on the tangent, draw an arc to intersect the tangent from 2. Continue this process around the circle, ending at the first drawn tangent. A smooth curve joining these points will be the locus of point *P* and is called the *involute of a circle*.

As the name implies, the value of an involute curve is to be found in the formation of involute gear teeth.

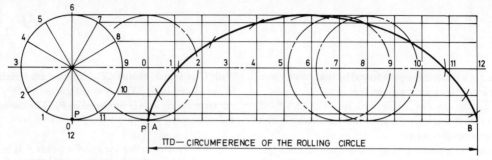

FIG. 9.6   A CYCLOID

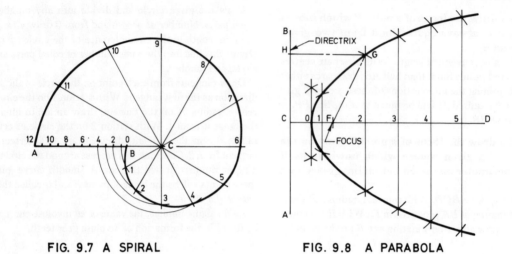

FIG. 9.7 A SPIRAL

FIG. 9.8   A PARABOLA

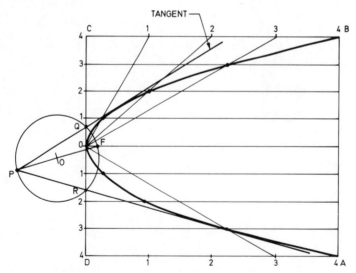

FIG. 9.9   A PARABOLA SHOWING TANGENT CONSTRUCTION

Fig. 9.6 To draw the locus of a point on a given circle which rolls uniformly along a given straight line

Draw the given circle and divide it into a convenient number of equal parts and number as shown. Mark on its circumference a point P. Draw the given straight line AB tangential to the lowest part of the circle and equal in length to the circumference of the circle. Divide AB into the same number of equal parts as the circle, numbering the parts as shown, and drawing vertical lines from these points extending a distance equal to the diameter of the circle.

From the numbered divisions around the circle project lines parallel to AB. The projected centre line is the locus of the centre of the circle as it rolls along AB.

With centre 1 on the horizontal centre line, radius equal to the radius of the circle, draw an arc to intersect the horizontal projector of point 1 on the circumference of the circle. With centre 2 on the centre line, the same radius, draw an arc to intersect the horizontal projector of point 2 on the circumference of the circle. Repeat this process for points 3, 4, 5, 6, etc. A smooth curve drawn through the points of intersection will produce the required locus of point P, that is, a *cycloid*.

To verify this construction, draw the rolling circle on a piece of transparent paper, marking the point P on its circumference. Place the centre of the circle on each of the numbered divisions on the horizontal centre line in turn, rotating the circle in a clockwise direction. The point P will be seen to be in contact with the cycloid as it travels from A to B.

Fig. 9.7 To draw the locus of a point which moves uniformly along a given line, the line rotating uniformly about a given fixed point

Let C be the given fixed point and AB the given line. From C draw twelve equally divided radial lines numbered 0 to 12. Divide the line AB into a similar number of equal parts for one revolution of the line. With centre C, radius $C1$, draw an arc to intersect radial line 1. With radius $C2$ and the same centre, draw an arc to intersect radial line 2,

..., etc. The intersection of 0 12 with AB indicates that the line has rotated through 360°. A smooth curve drawn through all the intersections will give the required locus of point B as it moves towards A in one complete revolution. The curve is called an *Archimedean spiral*.

Fig. 9.8 To draw the locus of a point which moves such that its distance from a given fixed point (the focus) is equal to its perpendicular distance from a given straight line (the directrix)

Draw the given straight line AB. Bisect and erect a perpendicular CD. Locate the focus F on CD and bisect CF at O. From O, along CD, draw any convenient number of dividing lines parallel to AB, numbering them as shown. With centre F, radius $C1$, draw arcs to cut the vertical dividing line 1 above and below CD. With centre F, radius C, draw arcs to cut vertical line 2, ..., etc. A smooth curve drawn through the points obtained will produce the required locus, which is a *parabola*. It will be seen that distance FG equals the distance HG.

Fig. 9.9 To construct a parabola within a given rectangle

Draw the given rectangle $ABCD$ any convenient size. Bisect CD at 0 and divide 0 to C and 0 to D into a number of equal parts. Erect perpendiculars. Divide AD and BC into the same number of equal parts as $0C$ and $0D$, numbering as shown. Join the divisions on AD and BC to point 0. The intersections of these radial lines with the perpendiculars on CD will produce points through which a smooth, parabolic curve can be drawn.

To produce tangents to a given parabola from a given external point

Let P be the given external point. Join P to the focus F and bisect FP at O. With O as centre draw a circle through F and P. The line CD acts as a principal vertex cutting the circle at Q and R. Straight lines through PQ and PR are the required tangents.

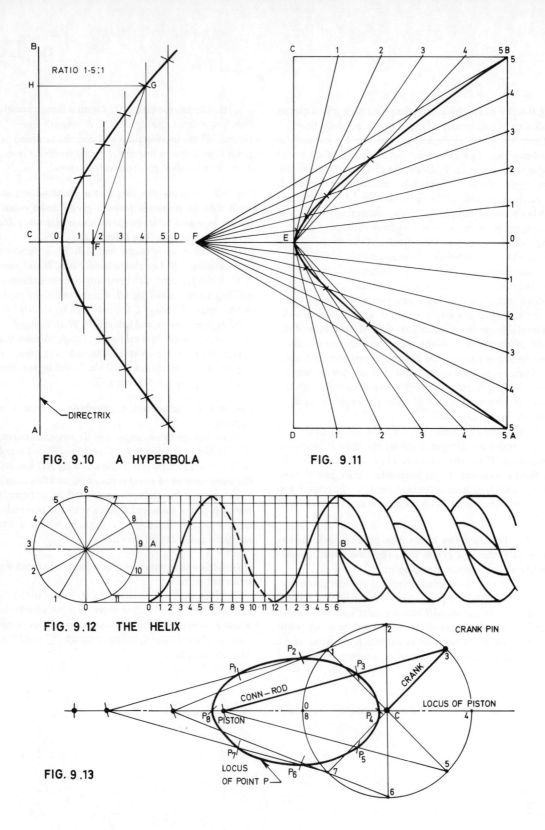

RATIO 1·5:1

H   G

C   0   1   2   3   4   5   D

F

DIRECTRIX

A

FIG. 9.10   A HYPERBOLA

C   1   2   3   4   5 B

E

D   1   2   3   4   5 A

FIG. 9.11

FIG. 9.12   THE HELIX

CRANK PIN

P_1 P_2 P_3

CONN–ROD   CRANK

LOCUS OF PISTON

P_8 PISTON   0   8 P_4 C

P_7 P_5

P_6 7

LOCUS OF POINT P

FIG. 9.13

42

9. Loci

A *hyperbola* may be defined as the locus of a point moving in a plane such that its distance from a fixed point, called the *focus*, is a constant ratio of its perpendicular distance from a given straight line called the *directrix; the ratio being greater than unity.*

Fig. 9.10 To plot the path of a point which moves such that its distance from a fixed point (focus) is a fixed ratio of its perpendicular distance from a given straight line (directrix). The ratio is greater than unity

Draw the given straight line *AB*. Bisect and erect a perpendicular *CD*. Locate the focus *F* on *CD*. Divide *CF* at 0 in the required ratio. From 0, along *CD* draw any number of convenient dividing lines parallel to *AB*, and number as shown. With centre *F*, radius *C1* multiplied by the ratio, draw arcs to cut division line 1. With centre *F*, radius *C2* multiplied by the ratio, draw arcs to cut division line 2, . . ., etc. Joining the intersections of division lines and arcs will produce a smooth curve called a *hyperbola*. Distance *FX* is in the fixed ratio of the perpendicular distance *XY*. (In the diagram *FG* is to *GH* as 1·5 is to 1.)

Fig. 9.11 To construct a hyperbola within a given rectangle, given the diameter *EF*

Draw the given rectangle *ABCD*. Bisect *AB at O* and erect a perpendicular *OF* (*OE* is called the *abscissa and EF* the *diameter*). Divide *AO, OB, AD,* and *BC* into the same number of equal parts, number as shown. Join the points on *AB* to *F* and the points on *AD* and *BC* to *E*. Intersection of these radial lines produces a series of points through which a smooth, hyperbolic curve can be drawn.

A *helix* is the locus of a point generated on the surface of a revolving cylinder as the point moves along a straight line parallel with the longitudinal centre line of the cylinder. The point thus wraps itself around the cylinder as it moves in a straight line along its surface.

Screw threads, coil springs and twist drills are examples of the application of helix construction. These will be dealt with more fully later in this book.

Fig. 9.12 To plot the path of a point moving horizontally along the surface of a rotating cylinder the longitudinal centre line of which is horizontal

Assume clockwise rotation of the cylinder and the point moving from *A* to *B*. Draw the centre line *AB* any convenient length. With *B* as centre, radius equal to the radius of the cylinder, draw a circle and divide it into twelve equal, numbered parts, as shown. Project the diameter of the semicircle towards *A* and complete a rectangle to represent the cylinder. Divide the rectangle into eighteen equal parts as 0, 1, 2, 3, . . . etc., and erect perpendiculars. Transfer the divisions of the circle horizontally across the rectangle. Commencing with 0, the intersections of the numbered divisions 0, 1, 2, 3, . . ., etc., vertically and horizontally, will give points through which a smooth helical curve may be drawn. It will be seen that in moving from 0 to 6 the point will have completed one-half a revolution of the cylinder; therefore, from 6 to 12 the line will be hidden and is shown dotted. The distance 0 to 12 is one complete revolution of the cylinder and is called a *pitch*.

Other valuable locus problems are those involving machines in which links play a part. It is sometimes necessary to know where a particular point on a link or rod is at given moment in the cycle of the machine, either to enable the designer to clear possible obstructions or to give precise data for the efficient operation of the machine (e.g. the tool movement on a shaping machine imparted by a quick-return motion).

Fig. 9.13 shows the locus of a point on an engine connecting rod.

With centre *C*, radius equal to crank length, draw a circle (locus of crank pin). Divide the circle into any number of convenient parts and number as shown. Extend the horizontal centre line (locus of the piston) and, from each crank-pin position, draw arcs equal in length to the length of the connecting rod, to intersect the centre line. Join crank-pin positions to corresponding piston positions and mark off points P_1, P_2, P_3, . . . etc., the required points on the connecting rod through which an elliptical curve may be drawn.

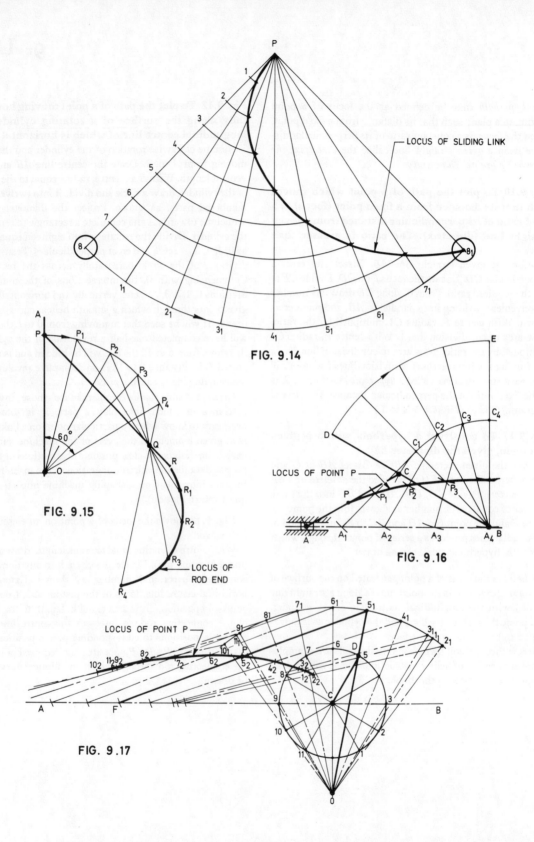

P

1
2
3
4
5
6
7
8

LOCUS OF SLIDING LINK

8₁

1₁
2₁
3₁
4₁
5₁
6₁
7₁

FIG. 9.14

A

P
P₁
P₂
P₃
P₄

60°

O

Q

R
R₁
R₂
R₃
R₄

LOCUS OF ROD END

FIG. 9.15

D

C₁
C₂
C₃
C₄

E

LOCUS OF POINT P

P
P₁
P₂
P₃

C

A   A₁   A₂   A₃   A₄   B

FIG. 9.16

LOCUS OF POINT P

7₁ 6₁ E 5₁
8₁
9₁   4₁
10₁ P   3₁ 1₁ 2₁
11 9₂ 8₂ 7₂ 6₂ 5₂ 7 6 D 5 4₁
10₂   4₂ 3₂
                        8 12 2₂
A   F   9   C   B
                    10   2
                    11   1
                        0

FIG. 9.17

44

Fig. 9.14 shows a pendulum pivoted at P which is free to swing through a given arc. During the time of the swing a block moves downwards from P, reaching point 8 at the end of the swing. It is required to plot the locus of the block.

With P as centre draw the given arc 8 8_1 and divide this into a convenient number of equal parts such as 1_1, 2_1, 3_1, etc. Join these points to the pivot point P. Divide $P8$ into the same number of equal parts numbering them 1, 2, 3, etc., commencing at P. With P as centre, radii successively $P1$, $P2$, $P3$, etc., draw arcs to intersect the radial lines $P1_1$, $P2_1$, $P3_1$, etc. A smooth curve drawn through the points obtained will produce the required locus.

Fig. 9.15 is a link mechanism in which an arm OA is pivoted at O and the arm moves through an angle of 60°. A rod PR is pivoted at P and passes through a fixed, swivelling block Q. It is required to draw the locus of the rod end during the the 60° movement of OA.

With centre O, radius OP draw an arc which subtends an angle of 60° from O. Divide the arc into a convenient number of parts and number them as shown. Join centre O to P_1, P_2, P_3, etc. Through each of these points successively, draw lines passing through Q that are equal in length to the rod PR. A smooth curve drawn through the points R_1, R_2, R_3, etc., will produce required locus.

Fig. 9.16 shows a link mechanism in which an arm BD, pivoted at B, moves through an angle of 60°. A connecting rod AC is pivoted at C and has attached at A a slider which is constrained to move horizontally along a line passing through B. It is required to draw the locus of a point P on the connecting rod midway between A and C.

With centre B, radius BD, draw an arc which subtends an angle of 60° from B. With centre B, radius BC draw an arc through the same angle. Divide the subtended angle into a number of equal parts and number as shown along the locus of C. Join centre B to C_1, C_2, C_3, etc.

With each of these points in turn as centres, radius CA, draw arcs to intersect AB at A_1, A_2, A_3, etc. Join these points. With centres marked C_1, C_2, etc. in turn, radius CP, draw arcs to intersect C_1, A_1, C_2, A_2, etc., at P_1, P_2, etc. A smooth curve drawn from P through P_1, P_2, etc. will give the locus of the point P.

Fig. 9.17 shows a diagram of a mechanism similar to that employed on a shaping machine. An arm OE oscillates about O. A crank CD rotates about C and is pivoted on the arm OE at D. A connecting rod EF is pivoted at E and constrained to slide horizontally along the line AB. It is required to find the locus of a point P situated on the connecting rod EF. Divide the circle swept out by CD into a number of equal parts, numbering as shown. With O as centre, radius OE, draw an arc. From O draw radial lines passing through the points on the circle swept out by CD which will also divide the arc through E into a number of equal parts. Number these division 1_1, 2_1, 3_1, etc., as shown. With each of these points in turn as centres, radius EF, mark the respective positions of F on the line AB. Join these points. Using the same successive centres as before, radius EP, draw arcs to intersect the lines representing EF and produce points 1_2, 2_2, 3_2, etc. A smooth curve from P through these points will produce the required locus.

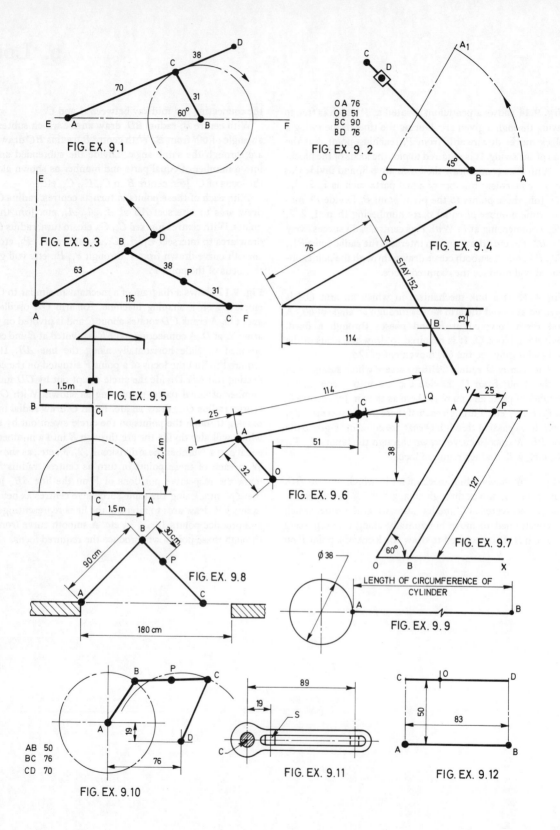

FIG. EX. 9.1

FIG. EX. 9.2

O A 76
O B 51
B C 90
B D 76

FIG. EX. 9.3

FIG. EX. 9.4

STAY 152

FIG. EX. 9.5

FIG. EX. 9.6

FIG. EX. 9.7

LENGTH OF CIRCUMFERENCE OF
CYLINDER

∅ 38

FIG. EX. 9.9

FIG. EX. 9.8

AB 50
BC 76
CD 70

FIG. EX. 9.10

FIG. EX. 9.11

FIG. EX. 9.12

Exercises for Chapter 9

1. A point moves in a plane in such a way that its distance from a fixed point is equal to its shortest distance from a fixed straight line.

   Plot the locus of the moving point when the fixed point is 44 mm from the fixed line. The maximum distance of the moving point is 127 mm from the fixed point. State the name of the locus, the fixed point, and the fixed line. *(AEB)*

2. A wheel of 70 mm diameter rolls without slipping along a straight path.
   (a) Plot the locus of a point *P*, on the rim of the wheel and initially in contact with the path, when the wheel makes half a revolution along the path.
   (b) Construct the normal, tangent, and centre of curvature at the position reached by point *P* after one quarter of a revolution of the wheel along the path. *(Camb.)*

3. Draw a part of the involute of a circle of 44 mm diameter, stopping the involute at *P* which is a point 86 mm distant from the centre of the circle. Construct also the tangent to the involute at *P*. *(Camb.)*

4. **Fig. Ex. 9.1** shows a link mechanism. *AD* and *CB* are links pinned together at *C*. The pivoted joint *B* allows the link *BC* to travel along the line *EF*. Plot the locus of *D* for one revolution of link *BC* *(CSE)*

5. **Fig. Ex. 9.2** shows that the rod *OA* rotates about *O* to OA_1. Rod *BC* is pin joined at *B* and is free to slide through the fixed pivot block *D*. Trace the locus of *C* as *OA* moves to the position OA_1. *(CSE)*

6. **Fig. Ex. 9.3** shows a link mechanism. Points *A* and *B* are pivoted. *C* slides along *AF*. Rotate *D* to *E*, trace the locus of point *P*. *(CSE)*

7. **Fig. Ex. 9.4** shows a 152 mm desk-stay fitted to a box. The stay is fixed to the lid at *A*, about which it is free to pivot, but always passes through a sleeve at point *B*. Plot the path traced out by end *C* of the stay as the lid moves from the closed position to its fully opened position. Indicate the position of the lid when fully opened. *(CSE)*

8. A sketch of a jib crane is shown in **Fig. Ex. 9.5**. The end of the crane jib *A* moves in a semicircular arc in the direction shown. During the time taken for the jib to travel 180° the crane moves along a track *CC* to deposit the load at *B*. Both motions are uniform. Draw, on the plan only, the locus of the tip of the jib *A*. Scale 1 cm represents 2·5 m. Dimensions shown are in metres. *(CSE)*

9. A mechanism is shown diagrammatically in **Fig. Ex. 9.6**. The rod *PQ* is connected to a pin joint at *A* whilst it is free to slide and oscillate in the rotatable support at *C*. The pin joint at *A* is connected to one end of the crank *OA* which rotates about *O*. Plot the loci of *P* and *Q* for one revolution of the crank *OA*. *(Camb.)*

10. A point *P* moves in a plane containing the axes *OX* and *OY*, shown in **Fig. Ex. 9.7**, in such a way that the products of the distances corresponding to *PA* and *PB* are constant. Draw the locus of *P* as it moves between the position shown and a point 152 mm from *OY*. *(Camb.)*

11. The plan of a folding door *ABC*, shown partly open, is given in outline in **Fig. Ex. 9.8**. The door is hinged to the wall at *A*, folds at *B*, and travels in a straight track at *C* to the closed distance of 180 cm. In the fully open position the door folds flat against the wall.

    Draw, to a scale of 1 cm represents 10 cm, the locus of *P* for one complete opening movement of the door. *(AEB)*

12. **Fig. Ex. 9.9** shows a string *AB* being equal to the length of the circumference of the cylinder. Calculate length *AB* and plot the path of the end *B* as the string is kept taut and wound clockwise on the cylinder. *(AEB)*

13. The mechanism, shown in **Fig. Ex. 9.10**, consists of a crank *AB* which rotates about centre *A*, an arm *CD* which oscillates about centre *D* and a link *BC* which connects the crank and the arm. Plot the locus traced out by the mid-point *P* of link *BC* for one complete revolution of crank *AB*. *(AEB)*

14. **Fig. Ex. 9.11** indicates a slotted lever mounted on a shaft, centre *C*, and carrying a slider *S*. The lever makes one revolution clockwise at constant speed about *C* while the slider moves with constant speed from its minimum position from the shaft to its maximum position. Plot, full size, the path traced out by *S*. *(AEB)*

15. **Fig. Ex. 9.12** shows two parallel lines *AB* and *CD* which are 50 mm apart. Plot the locus of a point *E* passing through *O* on line *CD* such that the distance of *E* from *A* and *B* respectively is in the ratio of 3 : 2 for all positions of the point *E*.

    The locus, which is the arc of a circle, is to extend approximately 50 mm on either side of point *O*. Find and state its radius. *(Camb.)*

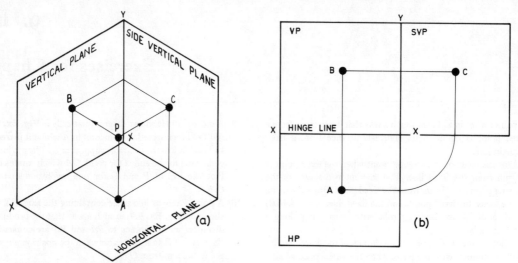

FIG. 10.1   PROJECTIONS OF A POINT IN SPACE

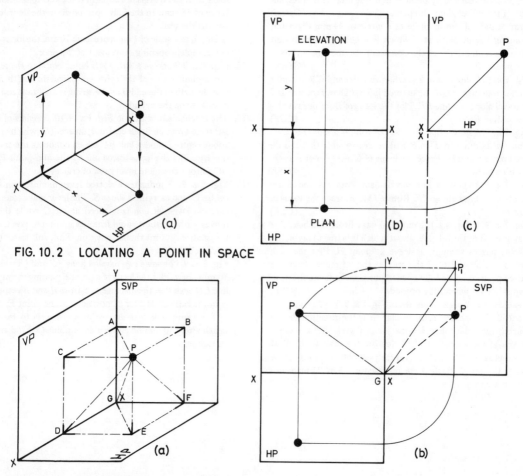

FIG. 10.2   LOCATING A POINT IN SPACE

FIG. 10.3   ANALYSIS OF A POINT IN SPACE

The principal planes of projection are the vertical plane or VP and the horizontal plane or HP. These are arranged so that they intersect at right angles to one another and divide space into four quadrants.

The planes extend in all directions to infinity—but for drawing purposes and to assist in understanding the related theory they are usually shown as having boundaries. The planes should be considered as thin sheets of transparent material hinged along the lines of intersection so that they can be opened out to form a flat sheet.

Consider **Fig. 10.1 (a)** which shows a point P lying in space between three coordinate planes, namely the vertical plane, the horizontal plane, and a side vertical plane. Lines parallel to these planes project from the point as shown by the arrows. Each projection line should be imagined as a line of sight. It will be seen that where these projection lines intersect with a plane, an image of the point appears in that plane. This image is a true picture of what is seen when viewing the point along the line of sight.

In order to locate the point in any one plane, more than one projection is required. For example, location of the point in the VP and SVP first requires a projection vertically downwards into the HP. Having fixed the position of the point in the HP, projections parallel to the VP and the SVP, turning at right angles at the hinge lines of the planes, will intersect in those planes with the arrowed projection lines from the point in space. These intersections define the positions of the point in the VP and the SVP.

The lines PA, PB, and PC are called the *rectangular coordinates of the point P*.

In **Fig. 10.1 (b)** the planes are opened out along their hinge lines XX and XY to form a flat sheet divided into three parts. The position of the projected point in each division is recorded. Points B and C are the elevations located in the vertical planes, while point A is a plan located in the horizontal plane.

Fig. 10.2 (a) uses only the two principal planes but in this case the projections of the point in space are dimensioned to give accurate location.

Fig. 10.2 (b) shows the plan and elevation of the point P.

A continued projection in **Fig. 10.2 (c)** determines the diagonal distance of the point P from the hinge line XX. In this diagram the principal planes are viewed edge-on. The point P is located dimensionally between the VP and the HP and a diagonal is drawn from the point to the hinge line XX.

Fig. 10.3 (a) shows a point P suspended in space between three planes. Projections from P into the planes produces the box $PABCDEFG$. Diagonals are drawn from P to B, P to D, P to F, P to G, and E to G. As in Fig. 10.1 (a), it will be seen that the point P lies in a corner of the box and all the lines drawn bold indicate right angles. It is also of interest to note that $PBGE$ forms a plane called an *auxiliary plane*.

Fig. 10.3 (b) shows the principal planes opened out along the hinge lines and the point P located in each of the three divisions representing these planes.

When it is necessary to determine the diagonal distance of point P from the hinge line XX and also the corner point G, the following procedure is adopted.

Join P to G (as shown by the long dash line) and measure directly to give the diagonal distance from P to XX. With G as centre and GP in the VP as radius, draw an arc to intersect with a vertical projector from P in the SVP at P_1. The length of P_1G is the diagonal distance of P from corner point G.

The *projections* of a straight line suspended in space between principal planes, are the lines drawn as plans and elevations which join points projected from the ends of the line on to the principal planes.

The *traces* of the straight line are the points at which the line intersects the VP and HP, the line being produced beyond its ends if necessary. The point of intersection in the VP gives the *vertical trace* (VT) and the point of intersection in the HP gives the *horizontal trace* (HT).

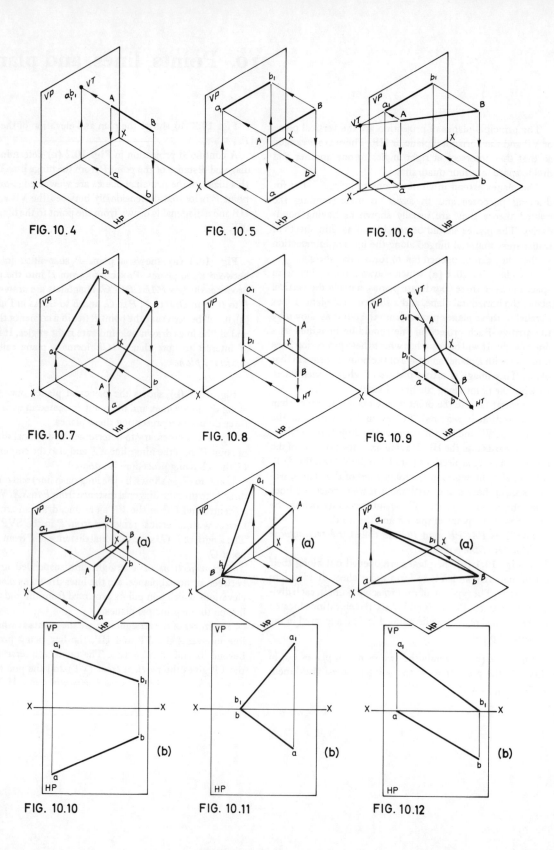

FIG. 10.4

FIG. 10.5

FIG. 10.6

FIG. 10.7

FIG. 10.8

FIG. 10.9

FIG. 10.10

FIG. 10.11

FIG. 10.12

10. Points, lines, and planes

Fig. 10.4 shows a straight line *AB* suspended in the first quadrant, lying above and parallel to the HP and at right angles to the VP. The projections of the ends of the line in the principal planes are given by *ab* and a_1b_1 which is also the vertical trace produced as a point. There is no horizontal trace because the line does not intersect with a horizontal plane.

Note the method of projection of the line and its trace in the HP to produce the trace in the VP.

Fig. 10.5 shows a straight line *AB* suspended in the first quadrant, lying above the HP and parallel to both principal planes. The projections of the ends of the line in the principal planes are given by *ab* and a_1b_1. Because the line does not intersect with either plane there are no traces.

Fig. 10.6 shows a straight line *AB* suspended in the first quadrant, lying above and parallel to the HP, and at an angle to the VP. The projections of the ends of the line in the principal planes are given by *ab* and a_1b_1. There is no HT, but producing the ends of the line to intersect in the VP gives the VT as a point.

Fig. 10.7 shows a straight line *AB* suspended in the first quadrant, lying above and inclined to the HP and parallel to the VP. The projections of the ends of the line in the principal planes are given by *ab* and a_1b_1. There is no VT, but producing the ends of the line will give an HT external to the sketch and similar to the previous example.

Fig. 10.8 shows a straight line *AB* suspended in the first quadrant, lying parallel to the VP and above and at right angles to the HP. The projections of the ends of the line in the principal planes are given by *ab* and a_1b_1. There is no VT, but producing the ends of the line give the HT as a point.

Fig. 10.9 shows a straight line *AB* suspended in the first quadrant, lying above the HP and inclined to both planes. The projections of the ends of the line in the principal planes are given by *ab* and a_1b_1. Producing the ends of the line to intersect in both principal planes gives the VT and HT as points.

Fig. 10.10 (a) and (b) show a straight line *AB* lying above the HP and inclined to both the HP and VP. Projection of the ends of the line in the principal planes are given by *ab* and a_1b_1. The orthographic projections of the line are shown at (b).

Fig. 10.11 (a) and (b) show a straight line *AB* lying above the HP and inclined to both the HP and VP and with one end in the join line *XX* of the principal planes. Projection of the free end of the line in the HP and VP and the pivot end are given by *ab* and a_1b_1. The orthographic projections of the line are shown at (b).

Fig. 10.12 (a) and (b) show a straight line *AB* lying above the HP and inclined to both the HP and VP. One end is in the HP and the other in the VP. Projection of the ends of the line in the principal planes are given by *ab* and a_1b_1. The traces are at *A* and *B*. The orthographic projections of the line are shown at (b).

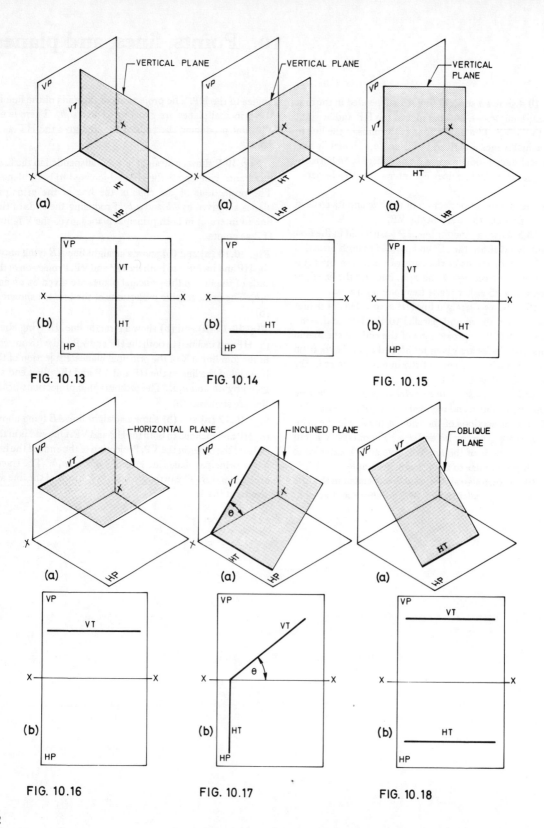

FIG. 10.13

FIG. 10.14

FIG. 10.15

FIG. 10.16

FIG. 10.17

FIG. 10.18

Planes, other than the principal planes of reference, can be used for projection purposes. They lie between the principal planes and are called auxiliary planes. Such planes are generally of three forms: *perpendicular, oblique*, and *inclined*. Perpendicular and inclined planes are perpendicular to either or both of the principal planes. Oblique planes are set an an angle to both the principal planes. The orthographic representation of an auxiliary plane lying between the principal planes is by lines defining the edges of contact of the planes.

Consider the principal planes as two flat rectangular pieces of any suitable material, such as cardboard, lying at 90° to one another. Apply a thin film of ink to the edges of a set square and press lightly into the right angle of the planes. The set square becomes an auxiliary plane, and on its removal inked lines will remain which will be the traces of the plane.

Fig. 10.13 (a) and **(b)** show a plane which is perpendicular to, and in contact with, the HP and VP. The orthographic views at (b) show the traces of the plane as the edge lines of contact and are labelled VT and HT.

Fig. 10.14 (a) and (b) show a plane which is perpendicular to the HP and parallel to the VP. There is a horizontal trace but no vertical trace, as shown at (b). This demonstrates that when a plane is parallel to one of the principal planes there will be no trace in that plane.

Fig. 10.15 (a) and **(b)** show a vertical plane which is perpendicular to the HP and inclined to the VP. The orthographic views at **(b)** show the traces and also that the angle of inclination of the plane to the VP is given by the angle between *XX* and the HT.

Fig. 10.16 (a) and **(b)** show a horizontal plane lying above and parallel to the HP and perpendicular to the VP. As one edge lies in the VP there is a VT but no HT. This is shown orthographically at (b).

Fig. 10.17 (a) and **(b)** show a plane inclined at an angle to the HP and perpendicular to the VP. An edge lies in each of the principal planes and these give the HT and the VT. The angle of inclination of the plane to the HP is given by the angle θ between the VT and *XX*. The orthographic projection is given at (b).

Fig. 10.18 (a) and **(b)** show an oblique plane, i.e. a plane inclined to both principal planes. The edges in contact with the HP and the VP give the HT and VT both of which are parallel to the hinge line *XX*. The traces are not true edge views when seen in orthographic projection because the full edges of the plane are not in contact with the principal planes.

In each of these examples, all of which are located in the first quadrant, the method of producing an orthographic projection from the pictorial drawing must be carefully studied. Problems set by examining boards do not provide the three-dimensional view. This means that students must be able to visualize the pictorial layout from the orthographic drawings printed on the question papers. When tackling problems of this nature, it is often helpful to make a pictorial sketch before making a serious attempt to find a solution. The extra time taken to draw the three-dimensional view can often be saved later because it is easier to read the drawing and it provides an easy route to the solution. When studying lines in particular, it must be remembered that the pictorial view usually contains three lines: the suspended line and its projections in the HP and VP. Traces are given by the intersection points of all three lines.

The orthographic drawing, on the other hand, contains only two lines, the elevation and plan. This is where the hinge line *XX* plays an important part. It is a turning point for all projection lines and provides a means of locating the traces.

There is a considerable difference in the methods of finding the traces of lines and planes. A line, having no thickness, can be extended indefinitely until its projection lies in a principal plane. Its trace will always be a point. A plane, on the other hand has height and width and its traces are edge lines often having angles formed between them which require projection and solution.

The understanding of the geometrical principles involved in the examples has important practical applications. Machine tool tables, and hence the cutting tools themselves, move in planes, and the geometry used to determine the angles at which the tools or the job must be set often involves lines and planes in space.

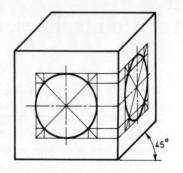

FIG. 11.1

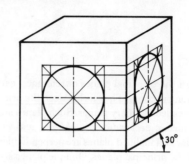

FIG. 11.2

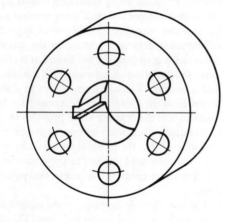

FIG. 11.3

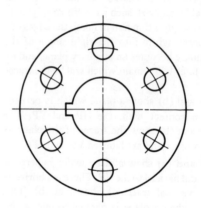

FIG. 11.4

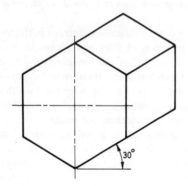

FIG. 11.5

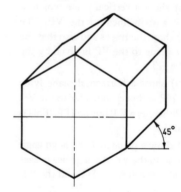

FIG. 11.6

11. Oblique projection

Pictorial projections are becoming increasingly used in modern drawing offices, not only to give an instant three-dimensional view of components and assemblies but also as fully dimensioned working drawings used for manufacture on the shop floor. In particular, working sketches can be produced in this way very quickly, especially when carried out on squared paper, such as isometric paper, specially prepared for the purpose.

Apart from perspective drawing, which is a form of pictorial presentation confined mainly to architectural and illustrative work, there are two important types of pictorial projection; *oblique projection* and *isometric projection*.

Of the two, oblique projection is the simpler because the drawing has as its basis a view looking directly on one face, i.e. a true elevation. To give the impression of three dimensions the lines representing depth recede from the elevation at a constant angle. The length of these receding lines may be true length of the object, or they can be reduced to lessen the distortion which is evident in this form of projection. When the receding lines are drawn one half full size (or one-half of the scale chosen for all the other measurements on the drawing), irrespective of the oblique angle used, the drawing is known as *cabinet projection*.

When the receding lines are drawn to the full scale used on the remainder of the drawing and the oblique lines are 45°, the drawing is known as *cavalier projection*.

The angle of the oblique axis can be any angle suited to the object, unless a particular type of projection, such as cavalier projection, is called for. Generally, however, the axis lines are confined to 45°, 30°, and 60° to the horizontal because these angles are readily available on the common set squares.

One big advantage of oblique projection is that curves and circles which appear on the front elevation can be drawn with compasses from their true centres, whereas with isometric projections special constructions must be made to enable compasses to be used and, in many cases, curves must be constructed using ordinate plotting of points through which freehand curves are drawn.

Figs 11.1 and 11.2 show oblique projections of a cube with circles on two faces. The depth lines are reduced to one-half true length. The circle is enclosed by a square which is divided into eight equal parts; the intersection of the circle and the diagonals is transferred vertically and horizontally to the square. These points are projected or transferred on to the sloping face to produce the ellipse.

Fig. 11.3 shows an oblique drawing of a half coupling and **Fig. 11.4** shows the end elevation alone. The effect of introducing relatively few additional lines to give a reasonable pictorial view of an object is clearly illustrated. The longitudinal axis of the coupling is drawn at 45°. The circle centres are therefore transferred along a 45° line to give the required plate thickness.

As will be seen in **Fig. 11.5** and **11.6**, where the same object is shown projected at 30° and 45°, care must be taken to ensure the correct choice of projection angle in order to achieve the maximum effect: 45° projection is obviously more suited to a hexagonal prism than a 30° projection, the amount of distortion being less in the former than in the latter.

This method of three-dimensional drawing is probably the most simple to adopt for freehand sketching. Students are advised to commence sketching simple features or components on squared paper, indicating depth along lines projected at 45° from the front face, as in oblique drawing. Gradually, as confidence in freehand drawing builds up, the squared paper may give way to cartridge paper.

Always commence a sketch by building a lightly lined framework into which the finished sketch will fit. There should be no need to erase the framework on completion, because the bolder, finished strokes will tend to 'fade' the lighter lines well into the background.

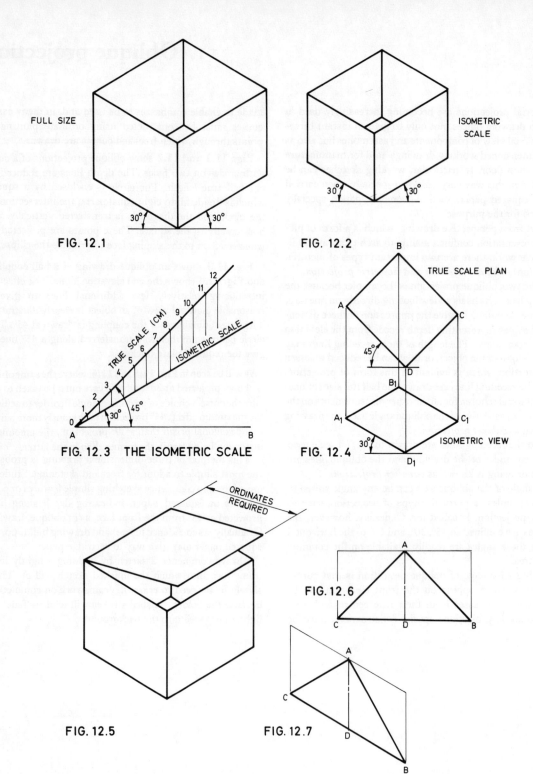

FULL SIZE

FIG. 12.1

ISOMETRIC SCALE

30°   30°

FIG. 12.2

TRUE SCALE (CM)

ISOMETRIC SCALE

12
11
10
9
8
7
6
5
4
3
2
1

30°   45°

0

A   B

FIG. 12.3   THE ISOMETRIC SCALE

TRUE SCALE PLAN

B

A   C

45°

D

B₁

A₁   C₁

30°

ISOMETRIC VIEW

D₁

FIG. 12.4

ORDINATES
REQUIRED

FIG. 12.5

FIG. 12.6

A

C   D   B

FIG. 12.7

A

C

D

B

56

Isometric projection can be considered as a special case of rotation of a figure. An edge is chosen to be directly in the line of sight and, although this edge is drawn vertically, it is in fact tilted towards the viewer on a point. This means that the line is foreshortened, i.e. it is not a true length. All lateral lines are at 30° to the horizontal and these too are foreshortened in the same way as the vertical lines.

Because the rotation of an object in isometric projection gives the same foreshortening to all the lines, any figure can be drawn to its true size or to a suitable linear scale. Although a drawing on the isometric axes to its full-size dimensions is often called an isometric projection, this is not strictly true because a correctly produced projection would have all its lengths reduced.

Fig. 12.1 shows an open box drawn full size on isometric axes.

Fig. 12.2 shows the same box drawn to isometric scale. The effect of using the scale is apparent.

It is not always necessary to use an isometric scale and, indeed, there is a growing tendency in industry to draw objects on the isometric axes full size; the saving in time more than outweighs the moderate degree of distortion which may be present. 'Exploded' views and sections, to show methods of assembly of mechanisms such as pumps and valves, complicated piping layouts and machined details, may be drawn in isometric projection to give a clear and immediate picture of the designers' intentions. This is of paramount importance when drawings are sent to a customer who may be hundreds of miles away and whose labour force may have difficulty in reading a 'flat' drawing.

Fig. 12.3 shows the method of constructing an isometric scale. Draw the horizontal line AB any convenient length. From A draw two angles, one of 45° and one of 30°. Along the 45° arm set off centimetres and divisions of centimetres as required, dropping these divisions vertically on to the 30° arm to give the isometric scale. When using the scale all dimensions directly measured are isometric dimensions.

Fig. 12.4 shows a method of direct projection of a plane surface from true size to isometric size without the use of an isometric scale. Draw the plane figure $ABCD$ set at an angle of 45°. Drop verticals from each corner as required. Locate D_1. Draw $D_1 A_1$ and $D_1 C_1$ at 30° until they intersect their corresponding projector from A and C. Draw $A_1 B_1$ and $B_1 C_1$ similarly. The lower plane figure is now to isometric scale.

Fig. 12.5 shows a partly open box. It is not possible to draw the sloping lid of the box to isometric scale, because it does not lie on the isometric axes. Ordinates are therefore necessary to complete the drawing. This is clearly demonstrated in **Fig. 12.7**, an isometric drawing of a triangle.

Fig. 12.6 shows a triangle ABC with a vertical AD bisecting the angle at A. This triangle is constructed in isometric projection in **Fig. 12.7**. Draw BC at 30° to the horizontal. Bisect and erect a perpendicular at D. Mark off the length of AD and join AC and AB. It will be seen that the sloping lengths AB and AC do not measure either their original length or isometric length. This clearly indicates that the sloping lengths cannot be directly measured and drawn.

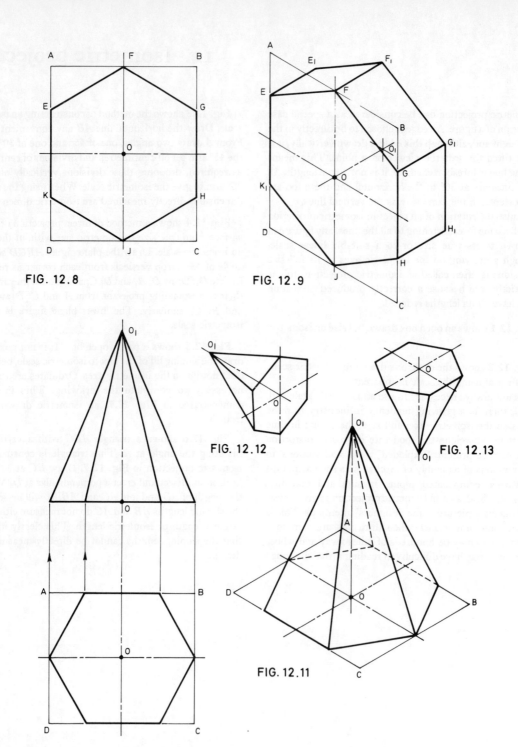

FIG. 12.8

FIG. 12.9

FIG. 12.12

FIG. 12.13

FIG. 12.11

FIG. 12.10

12. Isometric projection

Figs 12.8 and 12.9 show the method of drawing a piece of hexagon bar.

First draw the end elevation of the bar **(Fig. 12.8)** and enclose it within the rectangle *ABCD*. Mark the centre and the six points of the hexagon as shown.

Now draw the rectangle and the centre lines in isometric projection as shown in **Fig. 12.9.** The intersection of the vertical centre line and the rectangle will give two points *F* and *J.* Using compasses or dividers, transfer lengths *GH* and *EK* from **Fig. 12.8** and join the six points. To give depth to the drawing, draw lines at 30° through points *E, F, G,* and *H* for the required length to give E_1, F_1, G_1, and H_1. Join these points to form the rear 'face' of the bar. An alternative method of construction is to draw the front face of the hexagon bar within its rectangle and transfer the centre *O* to O_1 along the longitudinal centre line, equal to the length required, and erect a further rectangle within which the rear face may be drawn.

Fig. 12.10 shows two views of a hexagonal-based pyramid. The plane is drawn first and placed within a rectangle, the base of the pyramid in elevation being projected from this view and then to the apex O_1.

Fig. 12.11 shows an isometric projection of the elevation of the pyramid. Draw the rectangle *ABCD* and locate the centre *O*. Erect the longitudinal centre line from *O* and locate the apex O_1. Construct the base of the pyramid by the method shown in **Fig. 11.9.** It will be noticed that the hexagonal base is drawn as a plane figure, representing one face of the pyramid lying at right angles to the longitudinal centre line which gives the *direction* of the projection from this face and is the line along which the length or height of the pyramid is measured. The drawing may now be completed by joining the six points of the hexagon to the apex, showing hidden detail by dotted lines.

Figs 12.12 and 12.13 show further views of the same pyramid drawn to a smaller scale.

In drawing these various views the importance of obtaining the correct relationship between the base and the longitudinal centre line will be apparent.

The figures on the facing page have sloping lines in their constructions and it will be noted that in order to draw these lines, ordinate measurements are made. At no time is a sloping line used as a line of reference.

The importance of always making an isometric construction within a framework of squares or rectangles, cannot be over-stressed. This system will prove to be invaluable when using the isometric axes and constructions as a basis for good-quality freehand sketches. Students should practice by first copying the drawings shown in this chapter, and in a short while sketching along axes inclined at 30° will become an easy and natural method of freehand drawing.

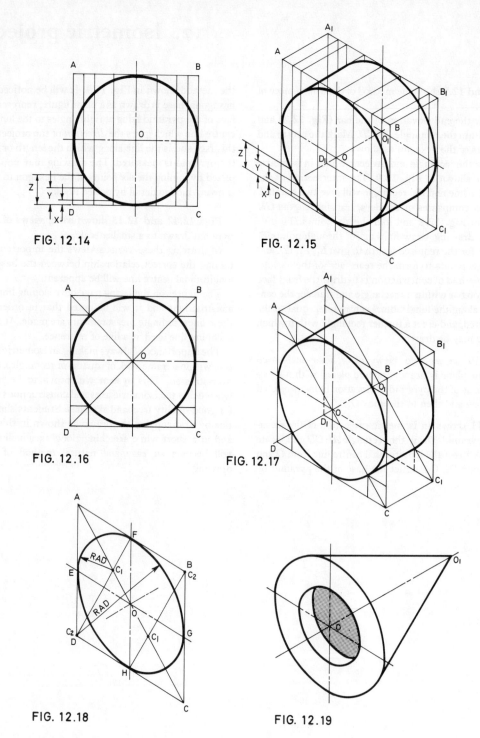

FIG. 12.14

FIG. 12.15

FIG. 12.16

FIG. 12.17

FIG. 12.18

FIG. 12.19

Figs. 12.14–12.19 show methods of drawing figures which are circular in section.

Draw a circle of convenient radius, centre O (Fig. 12.14) contained in a square $ABCD$. Divide the square into vertical strips which need not be equally spaced. Make an isometric drawing of the square as shown in Fig. 12.15 and transfer the vertical dividing lines. The points of intersection of these lines with the circumference of the circle, X, Y, Z, etc., may now also be transferred to the appropriate dividing vertical in the isometric square. A smooth curve joining these points will produce an isometric circle. This circle may be made into a cylinder by drawing a longitudinal centre line from O to O_1 of the required length and constructing another isometric square $A_1B_1C_1D_1$ on O_1 as centre, dividing it as before by projection of the division lines. Marking off the required intersection points X, Y, Z, etc., and drawing through them, will produce another circle which may now be joined to the front face by tangential lines at 30°.

Fig. 12.16 shows the same circle centre O enclosed in a square $ABCD$. Diagonals are drawn from corner to corner, and the intersections of these diagonals and the circumference of the circle are located by drawing vertical and horizontal lines from the points of intersection to the sides of the square. The isometric square is now drawn complete with diagonals (Fig. 12.17). The small corner squares are drawn to locate points on the diagonals which, together with the diameters formed by the vertical and horizontal centre lines, give eight points through which the circle may be drawn. The method of forming the circle into a cylinder by transferring the centre of the isometric square from O to O_1 along the longitudinal centre line is as previously described.

It will be noticed that the framework of lines required to produce a cylinder completely encloses it in what is sometimes referred to as an isometric box.

Fig. 12.18 shows a method of drawing isometric circles using compasses. This is not a true method, but is widely used in practice and is neat and easy to produce. Draw the isometric square $ABCD$ and locate centre O. Draw diagonals from corner to corner to join AC and BD. Join DF and BH to cut AC at C_1, the centres of arcs joining EF and GH. Points B and D are centres C_2 for arcs joining EH and FG.

Fig. 12.19 shows a cone drawn using this construction. The hole in the base is similarly constructed and the depth of the hole is effected by transferring the centres along lines at 30° for a distance equal to the depth of the hole.

This is another 'mechanical' method of pictorial drawing upon which freehand sketching may be based. In particular, the four-arc method of boxing-in circles is readily adapted to sketching. The freehand drawing of Fig. 12.18, where the three different axes of projection may be used, is strongly recommended.

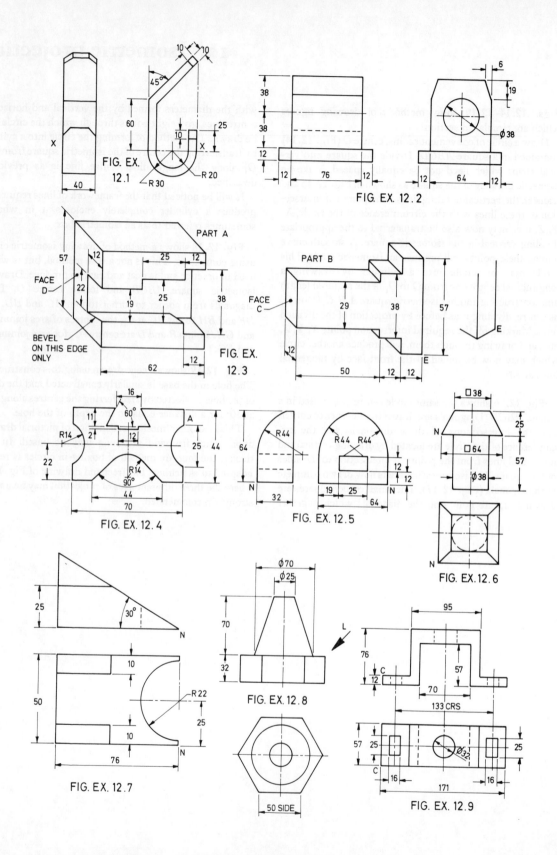

FIG. EX. 12.1

FIG. EX. 12.2

PART A

FACE D

BEVEL ON THIS EDGE ONLY

FACE C

PART B

FIG. EX. 12.3

FIG. EX. 12.4

FIG. EX. 12.5

FIG. EX. 12.6

FIG. EX. 12.7

FIG. EX. 12.8

FIG. EX. 12.9

12. Isometric projection

Exercises for Chapter 12

1. Draw, full size, an isometric view of the coat hook shown in **Fig. Ex. 12.1**, making edge X the nearest line. (*CSE*)
2. Orthographic views of a machine part are given in **Fig. Ex. 12.2**. Draw, full size, an isometric view to the dimensions given. Hidden edges need not be shown. (*CSE*)
3. **Fig. Ex. 12.3** shows two machined parts. Part B is to be fitted into part A. Part B is unfinished.

   Draw an isometric view of part B when it has been shaped to fit into part A.

   Note that face C is to be flush with face D.

   (The inset shows the position of point E on the finished drawing.) (*CSE*)
4. The outline of the cross-section of a dial-gauge stand is shown in **Fig. Ex. 12.4**. The stand is 102 mm long. Without using an isometric scale, draw an isometric view of the stand with corner A nearest to you. (*AEB*)
5. **Fig. Ex. 12.5** shows two elevations of a pawl in first angle projection. Produce an isometric drawing of the pawl showing hidden edges. An isometric scale is not to be used. N is to be the lowest point on your isometric drawing. (*Camb.*)
6. Make an isometric drawing of the rivet shown in **Fig. Ex. 12.6**. An isometric scale is not required. Make point N the lowest point on the isometric drawing and omit hidden edges. (*Camb.*)
7. Make an isometric drawing of the block shown in **Fig. Ex. 12.7**. An isometric scale is not to be used. Corner N is to be the lowest point on the isometric drawing and hidden edges must be shown. (*Camb.*)
8. Two views of a casting are shown in **Fig. Ex. 12.8**.
   Draw
   (a) the given views, and
   (b) an oblique pictorial view, looking in the direction shown by arrow L, using cabinet projection, that is with the third dimension at 45° and drawn half-full size. (*AEB*)
9. The plan and elevation of a special bridge piece are given in **Fig. Ex. 12.9**. Without using an isometric scale draw an isometric view of the bridge piece with corner C nearest to you.

   Hidden lines are not to be shown. (*AEB*)

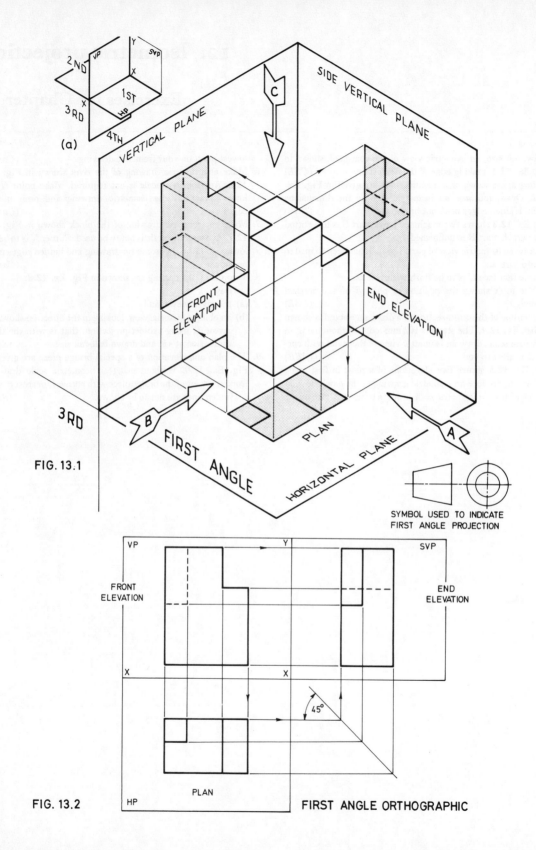

(a)

2ND

1ST

3RD

4TH

VP

SVP

Y

X

X

HP

C

VERTICAL PLANE

SIDE VERTICAL PLANE

FRONT ELEVATION

END ELEVATION

3RD

B

FIRST ANGLE

PLAN

HORIZONTAL PLANE

A

FIG. 13.1

SYMBOL USED TO INDICATE
FIRST ANGLE PROJECTION

VP

Y

SVP

FRONT
ELEVATION

END
ELEVATION

X

X

45°

PLAN

HP

FIG. 13.2

FIRST ANGLE ORTHOGRAPHIC

13. First and third angle projection

The two methods of projection acceptable as British Standards are known as *first angle* and *third angle*. First angle is the traditional British system of projection which is also widely used in other parts of Europe. It is commonly employed in architectural work in this country and also in the old-established or traditional fields of engineering. For these reasons it is referred to as 'European projection'.

Third angle projection, sometimes called 'American projection', is now gaining popularity in this country and a sound case can be made for its universal use by those who favour it. All government engineering establishments and their civilian contracting firms are required to use this form of projection. This has undoubtedly helped its case at the expense of the traditional British system.

The British Standards handbook, *BS 308, Part 1, General principles of engineering drawing practice*, quotes the use of either method of projection, giving examples of each. It does not, of course, explain the underlying geometrical theory.

The inset drawing, **Fig. 13.1 (a)**, shows that space can, for convenience, be divided into four quadrants. Each quadrant has two principal planes of projection as its boundaries, the vertical plane (VP) and the horizontal plane (HP). Other planes such as the side vertical plane (SVP) are introduced as principal planes where necessary to assist in the projection of all the views required of an object to make a complete drawing.

The join lines between the planes (*XX* and *XY* in the inset figures) allow the HP and SVP to hinge until all the planes form a flat sheet. As each separate part of this sheet contains a view projected from the object suspended between them when they were planes, the resulting 'flat' drawings are each in *orthographic* projection.

It will be seen that all elevations are situated in vertical planes while all plans are in horizontal planes. Later chapters will show how oblique, inclined, and auxiliary planes can be inserted between the principal planes to enable angled views to be produced.

First angle projection

The main characteristic of first angle projection is that any view of an object is drawn to represent the side of the object remote from it in the adjacent view. This means, for example, that the right-hand side of an elevation will be drawn to the left of that elevation, and all projection lines required to form the new view will pass through the elevation.

In theory the object to be drawn is suspended in the first quadrant as shown in **Fig. 13.1**. The directions of view are assumed to be along a beam of light, as indicated by the large arrows. The elevations and plan required will be outlined by the constant dimension shadows cast on the vertical, side vertical, and horizontal planes. Assuming these shadows to be fixed in their respective planes, and the planes opened out along their hinge lines, a three-view drawing will appear.

Fig. 13.2 shows the three-view orthographic drawing. The opened-out planes are labelled and the method of producing these views by straight line projection is indicated by the arrows on the projection lines.

Generally, the front elevation (viewed along arrow A in **Fig. 13.1**) is considered to be the main view and all heights and widths are taken from this view. Depth is decided in the plan and this measurement is transferred to an elevation by using an oblique line at 45° to turn the projection lines through 90°, thereby losing nothing dimensionally.

Close examination of this figure shows that the end elevation is produced from what is seen when looking at the left-hand side of the front elevation and the plan, that is, along arrows *B* and *C* in **Fig. 13.1**.

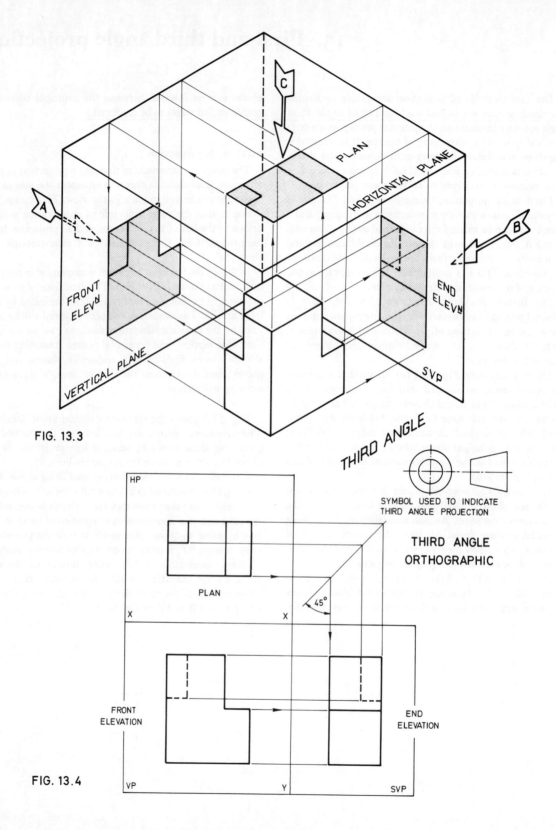

FIG. 13.3

THIRD ANGLE

SYMBOL USED TO INDICATE
THIRD ANGLE PROJECTION

THIRD ANGLE
ORTHOGRAPHIC

FIG. 13.4

The plan is produced from the front elevation by looking directly downwards from above. In both cases all projection lines are drawn through the work.

BS 308 says that when drawing long objects in first angle: 'it is not uncommon to place an end view adjacent to the face which it represents. The practice should be indicated by a note when it is adopted; a suitable note would be, "view in direction of arrow A".'

The number of views employed on a drawing should be kept to a minimum, but must be sufficient to ensure easy reading and manufacture with no misunderstanding. Hidden lines should also be kept to a minimum by careful selection of the views.

Scrap views can be used to clarify a particular part or feature where it is thought unnecessary to draw a complete view. Drawings should be clearly marked to indicate the method of projection used. Alternatively, the directions in which the views are taken should be indicated.

Third angle projection

The main characteristic of third angle projection is that any view of an object is drawn to represent the side of the object nearest to it in the adjacent view. This means that the right-hand side of an elevation will be drawn to the right of that elevation and all the lines required to form the new view will be projected away from the elevation.

Unlike first angle projection, there is no problem when drawing long objects because any end view relates directly to the end of the object nearest to it. This is one of the major advantages of third angle projection. The other advantage is that no projection lines pass through the work; they project away from the outside faces of the views of reference, with a consequent reduction in the number of lines crossing the work surface.

As with first angle projection, the number of views used should be kept to a minimum, but must be sufficient to ensure easy reading and manufacture with no misunderstanding. Hidden lines and detail should be kept to a minimum by careful selection of the required views. Scrap views and part sections can be used to clarify a particular part or feature where it is thought unnecessary to draw a complete view.

Drawings should be clearly marked as to the method of projection used either in the form of a note, or by showing the British Standards symbol. Alternatively, the direction in which the views are taken should be indicated.

Fig. 13.3 shows the object to be drawn suspended in the third quadrant. The principal planes should be imagined as consisting of transparent material.

It will be noted that, compared with the description of first angle projection, the horizontal plane now lies above the object instead of beneath it.

The directions of sight are exactly as before and are indicated by the large arrows. Looking at the object along arrow *A*, through the transparent VP, the only available method of producing a view is to draw in the VP exactly what is seen. This will produce the required front elevation. Similarly, looking along arrows *B* and *C* through the SVP and HP, it is clear that the only available planes in which to draw the end elevation and plan are the planes through which the line of sight passes. This means that whatever the eye sees from each point of view is drawn in the appropriate plane.

Fig. 13.4 shows the correct layout of the three views of the object as a 'flat' or orthographic projection. The join lines, *XX* and *XY*, of the planes are used as hinge points to allow them to lie flat. Compared with first angle projection, the relative position of the views has changed. The plan is now directly above the front elevation.

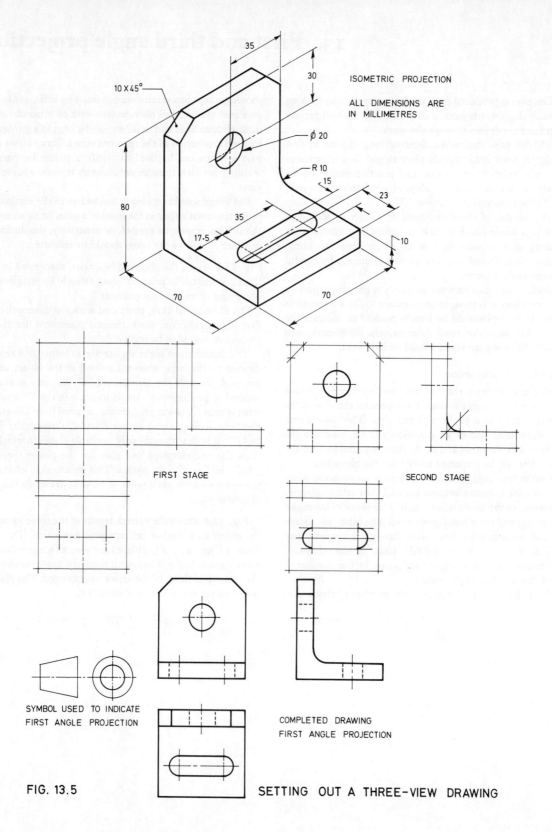

35

30

10 X 45°

ISOMETRIC PROJECTION

ALL DIMENSIONS ARE
IN MILLIMETRES

Ø 20

R 10

15

23

80

35

17·5

10

70

70

FIRST STAGE

SECOND STAGE

SYMBOL USED TO INDICATE
FIRST ANGLE PROJECTION

COMPLETED DRAWING
FIRST ANGLE PROJECTION

FIG. 13.5

SETTING OUT A THREE-VIEW DRAWING

Apart from the lines required to show hidden detail, no projection lines pass across the face of the work. This particular object is in the same position as that in the first angle projection examples, and could be positioned so that any dotted lines become unnecessary to the understanding of the geometry of the object. In plan view, the small corner cut-out would be in the bottom right-hand corner, and the full line across the depth of the object would be on the left-hand side instead of on the right. Dimensionally, this would be the correct method of positioning.

Note also the use of the line at 45° to transfer the depth of the object from the plan to the end elevation. As much work as possible should be done on all three views together to minimize dimension taking and to save time.

Fig. 13.5 shows the steps to be taken in the production of a three-view orthographic drawing in first angle projection of the cast bracket at the top of the page. The bracket is fully dimensioned in this isometric view but not in the orthographic views because dimensioning is a separate topic later in this book. It is much better to learn first the correct way in which to produce the views required and to progress in stages towards making the drawings complete in every detail.

The first step is to draw, in very faint outline, the three views using a hard pencil of, say, 3H grade sharpened to a chisel point. Commence with the front elevation, marking off the width and height, and transfer these dimensions appropriately to the plan and end elevation. Do not worry about ending the lines exactly at the corners of the bracket. If you keep the lines very faint like construction lines, any blemishes will tend to fade into the background as the

drawing progresses. Construction lines should not be erased, they should be kept so faint that the need for erasure should not arise.

Continue to project from one view to another as each dimension is taken. In this way any particular dimension need only be laid out once; much time is saved and the possibility of errors is reduced. For example, the 70 mm width should be marked out on the front elevation first of all. This dimension should then be projected downwards to determine the width in plan. No further projection of this dimension is required because the width is not required in the end elevation.

Mark out on all three views the centre lines of all holes and slots.

The second step is to determine the centres of all radii and draw in bold, finished outline, all curved features, using the appropriate compasses fitted with, say, an H grade lead. This is done first because it is much easier to join straight lines to curves rather than the other way round.

The third and last step is to complete the three views in bold outline and including any hidden detail using, where possible, the same grade of lead as that in the compasses. This is done so that the outline is as even as possible throughout. Sometimes a softer grade of lead is required in the compasses than is used in the pencil to achieve this result, because more pressure can be applied to the pencil, giving a greater degree of density.

The professional draughtsman can often be seen using a similar grade of pencil for all his work. He has discovered, after a great deal of experience, that variation of pressure is all that is required, and so he is able to draw very faint and bold lines at will.

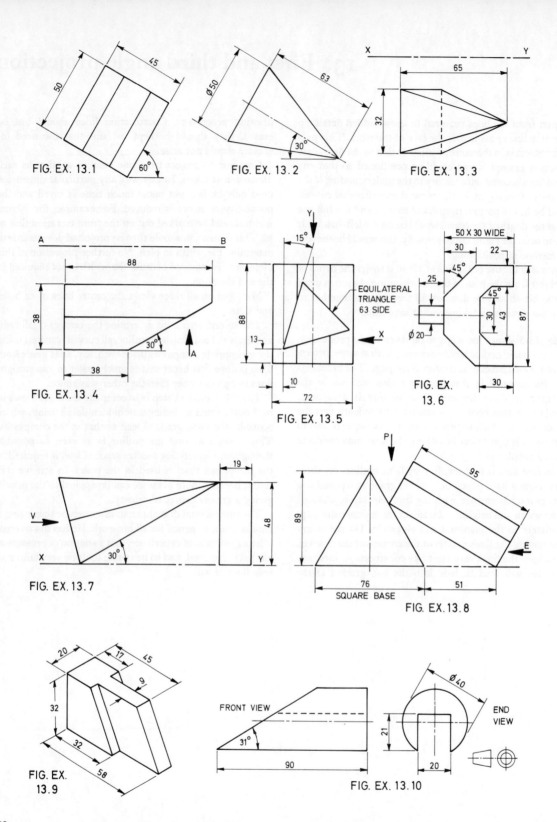

FIG. EX. 13.1

FIG. EX. 13.2

FIG. EX. 13.3

FIG. EX. 13.4

FIG. EX. 13.5

EQUILATERAL
TRIANGLE
63 SIDE

FIG. EX.
13.6

50 X 30 WIDE

FIG. EX. 13.7

FIG. EX.13.8

SQUARE BASE

FIG. EX.
13.9

FRONT VIEW

END
VIEW

FIG. EX. 13.10

13. First and third angle projection

1. **Fig. Ex. 13.1** shows a regular octagonal prism. Its axis is parallel to the VP. In third angle orthographic projection draw a plan and another elevation looking from the right. *(CSE)*
2. **Fig. Ex. 13.2** is a drawing of a cone. Its axis is parallel to the VP. In first angle or third angle orthographic projection draw a plan. State which projection you have used. *(CSE)*
3. **Fig. Ex. 13.3** is a plan view of a right square pyramid. Draw an elevation on *XY*. *(CSE)*
4. **Fig. Ex. 13.4** is the plan of an equilateral triangular prism with one end cut as shown. On *AB* draw an elevation looking in the direction of arrow A. *(CSE)*
5. **Fig. Ex. 13.5** shows the end elevation of a vertical regular octagonal-based right prism, 88 mm high, penetrated by a horizontal triangular prism 108 mm long. Draw
   (a) the given end elevation.
   (b) an elevation of the prisms as seen when looking in the direction of arrow *X*
   (c) a plan as seen when looking in the direction of arrow Y and projected under view (b).
   The length of the triangular prism is to be placed symmetrically about the vertical axis of the other prism.
   Show all hidden lines *(AEB)*
6. **Fig. Ex. 13.6** shows a forging of a fork to be used in a coupling. Draw the given view and project orthographically an end elevation and a plan in third angle projection. *(CSE)*
7. A regular hexagonal-based right pyramid resting with one edge of the base on the horizontal plane is tilted so that the apex just meets one of the top edges of a right rectangular prism as shown in **Fig. Ex. 13.7**

The length of side of the hexagonal base of the pyramid is 32 mm. The length of the rectangular prism is 50 mm. The axis of the pyramid is parallel to and 38 mm away from the vertical plane and cuts midway along the length of the rectangular prism.
Draw
(a) the given elevation,
(b) an end elevation as seen when looking in the direction of arrow *V*,
(c) a plan.
All hidden lines are to be shown. *(AEB)*

8. A square right pyramid and a regular pentagonal prism of 32 mm side both resting on the horizontal plane with their axes in the same vertical plane are shown in **Fig. Ex. 13.8**.
   Draw in third angle projection,
   (a) the given front elevation,
   (b) the plan, looking in the direction indicated by the arrow *P*,
   and
   (c) the end elevation, looking in the direction indicated by the arrow *E*.
   Show all hidden lines. *(CSE)*
9. Make a freehand orthographic drawing of the part shown in **Fig. Ex. 13.9** showing plan, front elevation and end elevation. You may use third angle or first angle projection, but you *must* state which system of projection you have used. Show hidden detail if required. *(CSE)*
10. **Fig. Ex. 13.10** shows two views of a part. Draw these two views and project a plan below the front elevation. *(CSE)*

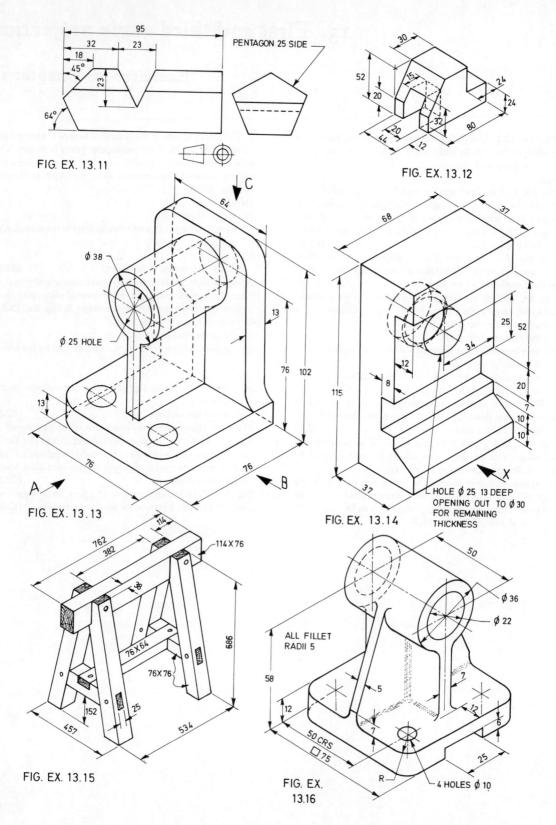

FIG. EX. 13.11

PENTAGON 25 SIDE

FIG. EX. 13.12

Ø 38
Ø 25 HOLE

FIG. EX. 13.13

HOLE Ø 25 13 DEEP
OPENING OUT TO Ø 30
FOR REMAINING
THICKNESS

FIG. EX. 13.14

FIG. EX. 13.15

ALL FILLET
RADII 5

Ø 36
Ø 22

50 CRS
□ 75

R
4 HOLES Ø 10

FIG. EX.
13.16

72

11. **Fig. Ex. 13.11** shows a pentagonal prism which has been machined. Draw the two given views and add a plan.

    (CSE)

12. **Fig. Ex. 13.12** depicts a block of metal that has been machined. In third angle orthographic projection, draw three views of the block with the face containing the rectangular hole as the front elevation.

13. An isometric projection of a bracket is shown in **Fig. Ex. 13.13**. Sketch *freehand*, and in projection, three orthographic views of the bracket as seen in the directions of the arrows *A*, *B*, and *C* respectively. First or third angle projection may be used, but the projection used must be stated. Hidden edges are *not* to be shown.

A scale is not to be used; the dimensions given are only a guide to the proportions and the approximate overall sizes of the views required. *(Camb.)*

14. Part of a stand for a scientific instrument is shown in **Fig. Ex. 13.14**. With the face in the direction of arrow *X* as the front elevation, draw three views in third angle orthographic projection, showing the hole only as hidden detail.

15. A wooden sawing stool is shown in **Fig. Ex. 13.15**. With the longest side as front elevation, draw three views in first angle orthographic projection.

16. A bearing bracket is drawn in **Fig. Ex. 13.16**. With the base edge containing the slot as front elevation, draw three views in third angle orthographic projection showing only the bearing hole and slot as hidden detail.

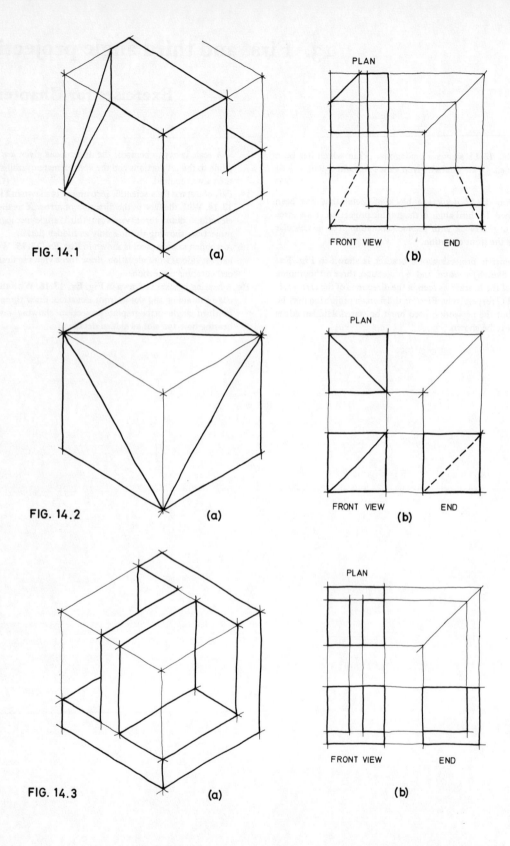

FIG. 14.1   (a)

PLAN

FRONT VIEW   END

(b)

FIG. 14.2   (a)

PLAN

FRONT VIEW   END

(b)

FIG. 14.3   (a)   (b)

The art of freehand sketching is most important, even to the accomplished draughtsman who is sometimes required to go to a factory site armed with a sketch pad and measuring instruments. It may be that new work is being undertaken, or modifications to existing plant or machinery are required. The draughtsman must be capable of producing reasonable freehand sketches that can be readily understood. He may be able to make only one trip to the site and his sketches must be made into working drawings, so there is little margin for error.

Many people shy away from sketching under the impression that it is very difficult to master the art. It is difficult, but following a few simple rules can help to ease the difficulties as they arise.

The first thing to do is to draw a faint scaffold or framework into which the finished outline can be drawn. The dimensions should be as accurate as possible whether the sketch is full size or drawn to scale. It is also frequently helpful to be able to sketch in pictorial or three-dimensional form so that anyone using the sketch can appreciate what it is meant to portray.

Figs. 14.1, 14.2, and **14.3** show pictorial sketches of machined blocks, all of which are the same size. Beside each large sketch are shown three views of the machined block: a plan, a front elevation and an end (or side) elevation.

The method of producing the sketches is the same for each one. Each figure labelled **(a)** is first lightly sketched within a framework of a cube. The finished, darker outline is drawn over the faint lines after all necessary detail has been accurately drawn. Three 'flat' views are the sketched in each area labelled **(b)**.

The three flat drawings are projected from one another to a scale which makes them half the size of the cube. This scale effect can be judged by eye or by using a pencil and a finger nail as a means of measuring. The faint lines which are sketched from one view to another in order to determine height, width and depth are called projection lines. These need not be erased; in fact it is a good rule to try and sketch the framework so lightly that any erasures become unnecessary once the correct shape has been finally settled.

It will be noted that the method of turning lines through 90° from plan to end elevation is to sketch them horizontally to a line lying at 45° and then vertically downwards, as described in the previous chapter.

Further examples of freehand sketching are shown on the next two pages.

Fig. 14.4 shows a woodworker's mallet. The sketch at **(a)** is the first step. Never try to make a finished drawing straight away. The light lines indicate that, initially, a rectangular block can be drawn. Mark off the position of the handle. The firm outline at **(b)** can now be produced.

Fig. 14.5 (a) and **(b)** show sketches of a screwdriver, while **Fig. 14.6 (a)** and **(b)** indicate a method of producing a sketch of a twist drill.

Fig. 14.7 shows a double-ended spanner lying within the sheet metal from which it is made.

Fig. 14.8 is a sketch of a spanner in which shading has been used to improve the three-dimensional effect. Shading should not normally be incorporated in an engineering sketch unless it is to be used as an illustration.

Fig. 14.9 shows a sketch of a woodworking chisel.

Fig. 14.10 is a sketch of a micrometer.

Fig. 14.11 shows a sketch of a cast bearing bracket including its dimensions. From such a sketch orthographic projections can be made, using drawing instruments. When fully dimensioned, the drawings produced from this sketch could be used as manufacturing drawings enabling the casting to be made in the foundry.

Fig. 14.12 shows the finished sketch of vernier calipers, the jaws of which are set for the measurement of an external feature of 30 mm length or diameter.

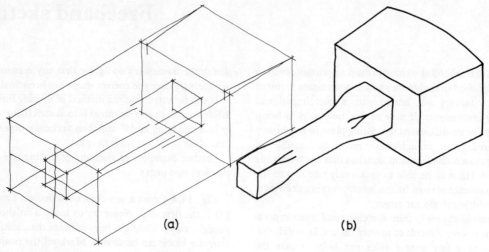

FIG. 14.4

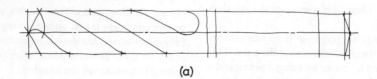

FIG. 14.5

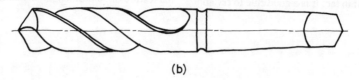

FIG. 14.6

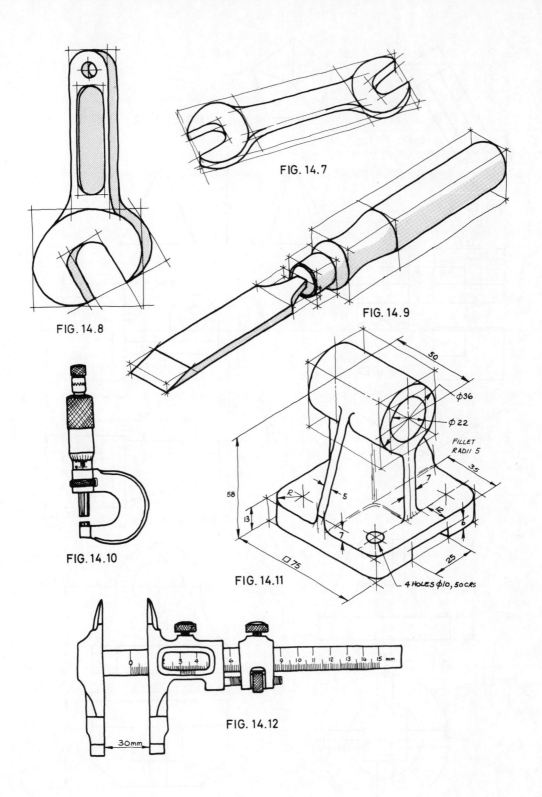

FIG. 14.7

FIG. 14.8

FIG. 14.9

FIG. 14.10

FIG. 14.11

50

φ36

φ22

FILLET
RADII 5

35

58

13

5

7

7

R

12

6

□ 75

25

4 HOLES φ10, 50 CRS

FIG. 14.12

30mm

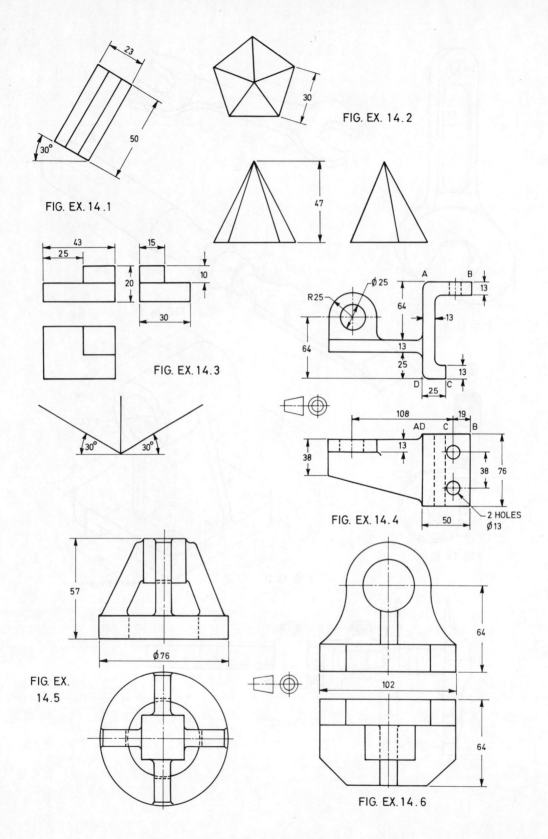

23

30°

50

FIG. EX. 14.1

30

FIG. EX. 14.2

47

43

25

15

20

10

30

FIG. EX. 14.3

30°   30°

Ø 25

R25

A   B

64

13

13

13

64

13

25

13

D   C

25

108

19

AD   C   B

13

38

38   76

50

2 HOLES
Ø 13

FIG. EX. 14.4

57

Ø 76

FIG. EX.
14.5

64

102

64

FIG. EX. 14.6

14. Freehand sketching

Exercises for Chapter 14

1. Given the front elevation of an inclined octagonal prism in **Fig. Ex. 14.1**, sketch **either,**
   (a) an end elevation, **or**
   (b) a plan.
   Hidden detail need not be added. (*CSE*)
2. Sketch the solid shown in **Fig. Ex. 14.2** in first angle projection.
   Give the name of the solid. (*CSE*)
3. Using the base lines given, make an isometric type sketch of the object in **Fig. Ex. 14.3**. (*CSE*)
4. Orthographic views of a bracket in first angle projection are shown in **Fig. Ex. 14.4**. Do **not** copy these views as shown, but sketch **freehand** and in good proportion an **isometric** view of the bracket with the face *ABCD* in the foreground. An isometric scale is not to be used and the dimensions are given as a guide to the general proportions. (*Camb.*)
5. Make a pictorial freehand sketch of the valve guide casting shown in first angle orthographic projection in **Fig. Ex. 14.5**. Hidden edges are **not** required. The freehand sketch must be in good proportion and approximately full size. (*Camb*)
6. Make a pictorial freehand sketch of the block shown in first angle orthographic projection in **Fig. Ex. 14.6**. Hidden edges are **not** required. The freehand sketch must be in good proportion and approximately full size. (*Camb.*)

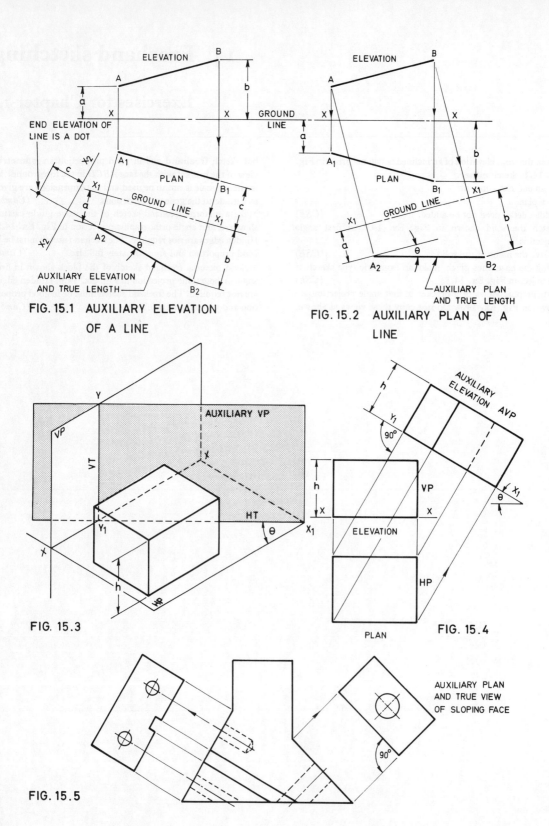

FIG. 15.1 AUXILIARY ELEVATION
OF A LINE

FIG. 15.2 AUXILIARY PLAN OF A
LINE

FIG. 15.3

FIG. 15.4

AUXILIARY PLAN
AND TRUE VIEW
OF SLOPING FACE

FIG. 15.5

15. Auxiliary projection

The principal planes of projection are the *vertical plane* and the *horizontal plane* (VP and HP). Any other imaginary plane, or auxiliary plane, may be introduced, provided it is inserted at right angles to the direction of view, in the same way that normal elevations and plans are at right angles to the horizontal and vertical planes.

An auxiliary view projected from an elevation will produce a plan, and an auxiliary view projected from a plan will produce an elevation. It will also be noted that any point in an elevation, resting on a ground line, must also be resting on the new ground line of an auxiliary elevation; and vertical heights in an auxiliary elevation are the same as the vertical heights in the normal elevation.

The practical value of auxiliary projection is to be found in the presentation of a true view of an object which is at some angle to either or both normal planes. These true views will give true length for direct dimensioning. An appreciation of the methods employed in projecting true lengths of lines, is therefore, of considerable importance.

Fig. 15.1 shows an elevation and a plan of a line *AB*, together with an auxiliary elevation and an end elevation. The original elevation is lying above the HP and inclined at an angle to both principal planes.

To draw the auxiliary elevation, first introduce a new ground line X_1X_1 at a convenient distance C from the plan and parallel to it. Project the ends of the line A_1B_1 through X_1X_1, at right angles to A_1B_1. Locate the points A_2B_2 by marking out from X_1X_1 the distance a and b given in the elevation. Join A_2B_2 to give an auxiliary elevation and the true length of the line *AB*. The angle of inclination to the HP is obtained by measuring the angle θ, the angle contained between A_2B_2 and a line drawn through A_2 parallel to X_1X_1.

To obtain an end elevation of the line, first produce the line B_2A_2 and insert a new ground line X_2X_2 at right angles to it. Along the extension mark out from X_2X_2 a distance c taken from the plan view. A dot at this point will represent the end elevation of the line.

Fig. 15.2 describes the same line *AB* as before. It is required to produce an auxiliary plan and determine its true length. The method of projection is similar to the previous example, except that the new plan is projected from the elevation. The projection lines are at right angles to *AB* and a new ground line X_1X_1 is inserted at a convenient place. The distances a and b measured from *XX* to the ends of the line in plan are marked out along the projectors passing through X_1X_1. These will give points A_2B_2, the ends of the line in auxiliary plan and also the angle of inclination of the line to the VP.

When direct projection is made of a plan or elevation into auxiliary planes the subsequent drawing is known as *first auxiliary*. Further projection from a first auxiliary drawing produces a *second auxiliary* view.

Fig. 15.3 shows a box standing on the HP and in front of the vertical and auxiliary planes. The lines of intersection of the planes are called *traces* and plans and elevations of these traces alone may be drawn. In **Fig. 15.3** the elevation of the vertical trace would be a vertical line extending from *Y* to Y_1 and resting on the horizontal line *XX*. The plan of the horizontal trace would be a straight diagonal line extending from Y_1 to X_1 and joined to the vertical trace at Y_1 on the horizontal (or hinge) line *XX*.

The method of showing this arrangement on a drawing is illustrated in **Fig. 15.4**. Note the layout: the elevation is standing on the hinge line *XX*, the plan is set the correct distance from *XX* in the HP. The auxiliary ground line X_1X_1 is set at the correct angle and the projections are effected at 90° to that angle.

Fig. 15.5 shows a machined block with sloping faces which contain essential details. In order to show these as true views, auxiliary projections are used, and the faces can now be fully and accurately dimensioned. This is a practical application of auxiliary projections where the reader of the drawing is left in no doubt about the sizes and dispositions of the sloping faces and the features they contain.

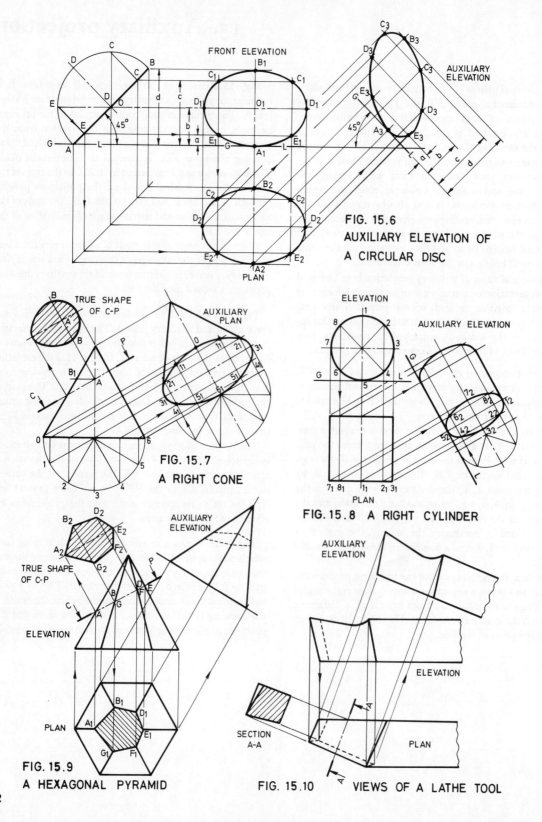

FRONT ELEVATION

FIG. 15.6
AUXILIARY ELEVATION OF
A CIRCULAR DISC

AUXILIARY
ELEVATION

PLAN

TRUE SHAPE
OF C-P

AUXILIARY
PLAN

FIG. 15.7
A RIGHT CONE

ELEVATION

AUXILIARY ELEVATION

PLAN

FIG. 15.8   A RIGHT CYLINDER

AUXILIARY
ELEVATION

TRUE SHAPE
OF C-P

ELEVATION

PLAN

FIG. 15.9
A HEXAGONAL PYRAMID

AUXILIARY
ELEVATION

ELEVATION

PLAN

SECTION
A-A

FIG. 15.10   VIEWS OF A LATHE TOOL

82

Fig. 15.6 shows a circular disc of diameter *AB*, standing on a horizontal ground line *GL* and inclined at 45° to that line. It is required to draw a plan, elevation, and an auxiliary elevation, projected from the plan on to a new ground line inclined at 45° to the horizontal. First locate the centre of disc, *O*. With *O* as centre draw a semicircle of radius *OA* or *OB*. Divide this semicircle (which is a true plan of the disc) into any convenient number of equal parts (four in this case) and label as shown. Project these points downwards at right angles to the disc, to divide the diameter *AB* into four parts. Now project the points on the disc horizontally. Locate centre O_1 and mark off distance O_1D_1 and O_1C_1 by using compasses or dividers extended to *OA* and *OE* on the disc. Draw vertical lines through O_1, D_1, and C_1. The intersections of these lines and the horizontal projection lines will produce points through which a smooth curve, the required front elevation, may be drawn. Next drop vertical lines from the points on the disc to intersect with a line at 45° and project horizontally to intersect with verticals dropped from the front elevation. A curve drawn through these intersections will produce a plan identical in shape to the elevation. Now draw the new ground line for the auxiliary elevation and project the points produced in plan at right angles to that line. Mark off heights *a*, *b*, *c*, and *d* from the ground line and project to produce intersections to form the new auxiliary elevation.

Fig. 15.7 shows an elevation and auxiliary plan of a right circular cone. The cone is cut by a plane CP, and an auxiliary, or true view, of the effect of this cutting plane is also shown.

In this example the centre line of the cone is used in place of a ground line for ease of working. A new ground line would, of course, be parallel to the centre line passing through point 3_1. To obtain the auxiliary plan, first divide the base of the cone into a number of equal parts by using a half plan. Now draw the auxiliary centre line and, on a suitable line at right angles, produce another half plan and divide into the same number of equal parts. Project these points parallel to the centre line to intersect with lines projected from the equally divided base of the elevation.

The joining of these intersections will produce the elliptical base. Project the apex of the cone on to the new centre line and join to the base. The true shape is produced by projecting at right angles from the cutting plane CP, at the three points of intersection with the cone in elevation. Draw a centre line to locate the overall length of the view. To obtain the maximum width *BB*, draw a horizontal line from *A* to B_1 in elevation; as B_1 lies on a true length line and the cone is circular in section, the line AB_1 must be half the total width across the plane *A*. This width may now be marked off using the compasses or dividers. To obtain a more accurate profile, further points of projection should be taken as shown in later examples. Where the cutting plane CP passes through the cone it forms a 'section' or 'cross-section'; for this reason the true view is shown with lines at 45° extending across its area. This is variously called 'hatching', 'sectioning', or 'cross-sectioning'.

Fig. 15.8 shows a method of producing an auxiliary elevation of a cylinder resting on a ground line GL. The elevation is divided into eight equal parts, and these divisions are projected downwards on to the plan. The new ground line for the auxiliary elevation is drawn and the centre line is drawn parallel to it. Set up a half end view and equally divide it as before, projecting the points obtained parallel to the centre line. The intersections of these lines and the points projected from the plan will complete the auxiliary view.

Fig. 15.9 shows the treatment of a hexagonal pyramid. The effect of the cutting plane is shown in plan and an auxiliary true view, the widths for which may be taken from the plan. The points at which the cutting plane intersects the edges of the pyramid are projected vertically downwards to the corresponding edges in plan.

Fig. 15.10 shows the application of projection to the production of a drawing of a lathe cutting tool, in which the auxiliary view is also a true view and the section *AA* is also a true view at the point of the section.

It will be noted that the figures are drawn in first angle projection.

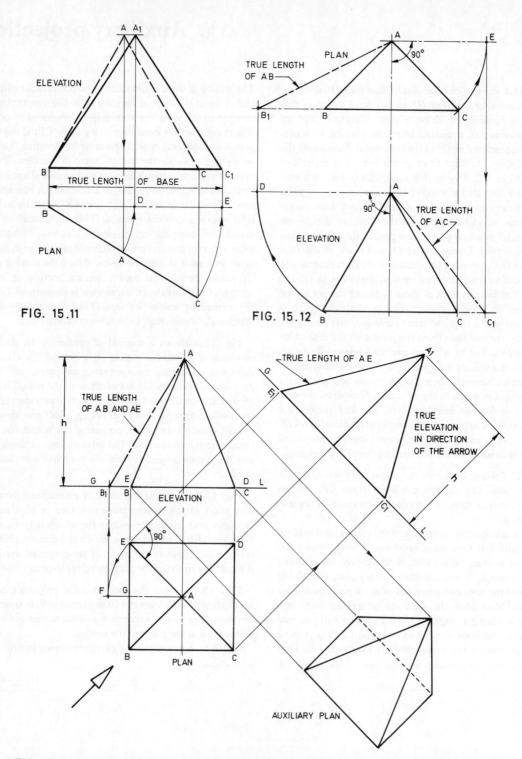

ELEVATION

TRUE LENGTH OF BASE

PLAN

FIG. 15.11

PLAN

TRUE LENGTH OF A B

90°

ELEVATION

90°

TRUE LENGTH OF A C

FIG. 15.12

h

TRUE LENGTH OF A B AND A E

ELEVATION

90°

PLAN

TRUE LENGTH OF A E

TRUE ELEVATION IN DIRECTION OF THE ARROW

AUXILIARY PLAN

FIG. 15.13   TRUE VIEW AND AUXILIARY PROJECTION

Fig. 15.11 shows a triangular plane lying at an angle to the VP and at right angles to the HP. It is required to produce a true elevation. With B in plan as centre and BA and BC as radii, draw arcs to intersect a line drawn parallel to VP in D and E. Project these points vertically to intersect the horizontal projectors of the apex A in A_1 and the base line BC in C_1. Join B, C_1, and A_1, the required true view.

Fig. 15.12 shows the plan and elevation of hip rafters of a roof, here depicted as two views of a triangle. It is required to find the true length of the roof rafters. With A in elevation as centre, radius AB, draw an arc to cut a horizontal projector from A in D. Project vertically upwards to intersect CB produced in B_1. AB_1 in plan is a true length. Alternatively, with A in plan as centre, radius AC, draw an arc to intersect a horizontal projector from A in E. Project from E vertically downwards to intersect BC produced in C_1. Join AC_1, the required true length.

Fig. 15.13 shows a plan and elevation of a square-based pyramid drawn in first angle projection. The drawing indicates two methods of finding the true length of the edge lines of the pyramid.

To find the true length and draw an auxiliary elevation, use the diagonal EC and draw a new ground line E_1C_1. Mark off the vertical height, taking the dimension from the front elevation, and locate the apex A_1. Join the edge lines seen when viewing in the direction of the large arrow. Because the projection has been made at right angles to the edges AE and AC, A_1E_1 and A_1C_1 are true lengths.

Alternatively, draw an arc EF in plan, with centre A and radius AE. Project from F vertically upwards to intersect with CB produced in B_1. Join AB_1 which will be a true length. The true length of the line AG in plan is given by direct measurement of AE in elevation.

From the elevation an auxiliary plan can be projected, as shown by the figure drawn at the lower right-hand of the diagram.

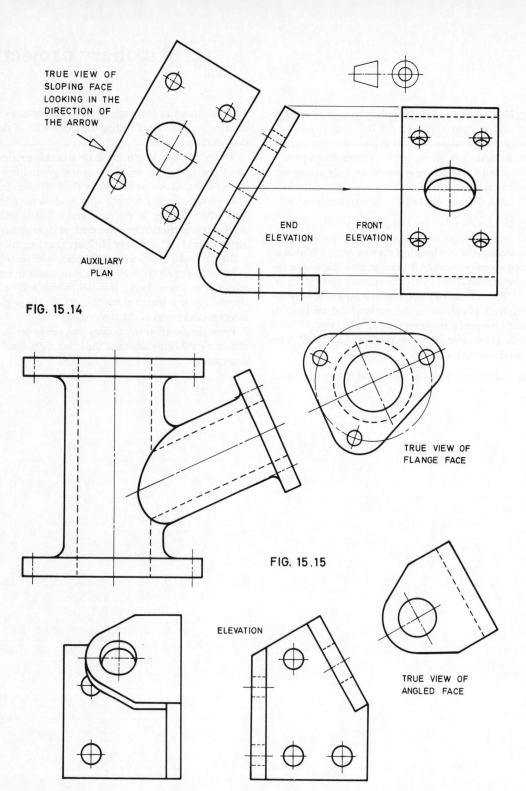

TRUE VIEW OF
SLOPING FACE
LOOKING IN THE
DIRECTION OF
THE ARROW

AUXILIARY
PLAN

FIG. 15.14

END
ELEVATION

FRONT
ELEVATION

TRUE VIEW OF
FLANGE FACE

FIG. 15.15

ELEVATION

TRUE VIEW OF
ANGLED FACE

FIG. 15.16

On the facing page are a number of practical applications of auxiliary projections.

Fig. 15.14 shows a piece of sheet metal bent to form a bracket and containing a number of drilled holes. The two normal elevations indicate the positions of the holes in the sloping face, and dimensions could be applied to these views. However, the true view of the sloping face would be a much more convenient drawing to use for this purpose.

Note that the true view is an auxiliary plan.

Fig. 15.15 is an illustration of a cast-iron pipe fitting.

The elevation gives no indication of the geometry of the flanges nor of any features which the flanges might contain. The true view, or auxiliary plan, of the flange on the sloping branch pipe is essential when its general shape is anything other than circular.

Fig. 15.16 shows two elevations and an auxiliary view of a special bracket. The two main views of the bracket are sufficient to enable complete understanding of the principal features of the component. The true view of the angled face would be necessary when undertaking the task of dimensioning the bracket for production.

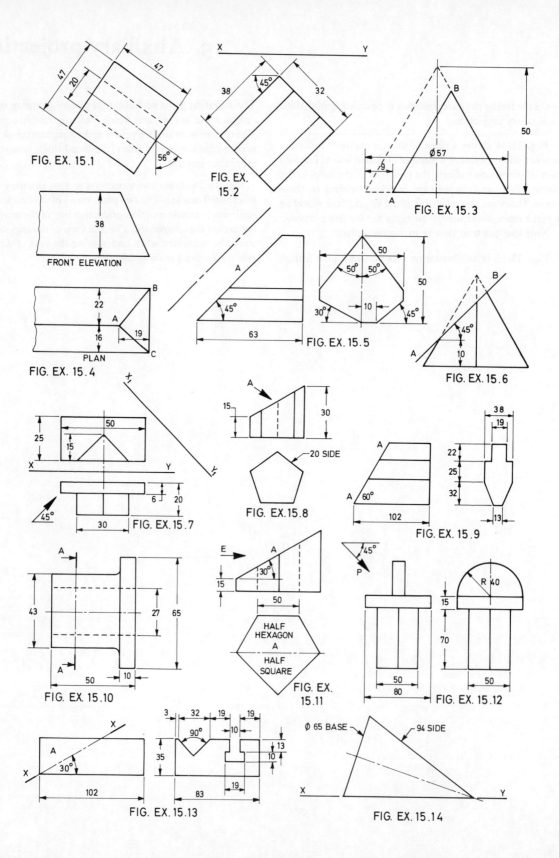

FIG. EX. 15.1

FIG. EX. 15.2

FIG. EX. 15.3

FRONT ELEVATION

PLAN

FIG. EX. 15.4

FIG. EX. 15.5

FIG. EX. 15.6

20 SIDE

FIG. EX.15.8

FIG. EX. 15.9

FIG. EX. 15.7

HALF
HEXAGON
A
HALF
SQUARE

FIG. EX.
15.11

FIG. EX. 15.10

FIG. EX. 15.12

FIG. EX. 15.13

Ø 65 BASE   94 SIDE

FIG. EX. 15.14

1. **Fig. Ex. 15.1** is a drawing of a cube. Draw a plan view.
   (CSE)
2. **Fig. Ex. 15.2** is the plan of a regular hexagonal prism. Project an elevation on XY. (Hint. Draw an auxiliary view of one end first.) This plan is drawn in first angle orthographic projection. *(CSE)*
3. **Fig. Ex. 15.3** shows the elevation of a cut cone. The true shape of AB is a parabola. Draw the parabola. The rectangle method may be used. *(CSE)*
4. From the elevation and plan in **Fig. Ex. 15.4** find the true length of AB and AC and the true shape of ABC. *(CSE)*
5. **Fig. Ex. 15.5** shows a machined block. Draw the true shape of the sloping face A. *(CSE)*
6. **Fig. Ex. 15.6** shows the elevation of a square-based pyramid cut by a plane AB. Draw the true shape made by the cut.
   (The outside shape of the elevation is in the form of an equilateral triangle of 63 mm side.) *(CSE)*
7. The plan and elevation of a shaped block are shown in **Fig. Ex. 15.7**. Project a new elevation on to the line X_1Y_1. *(CSE)*
8. Draw the true shape of the surface marked A in **Fig. Ex. 15.8**. *(CSE)*
9. **Fig. Ex. 15.9** shows two views of a short length of glazing bar. Draw in orthographic projection, first or third angle, full size,

(a) the given views,
(b) a plan,
(c) the true shape of the surface AA. *(CSE)*

10. Make a sectional view on the cutting plane AA drawn on **Fig. Ex. 15.10**.
    (The dimensions given do not indicate the shape of the figure, this has been left to the student to decide.) *(CSE)*
11. Draw, full size, the given views of the pentagonal prisms shown in **Fig. Ex. 15.11**, and add
    (a) an end elevation looking in the direction of arrow E,
    (b) the true shape of face A. *(CSE)*
12. **Fig. Ex. 15.12** shows two square prisms surmounted by a semicircular disc on edge.
    Draw the given views and add an auxiliary plan as seen in the direction of arrow P.
    Scale full size. *(CSE)*
13. The front and end elevations of a drill-jig base are given in **Fig. Ex. 15.13**. The front elevation is cut by the plane XX, the portion marked A being removed. Draw
    (a) the given views,
    (b) the plan, with portion A removed,
    (c) the true shape of the exposed face XX. *(CSE)*
14. **Fig. Ex. 15.14** shows the elevation of a cone lying on its side. Project the plan view. *(CSE)*

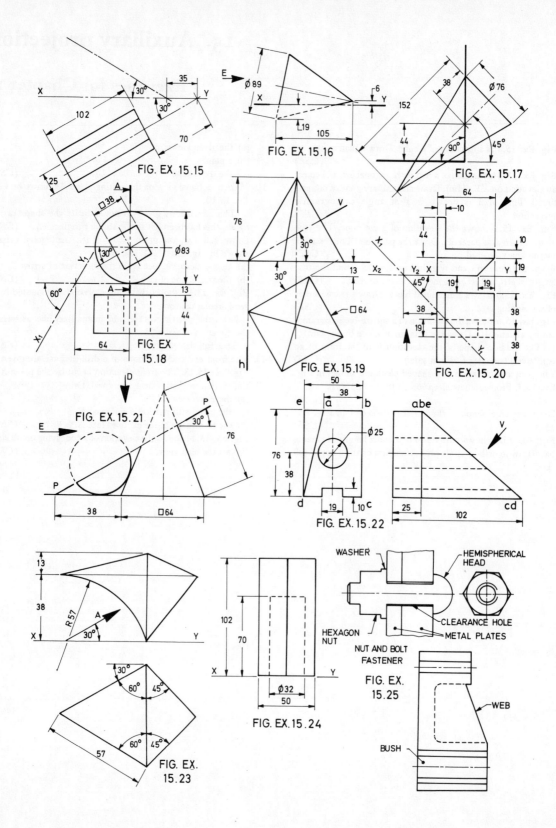

FIG. EX. 15.15

FIG. EX. 15.16

FIG. EX. 15.17

FIG. EX 15.18

FIG. EX. 15.19

FIG. EX. 15.20

FIG. EX. 15.21

FIG. EX. 15.22

FIG. EX. 15.23

FIG. EX. 15.24

WASHER

HEMISPHERICAL HEAD

CLEARANCE HOLE

HEXAGON NUT

METAL PLATES

NUT AND BOLT FASTENER

FIG. EX. 15.25

WEB

BUSH

15. A right regular hexagonal prism, 102 mm long, side of hexagon 25 mm, lies with one rectangular face on the horizontal plane and the axis of the prism inclined at 30° to the horizontal plane as shown in **Fig. Ex. 15.15**.

Draw, full size, an elevation of the prism projected on the new ground line sloping at 30° to the line XY whose point of intersection with the line XY is 35 mm from Y.

16. The elevation of the frustum of a right cone is shown in **Fig. Ex. 15.16**.

Draw in first angle projection, showing all hidden lines,
(a) the given elevation,
(b) the end elevation in the direction of arrow E, and
(c) the plan. (*AEB*)

17. **Fig. Ex. 15.17** shows two flat plates welded together at 90° and penetrated by a cone. Draw the shape of the larger hole to be cut in one of the plates to receive the cone. Neglect the thickness of the plates. (*AEB*)

18. The plan and elevation of a cylindrical blank with a square hole cut through it are shown in **Fig. Ex. 15.18**.
(a) Draw a sectional end elevation, the section being taken on the centre line and looking in the direction of arrows AA.
(b) Draw an auxiliary elevation on the ground line X_1Y_1.
All hidden lines to be shown. (*AEB*)

19. The plan and elevation of a square-base solid right pyramid are shown in **Fig. Ex. 15.19**. The pyramid is cut by a plane indicated by its traces vt and th. Draw, full size,
(a) the plan, elevation, and end elevation of the portion of the pyramid below the cutting plane,
(b) a true view of the plane vt.

20. The plan and elevation of a special angle bracket are shown in **Fig. Ex. 15.20**.
(a) Draw, full size, the given views and project an auxiliary plan on the ground line X_1X_1.

(b) Using the auxiliary plan in (a) above, project an auxiliary elevation on the ground line X_2Y_2).
All hidden detail to be shown. (*AEB*)

21. The elevation of a square right pyramid and a sphere of 38 mm diameter cut by a plane PP, is shown in **Fig. Ex. 15.21**. The axis of the pyramid and the centre of the sphere are in a plane parallel to the VP.

Draw, in first angle projection,
(a) the elevation of the two solids, below the cutting plane,
(b) the plan, looking in the direction indicated by the arrow D, and
(c) the elevation, looking in the direction indicated by the arrow E. (*AEB*)

22. Two elevations of a block in first angle projection are shown in **Fig. Ex. 15.22**. Draw the two views shown and project an auxiliary view in the direction of the arrow V, which is perpendicular to the face $abcd$. (*Camb.*)

23. Two views of a block are shown in first angle projection in **Fig. Ex. 15.23**. Draw the given views and project an auxiliary plan in the direction of arrow A. Hidden edges are to be shown. (*Camb.*)

24. **Fig. Ex. 15.24** shows the elevation of a hexagonal prism pierced by an axial cylindrical hole. Draw the true shape of the section made by a plane which bisects the axis of the prism and which is at 60° to the horizontal plane and perpendicular to the vertical plane. (*Camb.*)

25. **Fig. Ex. 15.25** shows two separate drawings, one of a nut and bolt fastener assembly, and the other of a bearing bracket.

Scale the drawings in the figure and draw them twice full size.

The details are to be shown as sections. Before sectioning, complete all the missing lines. (*CSE*)

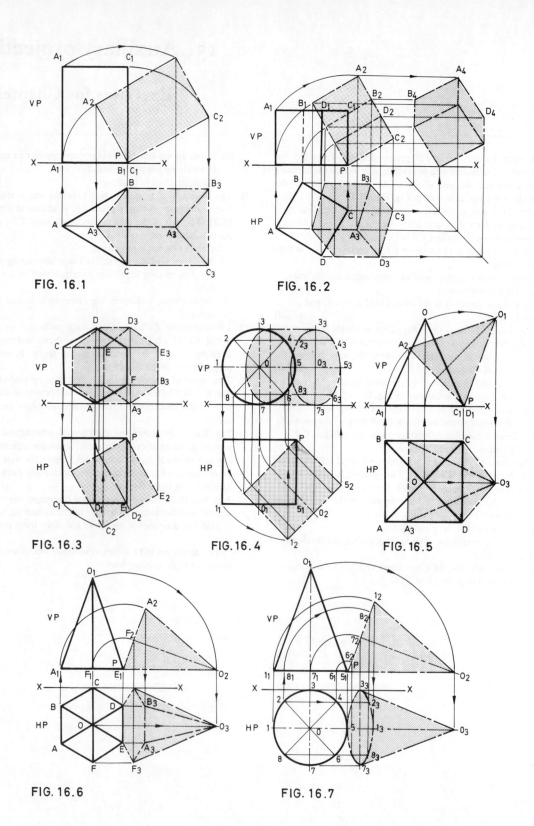

FIG. 16.1

FIG. 16.2

FIG. 16.3

FIG. 16.4

FIG. 16.5

FIG. 16.6

FIG. 16.7

16. Projections and sections of solids

To become proficient at projection it is often of great value to study the effect of tipping or *rotating* a solid object about one line or point and producing new views of the repositioned figure. The main difficulty usually is to be able to visualize what the rotated figure looks like when viewed from any particular direction.

Reference must be made to imaginary planes of projection and the location of these planes with the principal planes: the vertical and the horizontal.,

Fig. 16.1 shows a triangular prism standing on the HP (denoted by the bend line *XX*) in front of the VP, with one face at right angles to the VP. The figure is then inclined at an angle to the HP, pivoting about the base edge *BC*.
Draw the plan of the prism *ABC* in the HP and project an elevation on to the VP. Rotate about edge *BC* (point *P*) to the required angle and draw the new elevation. Project vertically downwards from this elevation and horizontally from the plan to give the new plan.

Fig. 16.2 shows a cube standing on the HP, in front of the VP and with one face at an angle to the VP. Draw the plan of the cube *ABCD* in the HP and project the elevation on to the VP. Rotate about corner *P* to the required angle and draw the new elevation. Project the new plan. An end elevation in the side vertical plane (SVP) may also be projected from these two views as shown.

Fig. 16.3 shows a hexagonal prism standing on the HP, in front of and at right angles to the VP. Draw the elevation and project a plan. One face is now inclined to the VP, rotating about point *P* in plan, and a new plan is drawn. The new elevation is projected vertically upwards from the plan and horizontally from the elevation.

Fig. 16.4 shows a cylinder lying on the HP in front of the VP and with its centre line at right angles to the VP. Draw the elevation and project a plan. Divide the circumference of the elevation into a number of equal parts and project downwards to intersect the nearest face of the cylinder in plan. Rotate the plan and the divisions about one diameter (point *P*). Projecting vertically from the new plan to intersect corresponding horizontal projections from the elevation will give the new elevation.

Fig. 16.5 shows a square base pyramid standing on the HP, in front of the VP and with base edge parallel to the VP.
Draw the elevation and plan. Incline the base at the required angle to the HP by rotating about the base edge *CD* (point *P* in elevation). Draw the new elevation. Project vertically downwards to provide the new plan.

Fig. 16.6 shows a hexagonal based pyramid. The base is parallel to and above the HP and square with the VP, with one base angle in contact with the VP. The pyramid is rotated until one triangular face is lying parallel to the HP.

Fig. 16.7 shows a right circular cone. The base is parallel to and above the HP and in contact with the VP. The cone is rotated about one point on the diameter until it is lying on its side parallel to the HP. The method of projection is similar to that involved in the cylinder (Fig. 16.4).

When drawing these figures students are advised to produce further projected views, as in Fig. 16.2, to assist in visualizing the elevations of the rotated objects.

It will be noted that all the figures are drawn in first angle projection.

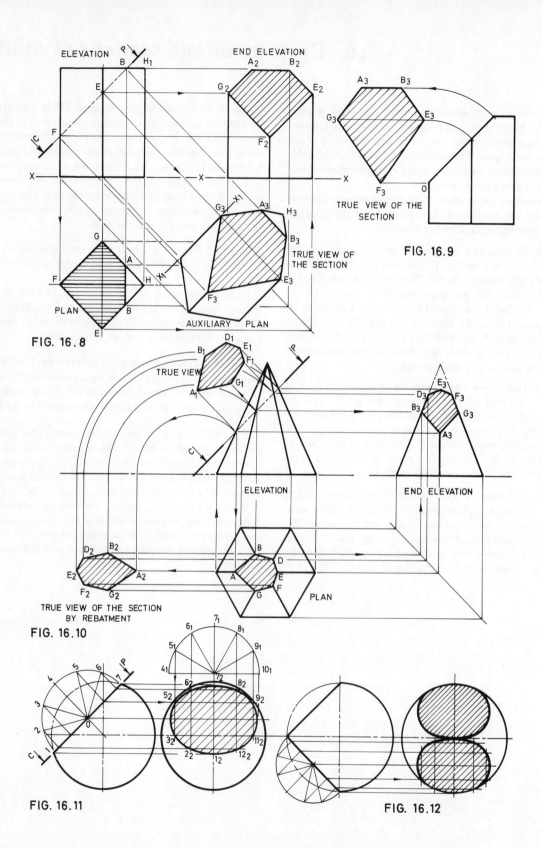

ELEVATION

END ELEVATION

TRUE VIEW OF THE SECTION

FIG. 16.9

TRUE VIEW OF THE SECTION

PLAN

AUXILIARY PLAN

FIG. 16.8

TRUE VIEW

ELEVATION

END ELEVATION

TRUE VIEW OF THE SECTION BY REBATMENT

PLAN

FIG. 16.10

FIG. 16.11

FIG. 16.12

94

16. Projections and sections of solids

Fig. 16.8 shows a square prism standing on the HP in front of the VP and cut by a plane CP.

The plan is drawn first and the elevation projected from it. The cutting plane is drawn in the required position on the elevation and its effect is projected on to the plan at *ABEFG*. An end elevation may now be orthographically projected (projection lines should be omitted for clarity), to include the cutting-plane points. An auxiliary plan is shown, drawn on the new ground line X_1X_1. The method of producing this view is as previously described, and, as the direction of view is at right angles to CP, this plan will also show a true view of the cutting plane.

An alternative method of drawing the true view is shown rebatted about point *O* in **Fig. 16.9**. If this construction is used in conjunction with the main drawings, the widths of the true view may be projected from the plan.

Fig. 16.10 shows a hexagonal pyramid standing on the HP in front of the VP and with one base edge parallel to the VP. The pyramid is cut by a plane CP.

The plan is drawn first and the base of the elevation projected from it. The apex of the pyramid is located and the base corners joined to it. The intersections of the cutting plane and the pyramid corners are projected downwards to intersect their corresponding corners in the plan at *ABDEF* and *G*. An orthographic projection is effected to produce an end elevation. Two methods of drawing a true view of the section are shown. One projected at right angles to the plane is as previously described. The other is by rebatment about point *O*, the point of intersection of the plane CP extended and the ground line *XX*. The widths are projected from the plan.

Fig. 16.11 shows a sphere cut by a plane CP, at a convenient angle to the horizontal: the line of sight. The front elevation is drawn and the cutting plane positioned at the required angle. Bisect the diameter of CP at *O*. With *O* as centre, draw a semicircle (half plan) on CP and divide into any convenient number of equal parts. Project these divisions on to CP. Draw an end elevation and above it, on centre, draw a divided semicircle equal to the first. The intersection of the horizontal and vertical projections from the plane CP and end view half plan will produce points through which an ellipse may be drawn.

Fig. 16.12 shows a sphere cut by two planes at right angles to one another. The method is similar to that adopted in **Fig. 16.11**.

It will be noted that the widths of the ellipses in the end elevation may be stepped off the corresponding half-plan widths, using compasses or dividers.

All the figures are drawn in first angle projection.

The result of a sphere being cut by any plane will be a circle, when viewed at right angles to the plane. If viewed at any other angle, the eye will see an ellipse.

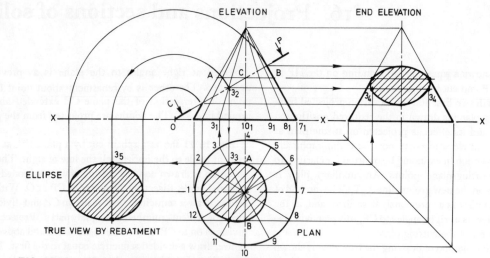

FIG. 16.13 CONIC SECTION PRODUCING AN ELLIPSE

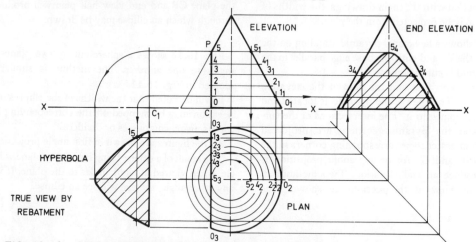

FIG. 16.14 CONIC SECTION PRODUCING A HYPERBOLA

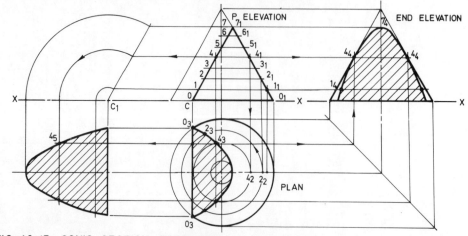

FIG. 16.15 CONIC SECTION PRODUCING A PARABOLA

16. Projections and sections of solids

Various sections through a cone will produce shapes already dealt with as plane figures earlier in this book. Three of these are shown in **Figs 16.13–16.15**. A cutting plane parallel to the base will produce a circle. A cutting plane passing through the vertical axis will produce a triangle.

A cutting plane inclined to the vertical axis and passing through both sides will produce an ellipse.

A cutting plane parallel to the vertical axis will produce a hyperbola.

A cutting plane parallel to one of the sides will produce a parabola.

Fig. 16.13 shows a cone cut by a plane CP, which is inclined to the vertical axis and which passes through both sides. The true view of the plan will be an ellipse. Draw the plan and divide into a number of equal generators, labelling as shown. Project upwards on to an elevation and draw the required cutting plane CP extended to ground line XX at O. The intersection of CP and the generators may now be projected downwards on to the appropriate generators in the plan. To obtain the plan at point C on the vertical generator, project through C to points A and B. This will be a diametral slice and will be the width of the plane at point C. Point A or B may be projected downwards to intersect the centre line 1–7, and, with C as centre, draw an arc to produce points A and B in plan. A smooth elliptical curve may now be drawn through the points obtained. As this is a section the curved area should be cross-sectioned. An end elevation may now be produced by projecting all the required points from the front elevation and the plan.

With point O lying on XX as centre, a true view of the effect of the plane may be produced by rebatment, the appropriate widths being taken directly from the plan as indicated. A true view may also be produced by projecting at 90° to CP, as previously described in Chapter 15.

Fig. 16.14 shows a cone cut by a vertical plane CP, parallel to the vertical axis of the cone. The true view of the plane will be a hyperbola.

Draw the plan and elevation in outline. It will be seen that the previous method of dividing the plan would be unsatisfactory in this case, as less than half the generators would contact the CP. For this reason labelled horizontal slices passing through and dividing CP and one side are employed. Any convenient number may be drawn and they need not be equally spaced. The intersections of the horizontal slices and the cone side are now projected downwards to the plan centre line, at $0_2, 1_2, 2_2, \ldots$, etc., and points are taken as radii from the cone centre and drawn as circles to intersect the cutting plane CP, which in plan appears as a straight line $0_3\, 0_4$. This line may now be used as the base line of the true view rebatted about point 0, the widths being projections of the intersections in plan. An end view may now be projected, the section also being a true view, identical to the rebatted plan. Smooth curves should be drawn through the points obtained.

Fig. 16.15 shows a cone cut by a plane CP, parallel to one side. The true view of the plane will be a parabola.

Draw the plan and elevation in outline. Divide the extent of the cutting plane into a number of horizontal slices and label as shown. Project the intersections of the slices and the cone side downwards on to the plan and draw as a series of circles. The points of intersection of CP and the slices may now be projected in plan to cut their respective circles, to produce the figure shown. The true view may now be rebatted about point C, but, for clarity, the base line $0_3\, 0_4$ has been projected to lie beneath point G in elevation, the new rebatment point. This procedure may be followed because the cutting plane is parallel to the side used for rebatment. An end elevation may be produced by projecting all the required points from the two views drawn. It will be noticed that CP cuts through the sides of the cone at points 5_4, 5_5 shown in end elevation.

A true view of the plane may also be shown as a direct projection at 90° from CP, as previously described.

Note that all the figures are drawn in first angle projection.

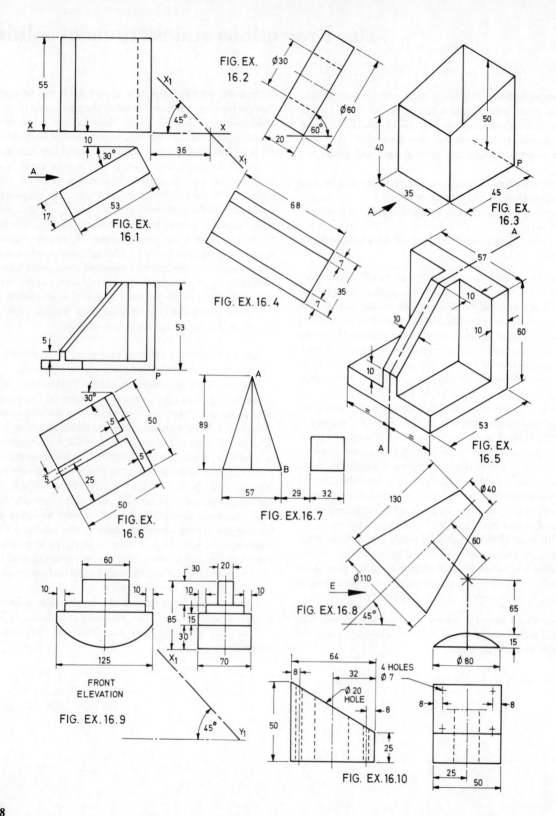

FIG. EX. 16.2

FIG. EX. 16.1

FIG. EX. 16.3

FIG. EX. 16.4

FIG. EX. 16.5

FIG. EX. 16.6

FIG. EX. 16.7

FIG. EX. 16.8

FRONT
ELEVATION

FIG. EX. 16.9

FIG. EX. 16.10

4 HOLES
Ø 7

Ø 20
HOLE

16. Projections and sections of solids

Not all the figures on this page describe problems related to Chapter 16. A number of them deal with sectioning and auxiliary projection.

1. **Fig. Ex. 16.1** shows two orthographic views of a rectangular block standing vertically in the HP and rotated at an angle of 30° to the VP.

   Draw the given views, project an auxiliary elevation on the ground line X_1X_1 and project an elevation in the direction of arrow A. State the method of projection.

2. **Fig. Ex. 16.2** is a drawing of a circular disc in elevation rotated through an angle of 30°. The disc has a hole through its centre.

   Project, from the given view, a front elevation and a plan in third angle projection.

3. **Fig. Ex. 16.3** shows a pictorial view of an open box. Draw, in third angle projection, three orthographic views of the box, making the front elevation that in direction of arrow A.

   Rotate the end elevation through 45° about the base edge labelled P and from it project a new plan.

4. **Fig. Ex. 16.4** is a channel section having a constant depth of 40 mm. The view given is a plan. Draw this view and project from it vertically an elevation in first angle projection.

5. **Fig. Ex. 16.5** depicts a cast bracket, omitting the corner radii. Draw a front elevation looking directly on the central web and project from it a plan and a sectional elevation on the plane AA.

6. **Fig. Ex. 16.6** shows a cast bracket, omitting the corner radii. The elevation is standing vertically in the HP and inclined at 30° to the VP.

   Draw two views and, from the left-hand side of the plan view, project a new elevation parallel to the VP.

7. **Fig. Ex. 16.7** shows the elevation of a hexagonal pyramid and a cube. The pyramid is tilted so that the side shown by the line AB rests against the cube. Edge B, and the cube, remain in their given positions.

   Draw the front elevation and plan of the two solids with the hexagonal pyramid in its new position. The axes are to be in line, parallel with the vertical plane. *(CSE)*

8. Draw, full size, the elevation of the table lamp shown in **Fig. Ex. 16.8**, and from this project an elevation looking in the direction of arrow E. *(CSE)*

9. The front elevation and end elevation of a wooden blotter are shown in **Fig. Ex. 16.9**. Draw the front elevation and plan of this and project an auxiliary elevation on the new ground line X_1Y_1. *(CSE)*

10. **Fig. Ex. 16.10** shows two views of a machined block which contains a central hole of 20 mm diameter and four holes of 7 mm diameter.

    Decide on the method of projection used and draw the given views, completing the end elevation by inserting the main hole, leaving centre lines to show the smaller holes.

    From the front elevation project a true view of the sloping face, showing all the holes correctly positioned.

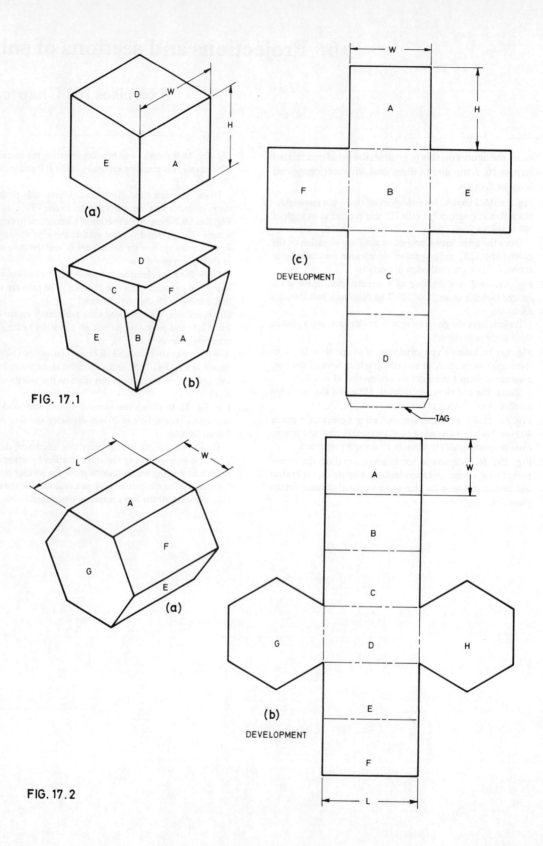

FIG. 17.1

FIG. 17.2

17. Developments

Sheet-metal parts, and components formed from thicker plate, are first cut out of the material of construction as a pattern in much the same way as cloth material is cut out to make clothing.

The stages in the production of a thin sheet-metal part, in the shape of an open box for example, can be broken down as follows.

The design of the part is decided in the drawing office and an orthographic drawing is made showing all the dimensions required of the finished article. During this stage the draughtsman will consider the methods of manufacture open to him in the factory.

As the part is to be cut out of flat sheet a *development* drawing, or pattern, is made. The draughtsman knows the size of sheet metal available and so he will ensure that the developed box-like component can be cut from this material in the most economical way, with the minimum of waste.

The development drawing is issued to the workshop and the craftsmen employed there follow the pattern laid out in the drawing office when cutting out the box.

After the cutting out operation, the sheet metal is folded along pre-determined bend lines. The box part is formed and the sides are joined together.

Sheet-metal parts can be soldered, welded, riveted, bolted or joined together using special adhesives. The method of joining will depend on the type of material, its thickness, and the intended use of the part in service.

It is often useful to be able to develop the surfaces of solid objects. When carrying out such work it is usual to assume that the surface of the solid is covered with a very thin film and it is this film which is the subject of the development exercise. In practice, thin sheet metal is sometimes cut out and used to sheath solid objects, especially architectural features such as roofs, domes, and spires. The metal used may be copper, lead, aluminium, or gilding metal which is a richly coloured brass containing a high percentage of copper.

Fig. 17.1 (a) shows an isometric drawing of a closed box in the shape of a cube, while the diagram at **(b)** is a drawing of the box showing the labelled sides prior to joining. **Fig. 17.1 (c)** is the development or pattern of the box laid out as a flat sheet. Following the system of labelling at (b), the position of the sides in the flat sheet are as indicated. The chain-dotted lines are the bend lines between the six sides.

It is intended that the edges of this box should be joined by soldering. In order to make the box very secure extra material could be left on adjoining sides to form tags. These would give an additional area of solder and the joints would be stronger. The shape of a typical tag is shown chain-dotted on the outer edge of side *D*.

It will be noted that the side pieces *E* and *F* in the development could be positioned adjoining any of the other sides and they need not be opposite one another.

Fig. 17.2 (a) is an isometric drawing of a hexagonal part made in thin metal. The development is shown in diagram **(b)**. Notice that the sides of the part are formed from rectangles having one side length equal to the side length of the hexagon.

The hexagon ends can be positioned adjoining any of the side rectangles.

Assuming that both of these examples were concerned with solid figures instead of hollow ones the method of developing the surfaces, neglecting the thickness of the metal, would be exactly the same.

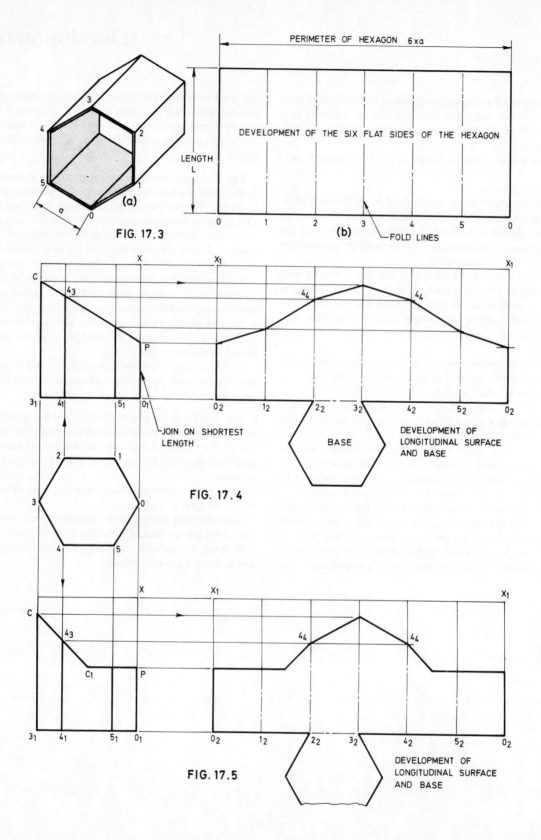

PERIMETER OF HEXAGON 6×a

DEVELOPMENT OF THE SIX FLAT SIDES OF THE HEXAGON

LENGTH
L

0   1   2   3   4   5   0

(b)

FOLD LINES

FIG. 17.3

(a)

JOIN ON SHORTEST
LENGTH

BASE

DEVELOPMENT OF
LONGITUDINAL SURFACE
AND BASE

FIG. 17.4

DEVELOPMENT OF
LONGITUDINAL SURFACE
AND BASE

FIG. 17.5

102

Fig. 17.3 (a) is an oblique drawing of a tube having an hexagonal section. The edge lines of the tube are numbered from 0 to 5, and the width of the flat strips making up the tube is a.

Fig. 17.3 (b) shows the development of the tube, the join line being that numbered 0. As the length of the tube is L, the development consists of six equal rectangles of length L and width a. The fold lines are indicated by the appropriate edge line number and by the chain-dotted lines.

Fig. 17.4 shows a hexagonal prism cut by a plane CP at any convenient angle. It is required to produce a development of the six faces of the complete prism, and also the effect of the cutting plane on this developed surface.

Draw the prism in plan and elevation, numbering the six base corners as shown in plan.

Imagining the figure to consist of a very thin film, marked with six equally spaced lines at each edge, it is intended to cut along edge line $P0_1$ in elevation and open out the film to form a flat figure.

Draw a line X_1X_1 equal in length to the perimeter of the hexagon and project the height of the prism from the elevation, to give the rectangle $X_1X_10_20_2$.

Draw vertical divisions to represent the corners of the hexagon and number as shown. This gives a development drawing of the complete prism. Draw the cutting plane CP at any convenient angle on the elevation. The intersections of CP and the hexagonal corners may now be projected on to the appropriate vertical lines on the development drawing, to give the required developed surface of the prism below the cutting plane.

Fig. 17.5 shows another hexagonal prism cut by a cranked plane CC_1P. For the purposes of division the elevation shares the plan drawn for **Fig. 17.4**. The method of setting out the development is as previously described.

Note in both of these latter drawings the bases are included as part of the development. The hexagon can be positioned on any face of the development, and its geometry will coincide with the plan view.

It is often useful to draw these developments on cartridge paper, or thin card, and then cut them out and fold them into the shapes from which the developments were derived. Transparent adhesive tape can be used to hold the folded sheet in place. This exercise will underline the need for accuracy in drawing, the use of bend lines and the reasons for choosing the shortest length as the join line.

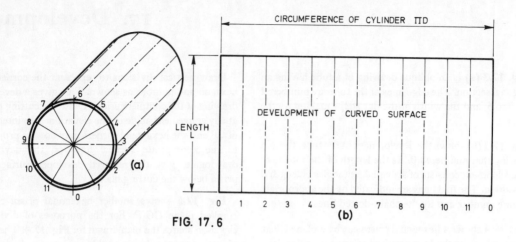

CIRCUMFERENCE OF CYLINDER ΠD

DEVELOPMENT OF CURVED SURFACE

LENGTH L

0 1 2 3 4 5 6 7 8 9 10 11 0

(b)

FIG. 17.6

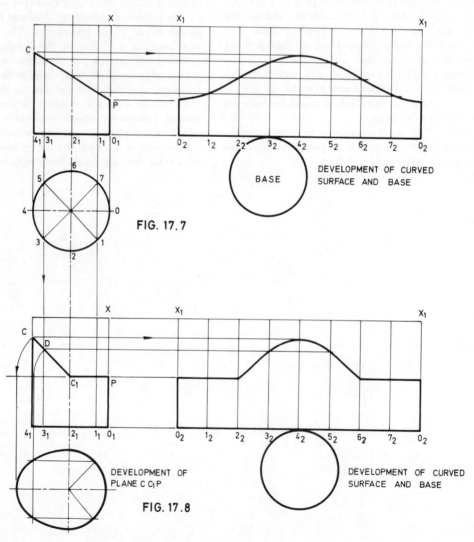

DEVELOPMENT OF CURVED SURFACE AND BASE

BASE

FIG. 17.7

DEVELOPMENT OF PLANE C C₁P

DEVELOPMENT OF CURVED SURFACE AND BASE

FIG. 17.8

17. Developments

Fig. 17.6 (a) is an oblique drawing of a circular tube, divided around its circumference into twelve equal and numbered parts. From each numbered point, chain-dotted generators are marked along the length of the cylinder. Fig. 17.6 (b) is the development of the tube, produced by cutting along the generator at 0 and opening out the sheet metal until it is flat. The developed sheet is a rectangle whose length is equal to the circumference of the cylinder and whose width is L, the length of the tube. A quick and acceptable method of producing the developed length of the circumference of the cylinder is to step out twelve times a distance equal to the chordal distance between any two of the numbered divisions. The alternative to this is to calculate the circumference by multiplying the diameter of the tube by π. As the tube is circular in section, bend lines are not required; the chain-dotted lines drawn in the figure indicate the positions of the generators on the flat sheet.

Fig. 17.7 shows a cylinder cut by a plane CP at any convenient angle. It is required to produce a development of the curved surface and the base of the cylinder. Draw the required plan and elevation. Divide the plan into any convenient number of equal parts, and project these on to the elevation as generators. Number as shown.

The full development will be a rectangle whose length is equal to the circumference of the cylinder. Divide the rectangle vertically into the same number of equal parts as the cylinder and number as shown. Projecting the intersections of the cutting plane and the generators on to the developed surface as before will produce the development of the portion of the cylinder below the cutting plane. It is assumed that the split line occurs along generator $X0_1$. The base will be a circle drawn touching the developed circumference at any convenient point.

Fig. 17.8 shows another cylinder cut by a cranked plane CP. The plan projections are obtained from Fig. 17.7 and the method of setting out the development is as previously described.

The plan view drawn in the bottom left-hand corner of the figure shows the development of the surface along the cutting plane CC_1P. That part of this plane to the right of C_1, when developed, is a semicircle. The sloping face must be rotated into the same plane as C_1P and then projected into the plan. To assist in producing the correct shape, point D is also rotated and projected, to provide two points which can be used to give the required egg-shaped development.

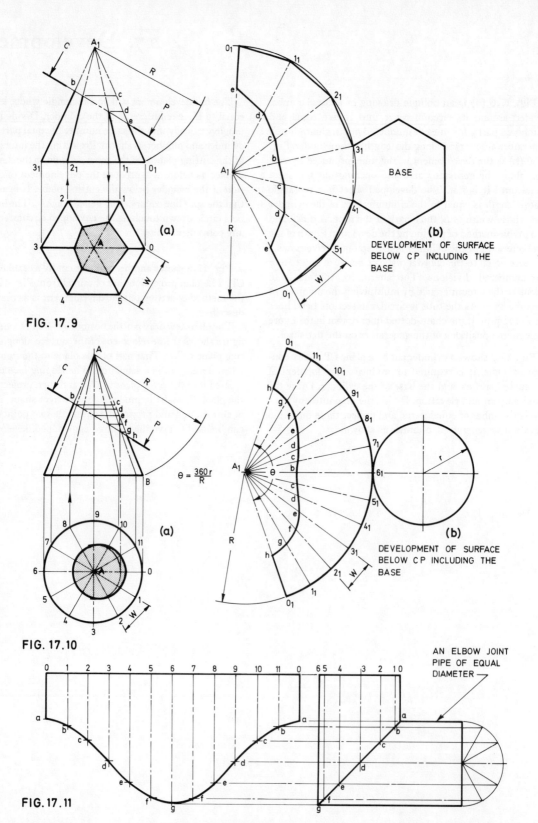

FIG. 17.9

$$\theta = \frac{360 r}{R}$$

(a)

(b)

DEVELOPMENT OF SURFACE
BELOW C P INCLUDING THE
BASE

BASE

FIG. 17.10

(a)

(b)

DEVELOPMENT OF SURFACE
BELOW C P INCLUDING THE
BASE

AN ELBOW JOINT
PIPE OF EQUAL
DIAMETER

FIG. 17.11

17. Developments

Fig. 17.9 (a) shows two views of an hexagonal based pyramid in first angle projection. The pyramid is cut by a sloping plane CP, the effect of which is indicated in plan by the shaded area. This is obtained by direct projection of the points of intersection of the cutting plane and the edge lines of the pyramid.

Fig. 17.9 (b) is the development of the surface area of the part of the pyramid lying below CP, including the base.

At any convenient point locate A_1 and with this point as centre, radius $A0_1$ or $A3_1$ taken from the elevation at (a), draw an arc through an angle of approximately 180°. From A_1 draw a vertical line and locate 0_1. From 0_1 step off inside the arc six widths equal to W in the plan view at (a). Number the points obtained to coincide with the numbering system adopted for the plan, i.e. 1_1, 2_1, 3_1, etc. Join these points to A_1, using chain-dotted lines and to one another around the inside of the arc.

It is now necessary to obtain the true length of the edge lines of the pyramid. $A_1 0_1$ and $A_1 3_1$ in elevation ($A0$ and $A3$ in plan) are the only true length lines that can be measured directly. The other edge lines must be rotated into the same plane as these in order to obtain their true lengths. The lengths required for development can be found by projecting the points of intersection of the edge lines and the cutting plane in elevation to the true length line $A_1 0_1$, to give points c and d. Using the compasses, mark off successively the lengths $A_1 b$, $A_1 c$, $A_1 d$, and $A_1 e$ on the development. It will be noted that these lengths, except $A_1 b$, appear twice. Join with straight lines all the points obtained and add the base to complete the development.

Fig. 17.10 (a) shows a plan and an elevation of a right circular cone cut by a sloping plane CP.

Draw these two views, locate the cutting plane at any convenient point and divide the plan into twelve equal parts, numbering as shown. Project each point into the base of the cone and then produce generators from the base to the apex A. Project all non-true lengths in elevation to the true length line AB to give points c, d, e, f and g.

To complete the plan, project the points of intersection of the generators with CP directly, to intersect the plan generators. To obtain the points on the vertical centre line, project point e into the plan to cut line $A0$. With A as centre, draw an arc from this point to give the required points on plan generators A_3 and A_9.

Locate A_1 and with this point as centre, radius AB, draw an arc. Divide this arc into twelve equal parts of width W taken from the plan. Join each point to A_1 and mark off on these lines the true lengths Ab, Ac, Ad, etc. Join these points by a smooth curve, draw a base circle at any convenient point and complete the development.

The angle subtended by the developed sheet at A_1 can be found from the formula $\theta = 360r/R$, where r is the radius of the base and R is the total slant length of the cone. When this formula is used, the twelve equal divisions may be found by angular measurement.

Fig. 17.11 shows an elevation of a pipe elbow and the development of one of the pieces of equal diameter pipe forming the elbow. As the pipes are the same size, the curve of intersection between the two is drawn as a straight line.

The method of producing the development is as follows. Adjacent to one end of the pipe in elevation draw a half end elevation and divide it into six equal parts. Produce generators on the surfaces of the cylinders, numbering as shown, and indicate with letters the point where the generators meet the curve of intersection (a, b, c, d, etc.). Project a base line equal in length to the circumference of the pipe. Divide this into twelve equal parts, produce ordinates as chain-dotted lines from each point and number as shown. Project from points a, b, c, d, etc., in elevation to the appropriate ordinate, similarly lettered, in the development. A smooth curve drawn through the points will enable the development drawing to be completed.

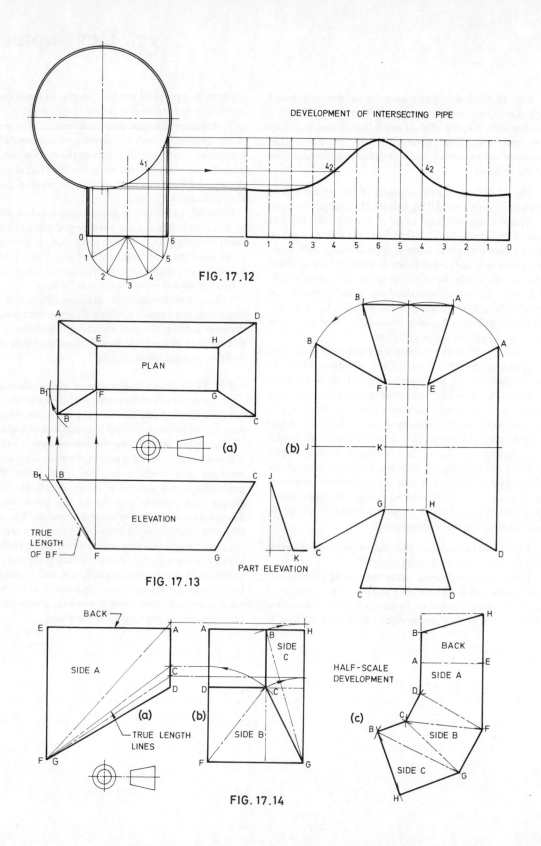

DEVELOPMENT OF INTERSECTING PIPE

FIG. 17.12

PLAN

ELEVATION

TRUE
LENGTH
OF BF

PART ELEVATION

FIG. 17.13

(a)

(b)

BACK

SIDE A

TRUE LENGTH
LINES

(a)

(b)

SIDE C

SIDE B

HALF-SCALE
DEVELOPMENT

BACK

SIDE A

SIDE B

SIDE C

(c)

FIG. 17.14

Fig. 17.12 shows a section through two intersecting circular pipes of different diameters together with the development of the smaller pipe. To produce the development it is first necessary to draw a half plan of the branch pipe, divide this into six equal parts, and number as shown. From each numbered division produce generators to intersect with the curve of the main pipe. Project the end of the branch pipe as a straight line and from any suitable point mark out a distance equal to its circumference. Divide this distance into twelve equal parts, number as shown, and draw vertical ordinates at each numbered division. From the points of intersection of the generators on the small pipe with the curve of the main pipe, project to cut the appropriately numbered ordinate in the development. Complete the outline of the development drawing by producing a smooth curve through the points obtained.

Fig. 17.13 (a) shows orthographic views of a sheet-metal dish with sloping sides and ends. It is required to produce a development in one piece. Before commencing the development drawing, it is necessary to determine the true length of the corner edges. As each one is the same length, one construction will do for them all.

With compasses centred on point F in plan, radius FB, draw an arc to cut GF produced in B_1. Project this point into the elevation, cutting CB produced in B_1. Join B_1F, which will be the true length of BF.

The development is shown in diagram (b). Draw the base rectangle $EFGH$, spaced about the two centre lines. With centres E, F, G, and H in turn, radius equal to the true length line B_1F, draw arcs. Each pair of arcs at the ends of the development will intersect on the centre lines. With these points as centre in turn, and radius half the distance between A and B in plan, draw arcs to cut the former

arcs at A, B, C, and D. Join AB and CD. Join AE, BF, CG, and DH.

Draw a part end elevation to show the sloping side, represented by the line JK. This part view, which can be projected directly from the two orthographic views, gives the true length of the centre of the longest sloping sides. Set this distance off along the horizontal centre line from K in the development. Join BC passing through J. Repeat the construction on the other side of the vertical centre line and hence complete the development.

Fig. 17.14 (a) and (b) show two views of a sheet-metal transformer piece having a rectangular base, a square opening at the top, and two sloping sides. The drawing at (c) is the development of the transformer piece drawn half scale.

The plan view at (b) is divided into convenient triangles, the corners and sides are labelled, and each sloping line is rotated about a corner into the same plane as the elevation at (a). True lengths of the sloping lines are produced on the elevation in the manner previously described.

Commence the development at H. Mark off HE and EF, which can be measured directly as length and width from (a) and (b). Using the compasses, mark off FC, FD, and FG in space. Produce AE and, with A as centre, draw arcs to give AB and AD. From D locate point C. Join FC and FD. From C locate G by drawing an arc of radius equal to the true length of CG. Join CG. With G as centre draw arcs in space of radius GB and GH. With C as centre locate point B. Join BG. With B as centre, radius BH taken from the other end of the development, locate H to complete the construction. Draw the development in firm outline and include the chain-dotted fold lines.

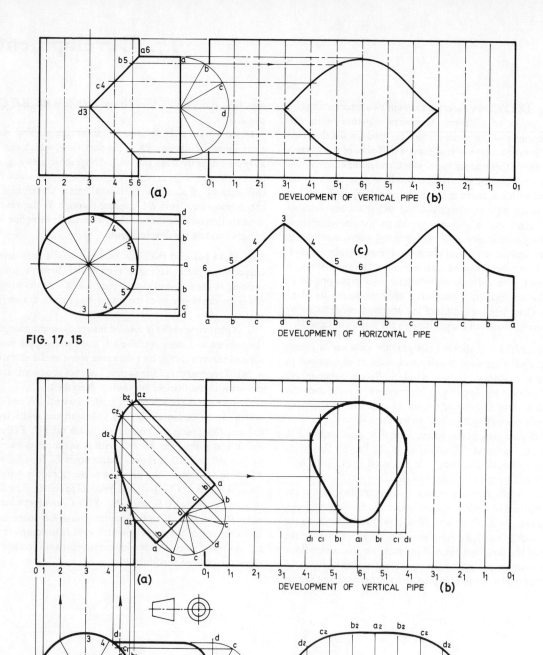

(a)

DEVELOPMENT OF VERTICAL PIPE **(b)**

(c)

DEVELOPMENT OF HORIZONTAL PIPE

FIG. 17.15

(a)

DEVELOPMENT OF VERTICAL PIPE **(b)**

DEVELOPMENT OF SLOPING PIPE **(c)**

FIG. 17.16

110

Fig. 17.15 (a) shows two views of pipes of equal diameter intersecting one another at 90° while Fig. 17.15 (b) and (c) show developments of the vertical and horizontal pipes respectively. Draw the elevation and plan of the complete tee piece, dividing the surfaces of both pipes into the same number of equally spaced generators. Number the generators, using a system which will clearly identify each generator on all views. Drawing lines through the points of intersection of the generators in the elevation will indicate the join line of the two pipes, or the curve of intersection. When the two pipes are of equal diameter and at 90° to one another, the intersection will appear as two straight lines forming an angle of 90°, whose apex coincides with the centre line of the vertical pipe.

To develop the vertical pipe, first draw a rectangle equal in length to the circumference of the pipe and whose breadth is equal to the length of the pipe. Divide the rectangle into the same number of equal parts as there are generators on the surface of the pipe. Produce ordinates 1_1, 2_1, 3_1, 4_1, etc. Project from each point on the curve of intersection to cut the appropriate ordinate; thus $a6$ cuts ordinate 6_1, $b5$ cuts ordinate 5_1, $c4$ cuts ordinate 4_1, etc.

To develop the horizontal pipe, first draw a line equal in length to the circumference of the pipe. Divide this line into the same number of equal parts as there are generators on the surface of the pipe. Produce ordinates a, b, c, d, etc., and commencing with the shortest length, mark off on them the appropriate length of each generator taken from either the plan or the elevation. A smooth curve drawn

through the points obtained will complete the development.

Fig. 17.16 (a) show two views of intersecting pipes whose diameters are unequal. The procedure for producing the curve of intersection is as previously described, except that the points projected from the plan into the elevation are those where the generators on the sloping pipe cut the vertical pipe, as indicated by a_1, b_1, c_1, etc.

To draw the development at (b), first produce a rectangle whose length is equal to the circumference of the vertical pipe and whose breadth is equal to the height. Locate the centre of the development sheet (as at 6_1) and draw a vertical centre line. To either side of this line draw vertical ordinates whose distances apart are taken from the developed distances in plan of the points a_1, b_1, c_1, and d_1. Project from the points lying in the curve of intersection (a_2, b_2, c_2, d_2, etc.) to cut the appropriate ordinate on the development drawing. A smooth curve drawn through the points obtained will give the hole required in the developed sheet.

To draw a development of the sloping pipe at (c), first produce a base line equal in length to the circumference of the pipe. Divide this into the same number of equal parts as there are generators and produce ordinates a, b, c, d, etc. Mark off along these ordinates distances equal to the lengths of the generator taken from either the plan or elevation. A smooth curve drawn through the points obtained will give the required development.

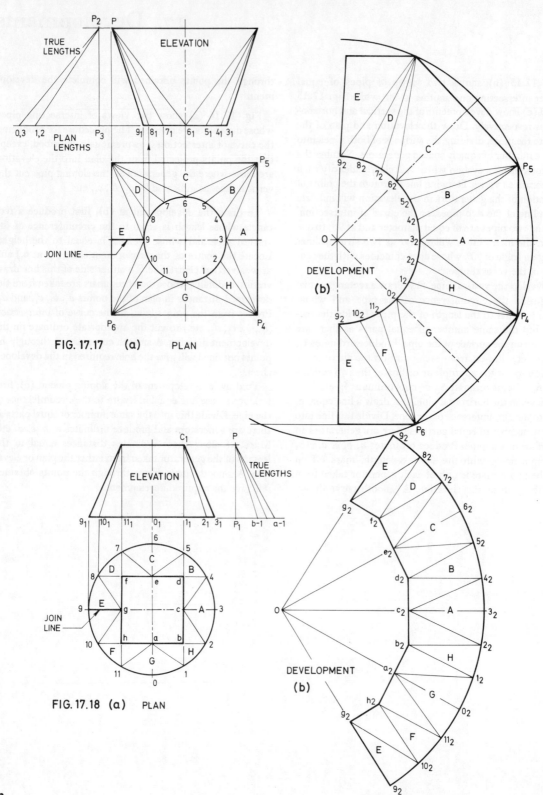

TRUE LENGTHS

ELEVATION

PLAN LENGTHS

JOIN LINE

DEVELOPMENT
(b)

FIG. 17.17   (a)   PLAN

TRUE LENGTHS

ELEVATION

JOIN LINE

DEVELOPMENT
(b)

FIG. 17.18 (a)   PLAN

17. Developments

The development of a sheet-metal square-to-round transition piece is shown in **Fig. 17.17 (a) and (b).** Components of this type are used in pipework or air ducting where a change of section is required.

Draw the plan and elevation. Divide the circular section in plan into any convenient number of equal parts, project on the elevation and label as shown. Join the equal divisions for each quarter of a circle to its appropriate corner in plan and elevation, as indicated at P, P_4, and P_5.

Set out the true lengths of the generators by transferring plan lengths on to a horizontal line and joining to a projected vertical height, as previously described ($P_4 1$, $P_4 2$, in plan becoming $P_3 1$, $P_3 2$, etc.). The development itself becomes a series of joined triangles, although, in fact, the curved portions which give the change of section of the transition piece are parts of oblique cones.

At any convenient point draw a horizontal centre line, and draw $P_4 P_5$ perpendicular to it and equally disposed about it, the length of this line being equal to the length of one side of the square.

With compasses set at the true length of $P_2 3$ in the true length diagram, and centre P_4, draw an arc to cut the horizontal centre line at 3_2. Join 3_2 to P_4 and P_5, to give the development of triangle A.

With centre P_4 and radius $P_2 2$ from the true length diagram, draw an arc. With centre 3_2 and radius equal to the length of the arc of a division on the circle in plan, draw an arc to intersect the first in 2_2. Join P_4 and 2_2. Repeat this process for points $P_4 1_2$, $P_4 0_2$, to obtain the development of segment H.

With P_4 as centre and the length of one side of the square as radius, draw an arc. With 0_2 as centre and $0_2 P_4$ as radius draw another arc to intersect the first in P_6. Join $P_4 P_6$ and bisect. Erect a perpendicular passing through 0_2 to locate 0, the centre of a circumscribing circle for the figure.

Develop triangle G and segment F as previously described.

Continue the development, drawing a smooth curve through the points obtained in developing the curved segment.

The triangulation method of development is again used for the round-to-square transition piece shown in **Fig. 17.18 (a) and (b).**

Draw the plan and elevation and divide the circular base into twelve equal parts, numbering as shown. Join these twelve points to the corners and centre points on the square, to form a series of curved-based triangles. Project generators on to the elevation as in the previous example, and also produce a true length diagram.

At any convenient point draw a horizontal centre line and mark off $c_2 3_2$ along it, this distance being the true length $c_1 3_1$ in elevation. At c_2 erect a perpendicular $b_2 d_2$, equal in length to one side of the square and disposed equally about the centre line. Mark off $c_2 2_2$ and $c_2 4_2$ using dividers or compasses and taking the length from the true length diagram. Join 2_2 and 4_2 to b_2, c_2, and d_2 as shown to give segment A.

With b_2 as centre and $b_2 2_2$ as radius, draw an arc, and with 2_2 as centre and the length of the arc of one of the twelve circumferential divisions in plan as radius, draw another arc to intersect the first in 1_2. Join $b_2 1_2$ to give segment H.

With b_2 as centre, radius ab in plan, draw an arc, and with 1_2 as centre, radius $c_2 2_2$, draw an arc to intersect the first in a_2. Join $a_2 1_2$.

Using compasses mark off $a_2 0_2$, making it equal in length to $c_2 3_2$.

Draw a line from 0_2 passing through a_2 to intersect the horizontal centre line in 0.

With 0 as centre, radius $0 3_2$, draw the base arc to pass through 6_2 and 0_2.

The development may now be completed, all the lines required having been drawn at least once.

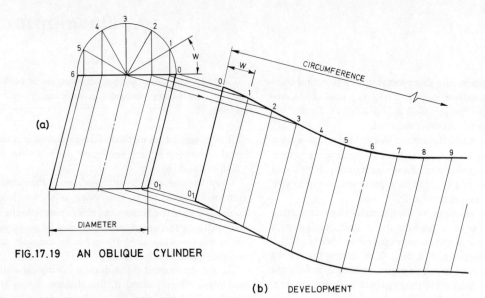

FIG.17.19   AN OBLIQUE CYLINDER

(a)

(b)   DEVELOPMENT

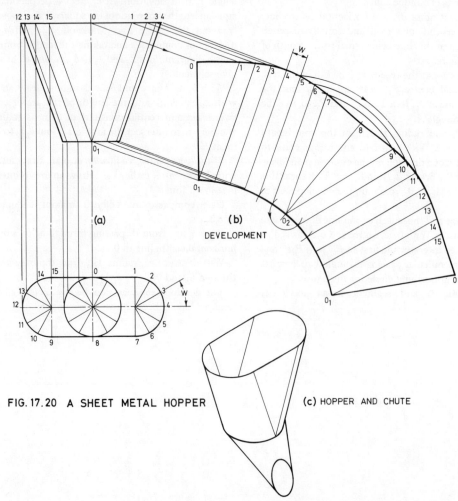

(a)

(b)   DEVELOPMENT

FIG. 17.20 A SHEET METAL HOPPER

(c) HOPPER AND CHUTE

Fig. 17.19 (a) shows the elevation of an oblique cylinder, that is a cylinder whose plan is a true circle but whose axial centre line is not perpendicular to the base diameter. Fig. 17.19 (b) is the development of most of the cylinder, which is projected from the elevation. This method of producing the development drawing has taken all the available space, making the drawing incomplete. However, there is sufficient detail to enable students to follow the method because the development is symmetrical about its centre line (line 6).

Draw the elevation and half plan, as shown in Fig. 17.19 (a), dividing the half plan into six equal parts and numbering. Project the equal divisions downwards, parallel to the longitudinal centre line, so that the cylinder may be considered as having twelve equally spaced lines drawn on its surface. Each of these lines is true length.

Projecting at right angles to the longitudinal centre line, draw the split line 00_1 at a convenient point, to become the first edge line of the development. Similarly project the other equal divisions at each end of the cylinder as shown.

With compasses set at width W, taken from the half plan, mark off from 00_1 twelve equal divisions successively at 1, 2, 3, etc., each arc cutting the appropriate line projected from the elevation. Draw a smooth curve through the points obtained, to give the development.

The hopper shown in Fig. 17.20 (a) consists of two halves of oblique cylinders joined by two triangular flat sheets.

The elevation and plan, here drawn in third angle projection, should be self-explanatory.

Divide the central hole and the two semicircular ends, as shown in the plan, and number the divisions obtained. Project these divisions vertically upwards on to the elevation, to give the required surface divisions.

To produce the development, commence by projecting $0,0_1$, the split line and first edge line, at right angles to the sloping side of the elevation. Similarly project the other equal divisions at each end of the cylinder as shown. The triangle $0,1,0_1$, being composed of true length lines, is the same in both elevation and development.

Divisions 1, 2, 3, etc., in the development are drawn as previously described for the oblique cylinder, until line $7,0_2$ is reached. With 0_2 as centre and 0_27 as radius, draw an arc to intersect the projector 1, 7 from the elevation, to give point 9. Join $9,0_2$. Join 7 and 9 with a straight line which, when bisected, gives point 8, marking the centre of the development.

With 0_2 as centre, continue to mark off points 6, 5, 4, etc., on the opposite side of the centre line 0_28, to give points 10, 11, 12, etc.

Smooth curves drawn between the points obtained will give the development of the hopper.

A typical example of the application of this type of hopper is shown in Fig. 17.20 (c). The chute depicted in this isometric sketch is a frustum of an oblique cone.

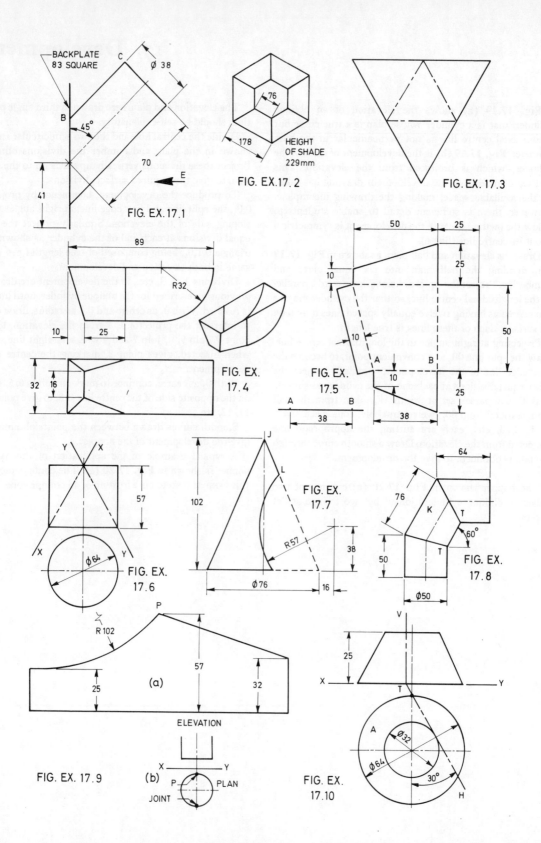

BACKPLATE
83 SQUARE

C

Ø 38

B

45°

70

41

E

FIG. EX.17.1

76

178

HEIGHT
OF SHADE
229mm

FIG. EX.17.2

FIG. EX. 17.3

89

R32

10

25

32

16

FIG. EX.
17.4

50

25

10

25

10

50

10

A

B

25

A

B

38

38

FIG. EX.
17.5

Y

X

57

X

Y

Ø 64

FIG. EX.
17.6

J

L

102

R57

38

Ø 76

16

FIG. EX.
17.7

64

76

K

T

50

60°

T

Ø50

FIG. EX.
17.8

P

R 102

57

25

32

(a)

ELEVATION

X

Y

P

PLAN

JOINT

FIG. EX. 17.9

(b)

V

25

X

Y

T

A

Ø32

Ø64

30°

H

FIG. EX.
17.10

116

17. Developments

Exercises for Chapter 17

1. The elevation of a socket and backplate, for supporting a flagpole, is shown in **Fig. Ex. 17.1**. Draw the given elevation and either,
   (a) an end elevation from *E* including all hidden detail,
   or
   (b) a development of the socket with the seam at *BC*.
   Dimensions in millimetres. (*CSE*)
2. **Fig. Ex. 17.2** shows the plan of a lamp shade which is in the form of a truncated pyramid. Both top and bottom hexagons are regular. Draw the following views to a scale of $\frac{1}{4}$:
   (a) a plan,
   (b) a front elevation,
   (c) an end elevation,
   (d) a development of the lamp shade. (*CSE*)
3. **Fig. 17. 3** shows the development of a tetrahedron. Sketch the three orthographic views of this solid. (*CSE*)
4. The drawings in **Fig. Ex. 17.4** show the bucket for a model dredger. Draw, full size, a one-piece development. Tabs are not required.
   All dimensions are in millimetres. (*CSE*)
5. On a line *AB*, in first angle projection, draw a plan and project a front view of the development of a metal container, shown in **Fig. Ex. 17.5**. (*CSE*)
6. The plan and elevation of a solid cylinder, 64 mm diameter and 57 mm high, are shown in **Fig. Ex. 17.6**. The cylinder is cut by two planes *XX* and *YY* to form a wedge with a circular base. Draw, full size,
   (a) the plane and elevation of the wedge,
   (b) the true shape of one of the sloping faces of the wedge,
   (c) the development of the curved surface of the wedge.

(Note: the length of the circumference of a 64 mm diameter circle may be assumed to be 201 mm.) (*AEB*)
7. **Fig. Ex. 17.7** shows an elevation of a cone from which a portion has been cut away by a cylindrical surface.
   Draw, full size,
   (a) the given elevation, and
   (b) the development of the curved surface taking *JL* as the joint line. (*AEB*)
8. **Fig. Ex. 17.8** shows three pipes, each of 50 mm diameter and of negligible thickness, with their axes in the same plane and forming a bend through 90°.
   Draw, full size,
   (a) the given view, and
   (b) the development of pipe *K*, using *TT* as the joint line. (*AEB*)
9. **Fig. Ex. 17.9 (a)** shows the development of the cylindrical surface of a portion of a 50 mm diameter right circular cylinder. Draw the given development accurately and use it to produce a plan and elevation of the incomplete cylinder. The views are to be in first angle projection and arranged as shown in **Fig. Ex. 17.9 (b)**. (*Camb.*)
10. **Fig. Ex. 17.10** shows the plan and elevation of a solid which is divided into two parts by the auxiliary vertical plane *VTH*. Draw a development of that part of the sloping surface of the solid which is indicated by the letter *A* in the plan view. (*Camb.*)

Further development exercises are to be found at the end of the next chapter, where problems dealing with the intersections of solids and development of the surfaces of solids are combined.

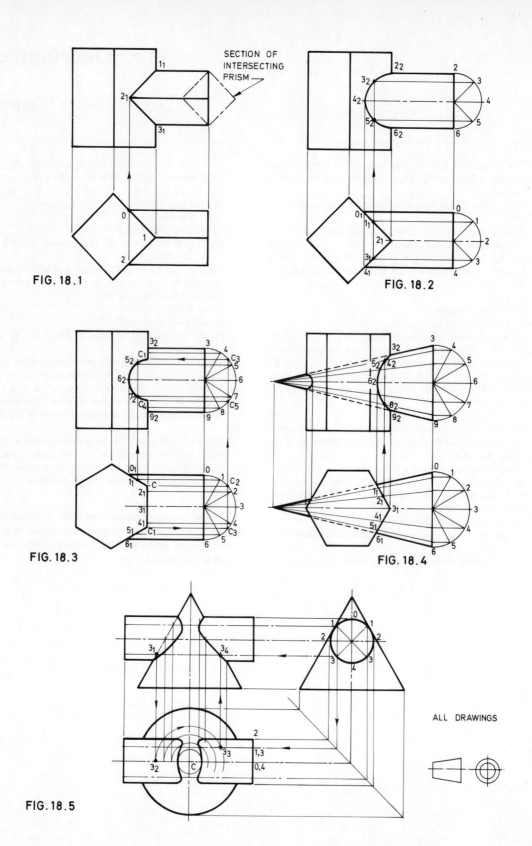

SECTION OF
INTERSECTING
PRISM

FIG. 18.1

FIG. 18.2

FIG. 18.3

FIG. 18.4

FIG. 18.5

ALL DRAWINGS

18. Intersections

The shape of the lines of intersection caused by the meeting of solid objects will depend upon the shape of the contacting surfaces. The intersection of two plane surfaces will be denoted by straight lines, and the intersection of curved surfaces will be denoted by curved lines.

At least two views of the intersecting solids will need to be drawn in order to produce the required shapes, and generally these views must be developed together because the shape of one depends so much on its projected shape.

Reference should be made to the previous chapter in which the intersection curves of pipes have been drawn prior to development. This will give an appreciation of the practical application of the exercises in this chapter.

Fig. 18.1 shows the intersection of two square prisms of different sizes. Draw the plan and lay out as much of the elevation as possible without showing the lines of intersection. In the plan view three intersecting angular edges are shown at 0, 1, and 2. In elevation points 0 and 2 become the limits of penetration on the centre line of the smaller prism shown at 2_1 and point 1 becomes the point of least penetration at 1_1 and 3_1. Joining 1_1, 2_1, and 3_1 by straight lines will give the required shape. Intermediate points may be marked and projected to verify that the intersection is shown by straight lines.

Fig. 18.2 shows a square prism intersected by a cylinder. Draw the plan and elevation in outline. Produce a part end elevation for the cylinder in both views and divide into a convenient number of equal parts, producing these as generators along the surface of the cylinder. The generators will contact the faces of the prism in plan as shown. The vertical projection of these points on to the corresponding generators in elevation will, when joined, produce the required curve.

Fig. 18.3 shows the intersection of a cylinder with a hexagonal prism. Draw the plan and elevation together in outline. Draw a part end elevation of the cylinder and divide into a number of equal parts and produce these as generators. No curve will be seen along face CC_1, but these points must be located in elevation to indicate the true point of the commencement of the intersecting curve. Project C and C_1 on to the part end elevation in plan, then vertically on to the elevation, finally to locate C_1C_4, the starting point for the curve. Continue the projection as previously described to produce the required curve.

Fig. 18.4 shows the intersection of a cone with a hexagonal prism. Draw the plan and elevation together. Divide the cone surface with generators in both views. Project the points of intersection of the generators, and the prism in plan, vertically on to the corresponding generators in elevation to give the points required to produce curves. The same procedure should be adopted for angular penetrations.

Fig. 18.5 shows the intersection of a cylinder with a cone. Draw the outline of the three views. Divide the cylinder into a number of equal parts and produce generators as shown. The points of contact of the generators and the sides of the cone in elevation may be treated as diametral slices and are used to produce the required curves in the following manner: project the point of contact 3_1 downwards on to the centre line of the cylinder in plan 3_2. With C as centre, draw an arc to cut the corresponding plan generator at the required point 3_3. Project this point upwards to intersect the appropriate generator in elevation 3_4, to give a point on the required curve. Continue this process for each generator.

119

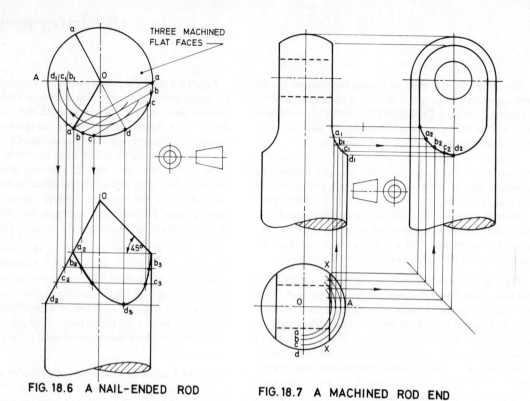

THREE MACHINED
FLAT FACES →

FIG. 18.6 A NAIL-ENDED ROD

FIG. 18.7 A MACHINED ROD END

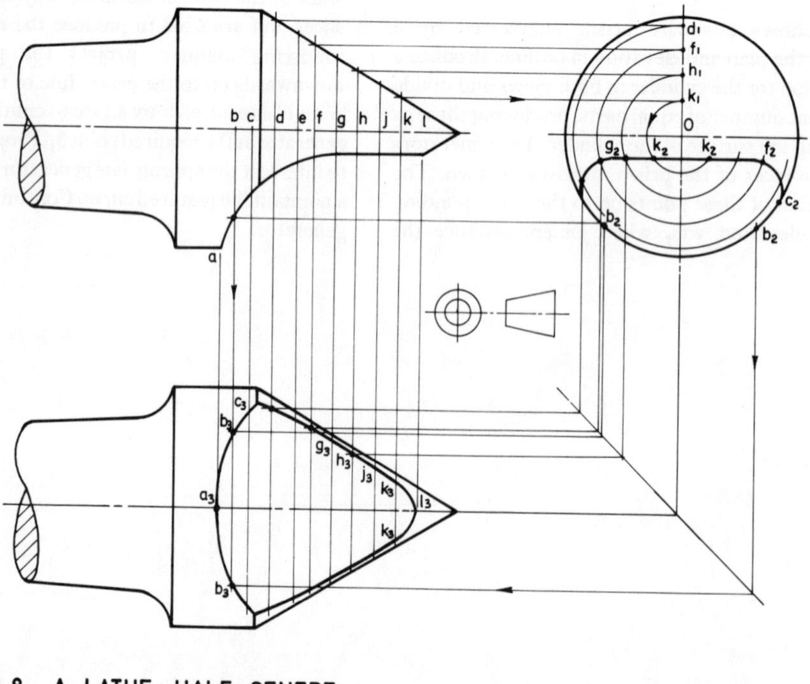

FIG. 18.8 A LATHE HALF-CENTRE

On the facing page are three examples of machined components. During the machining processes involved in producing these shapes there is contact between the components and the cutting tools, the result of which is curves of intersection. Machined parts of the type shown here represent the practical application of the principles of orthographic projection and the construction of curves of intersection.

Fig. 18.6 shows a circular rod which has three plane surfaces machined into it to form a nail point. It is required to determine the curve of intersection formed by the cutting during the nailing operation.

The orthographic views given are in third angle projection.

Draw the two views in outline, showing the three equally spaced plane surfaces in the plan view and labelling the edge lines Oa as shown.

Join two of the points aa across one of the faces and bisect this line to give Od as a continuation of the third edge line Oa. Draw, parallel to aa, any required number of lines such as bb and cc to act as generators in the plan. Each of these parallel lines contacts the line Od at a point and, with O as centre and each point in turn as radius, draw arcs to cut the horizontal centre line OA in b_1, c_1, and d_1. Project these points into the elevation.

In the elevation set out, the given 45° edge line as a true view of Oa. From the point of intersection of this inclined line and the diameter of the rod, project a horizontal line to meet at a_2 with a projector from a directly above it in plan. Draw a straight line from O through a_2 to give d_2 on the diameter of the rod. Project across the rod from d_2 to meet at d_3 with a projector from d in plan. This will give the lowest point on the required curve. Project downwards the points b_1, c_1, and d_1 in plan to intersect with the sloping face Od_2, to give b_2 and c_2. Generators produced across the face of the bar will contact projectors from the two sets of points labelled a, b, and c, and these points of contact will give b_3 and c_3 both of which lie in the required curve of intersection.

Fig. 18.7 shows three views in first angle orthographic projection of a rod machined to give what is called a *clevis*. The machining process consists of milling two flat surfaces into the circular bar, drilling a hole to take the clevis pin and

rounding the end of the bar. It is required to draw the curve of intersection produced as a result of the machining operations.

With the centre O in plan, draw a series of arcs which need not be equally spaced, to intersect one of the flats XX at two points for each arc. These arcs are labelled a, b, and c, the outside diameter being d. They intersect the centre line OA and from these points of intersection project vertically upwards to meet the given fillet radius at a_1, b_1, c_1, and d_1. Project these points horizontally across the end elevation to contact projectors from the arc points on face XX in plan.

These points of contact will give a_2, b_2, c_2, and d_2, all of which lie in the required curve.

Fig. 18.8 shows three views in third angle orthographic projection of a lathe half-centre. This is an example of the intersection of a milling cutter with a conical and cylindrical machined bar. A half-centre is a device which is used in a lathe to turn a component between centres. The cut-out portion allows the cutting tools to traverse the whole length of the bar before being run out.

Draw the three views in outline.

Divide the elevation into any number of slices at right angles to the longitudinal centre line, extending along the machined face. These are shown lettered a to l. Produce these divisions to divide up the plan.

Project the points of intersection of the slices and the cone face horizontally, to meet the end-elevation centre line at d_1, g_1, etc., and produce these points as circles struck from the centre, to give an end view of the slices.

The milled contour in elevation cuts through the vertical slices at given points, which must be projected horizontally to intersect the corresponding circle in the end elevation at b_2, c_2, f_2, etc. A smooth curve drawn through the points obtained will complete the end elevation.

All the points on the end elevation must now be projected on to the plan, as shown, to intersect with the vertical projections previously made to give points a_3, b_3, c_3, etc., through which a smooth curve should be drawn.

It will be particularly noted that, although the milled contour extends into the parallel portion of the bar, the effect of this will not be seen in the end elevation. The projections must still be made, however, to enable the plan to be completed.

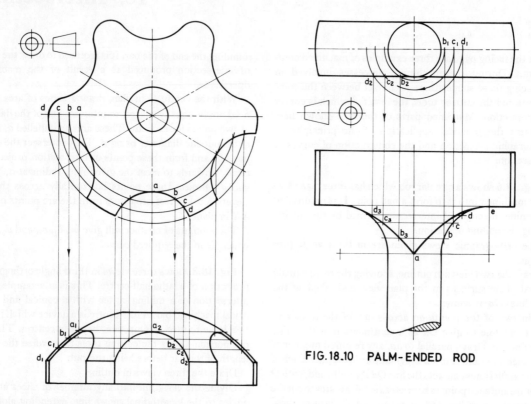

FIG. 18.9   VALVE HANDWHEEL

FIG.18.10   PALM-ENDED ROD

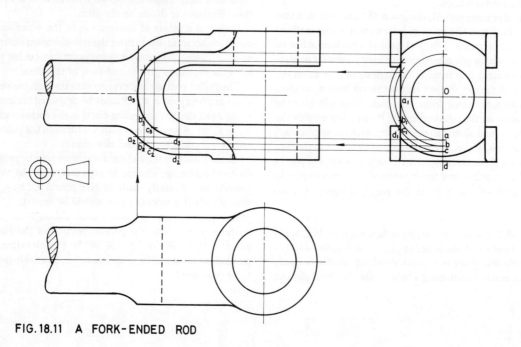

FIG. 18.11 A FORK-ENDED ROD

Fig. 18.9 shows a third angle orthographic projection of a valve handwheel of the type used on domestic hot water radiator installations. It is essentially a circular, domed component, with cutouts to fit the fingers of the hand. In practice the handwheel would not have sharp corners or edges at the extremities of the cut-outs. The shape would be more like that shown at the top. The sharp edges have been retained in this exmple so that the definition given to the projections is sharper and allows points of projection to be accurately located. It is required to draw a plan and elevation showing the curves of intersection.

In the plan view, draw any number of concentric arcs struck from the centre and extending inwards towards the centre for a distance equal to the depth of the finger cutouts. Where they meet the horizontal centre line label them a, b, c, and d as shown.

Project these points vertically downwards to meet the curve of the elevation at $_1$, b_1, c_1, and d_1. Draw horizontal slices across the elevation from these latter points.

From the intersections of the semicircular arcs and the finger cut-out radii in the plan project vertically downwards to meet the appropriate horizontal slices in the elevation as shown at a_2, b_2, c_2, and d_2. These points will lie on the required curve of intersection. Continued projection from plan to elevation will give the curves of intersection for three of the finger cut-outs.

This type of valve handwheel is usually moulded in a hard thermosetting plastics material such as phenol formaldehyde, or *Bakelite* as it is often called.

Fig. 18.10 shows two views in first angle orthographic projection of a palm-ended rod. This is a circular-sectioned bar flattened at one end by forging operations and having a width equal to the diameter of the bar. The forging processes produce intersection curves as the shape of the bar changes from circular to flat.

It is required to produce the curves of intersection. Draw the plan and the outline of the elevation.

Across the total depth of the blending radius ae draw a series of horizontal slices, which need not be equally spaced, labelling them b, c, d, and e, as shown.

Project the points of contact of the slices with the blending radius vertically upwards to meet the horizontal centre line in the plan at b_1, c_1, and d_1. Draw these latter points as arcs struck from the centre, to intersect with the flattened face at b_2, c_2, and d_2. Project b_2, c_2, and d_2 vertically downwards to locate the points b_3, c_3, and d_3, lying on the horizontal slices in the elevation.

Draw the required curve of intersection through the points obtained.

Fig. 18.11 shows a first angle orthographic drawing of a fork-ended rod treated as a practical exercise in determining curves of intersection. The fork-end is a forging and during the forging operations a series of hammer blows is delivered to the metal to make it flow into the desired shape. The basic shape of the fork-end is circular but the sides are flattened to give clearance when the fork swings during its working cycle. This flattening process produces curves of intersection owing to the changes in section.

Draw the outline of the three views.

With O in the end elevation as centre, draw a series of arcs such as those labelled a, b, c, and d. These arcs, which need not be equally spaced, will intersect the flattened face at the points labelled a_1, b_1, c_1, and d_1.

Project from the end elevation into the front elevation the points a, b, c, and d until they make contact with the outside curved surface of the fork at points a_2, b_2, c_2, and d_2. Erect perpendiculars from these points across the face of the front elevation to intersect the horizontal projectors from points a_1, b_1, c_1, etc., to give a final set of points a_3, b_3, c_3, and d_3 which all lie in half of the required curve of intersection.

In this method use is made of circular slices concentric with the centre of the rod being interrupted by the flat faces formed in the rod surface. As the interruptions take place at definite points in the arcs formed by the circular slices, they can be used to provide a means of projection into other views.

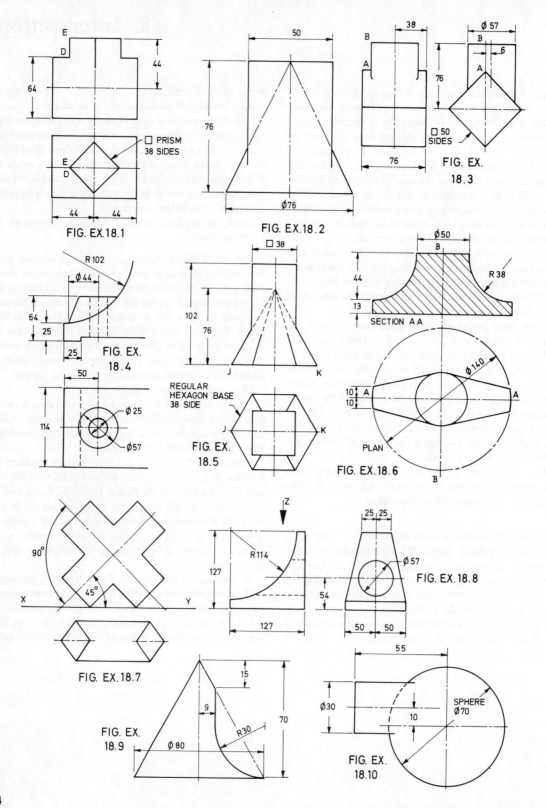

FIG. EX.18.1

FIG. EX.18.2

FIG. EX.18.3

FIG. EX.18.4

FIG. EX.18.5

FIG. EX.18.6

FIG. EX.18.7

FIG. EX.18.8

FIG. EX.18.9

FIG. EX.18.10

PRISM 38 SIDES

□ 50 SIDES

SECTION A A

PLAN

REGULAR HEXAGON BASE 38 SIDE

SPHERE Ø70

1. **Fig. Ex. 18.1** shows the plan and incomplete elevation of the junction of a hollow square prism with a cylinder.
   (a) Complete the elevation showing the curves of intersection properly constructed.
   (b) Draw the development of the outer surface of the square prism which is joined along the edge *DE*.   (*Camb.*)
2. **Fig. Ex. 18.2** shows the incomplete elevation of parts of a square prism and right circular cone whose axes coincide and whose outer surfaces intersect.
      Draw the complete elevation showing the lines of intersection properly produced.   (*Camb.*)
3. A length of a sheet-metal air duct is intersected by a circular tube manufactured from similar material. The arrangement of the duct and pipe is shown in **Fig. Ex. 18.3** by two elevations, one of which is partly completed. Draw
   (a) the views as given and complete the elevation by showing the entire of intersection of the outer surfaces of the duct and pipes—the hidden detail should be shown by a dotted line;
   (b) the development of the circular pipe with a butt joint along *AB*.
      Neglect the thickness of the sheet metal.   (*Camb.*)
4. A portion of the foot of a casting is represented in the first angle elevation and part plan shown in **Fig. Ex. 18.4**. The part represented takes the form of a truncated cone, with a diameter on the cut face of 57 mm and a base radius of 44 mm, intersecting a surface of single curvature of 102 mm radius.
      Draw the given elevation and the complete plan of the portion of the casting, *showing clearly the construction of the curve of intersection of the cone and the curved surface.*
                        (*Camb.*)
5. The first angle plan and the part elevation shown in **Fig. Ex. 18.5** represent a sheet-metal pyramid with a regular hexagonal base, intersected by a prism of square cross-section. Draw
   (a) the given plan and the complete elevation of the arrangement,
   (b) the development of that portion of the outer sloping surface of the pyramid, which lies below the line *JK* in the plan.   (*Camb.*)
6. The plan and sectional elevation of a lever end are shown in **Fig. Ex. 18.6**. The final shape is produced by removing those portions of a solid of revolution depicted by chain-dotted lines in the plan view.
      Draw, full size, that half of the plan which lies to the left of *BB* together with the corresponding half elevation showing the curve of intersection accurately constructed.   (*Camb.*)
7. The incomplete plan and incomplete elevation of two right square prisms, intersecting symetrically at 90°, are shown in **Fig. Ex. 18.7**. Each prism is 95 mm long and the length of the side of the square is 25 mm. Draw and complete the given views and add an end elevation. No hidden lines are to be shown.   (*AEB*)
8. Two elevations of a wheel stop are shown in **Fig. Ex. 18.8**. Draw, full size,
   (a) the given elevation,
   (b) a plan looking in the direction of arrow *Z*.   (*AEB*)
9. **Fig. Ex. 18.9** shows the elevation of a right circular cone with a portion cut away.
      Draw, full size, the given elevation and project a plan and end elevation, showing the curve of intersection between the milling cutter used and the cone surface.
10. **Fig. Ex. 18.10** shows a sphere penetrated by a cylinder. In plan the axis of the cylinder lies on the horizontal centre line of the sphere.
      Project sufficient views to show the curve of intersection, the drawings to be full size.

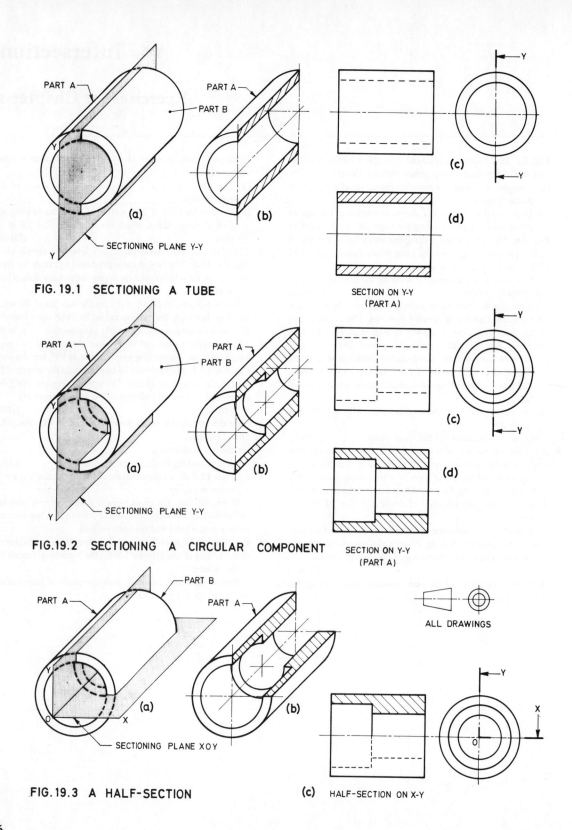

FIG. 19.1 SECTIONING A TUBE

PART A
PART B
SECTIONING PLANE Y-Y
(a)
(b)
(c)
(d)
SECTION ON Y-Y
(PART A)

FIG.19.2 SECTIONING A CIRCULAR COMPONENT

PART A
PART B
SECTIONING PLANE Y-Y
(a)
(b)
(c)
(d)
SECTION ON Y-Y
(PART A)

FIG. 19.3 A HALF-SECTION

PART B
PART A
SECTIONING PLANE XOY
(a)
(b)
ALL DRAWINGS
(c) HALF-SECTION ON X-Y

19. Sectioning and conventions

Sectioning a solid object is carried out to achieve a number of things.

1. By cutting open an object it is possible to see its inside construction.
2. Sectional views can dispense with the need to use dotted lines to represent hidden detail.
3. The number of views required to give a complete picture of the object are often reduced.
4. A sectional view of a mechanism can show much more easily how that mechanism works.

A section of an object is produced by cutting through it along a plane, or planes, removing one or more parts and drawing a view of the effects of the cutting plane on the parts remaining. Taking a piece of wood and sawing through it at any point produces a section. If one piece is removed and the cut end is looked at directly, the drawing of what is seen gives gives a sectional view. Generally, the area of this sectional view that contains material is cross-hatched, i.e. lines are drawn at 45° across the section to make it stand out and to help differentiate between the lines of a sectional view and an external view.

Sectional or hatching lines are thin lines having a similar density to projection and dimension lines. Unless used on a large area or when interrupted by a dimension, section lines should be continuous across the surface.

Fig. 19.1 (a) shows a circular tube cut along its length by a plane $Y-Y$ which divides the tube into two equal parts, A and B. The drawing at **(b)** is a pictorial view of part A when part B is removed. The path of the cutting plane is indicated by the sectioning lines drawn across the faces of the tube exposed by removing part B. The drawing at **(c)** shows two views of the complete tube, together with the method of indicating the cutting plane $Y-Y$ and the direction of view. The drawing at **(d)** is the method of indicating the sectioned tube on a normal orthographic drawing, viewing part A on its cut face.

Fig. 19.2 (a) shows a circular component containing a through hole and a counter-bore, cut by a vertical plane $Y-Y$ which divides it into two equal parts. The drawing at **(b)** is a pictorial view of part A when part B is removed. The faces cut by the plane are sectioned. The drawing at **(c)** shows two views of the complete component, together with the method of indicating the cutting plane and the direction of view. The drawing at **(d)** is the method of indicating the sectioned component on a normal ortho-graphic drawing, viewing part A on its cut face.

Fig. 19.3 (a) shows a component similar to that in the previous figure. It is cut by a plane XOY, part of which is vertical and part horizontal. The effect of this plane is shown at **(b)**, where it will be seen that the removed part B is a quadrant. The drawing at **(c)** indicates the method of presenting this information on an orthographic drawing, although it is not necessary to label the point where the plane changes direction, nor to include dotted lines to indicate hidden features. Half-sections of this type are used on symmetrical components and assemblies in order to save time drawing and sectioning the whole component.

Another example of half-sectioning is shown in **Fig. 19.10**.

Section planes may be vertical, horizontal, or at any angle. They may also be a combination of these dispositions. Their purpose is to show sufficient detail to enable the drawing to be clearly understood and the object to be manufactured or assembled.

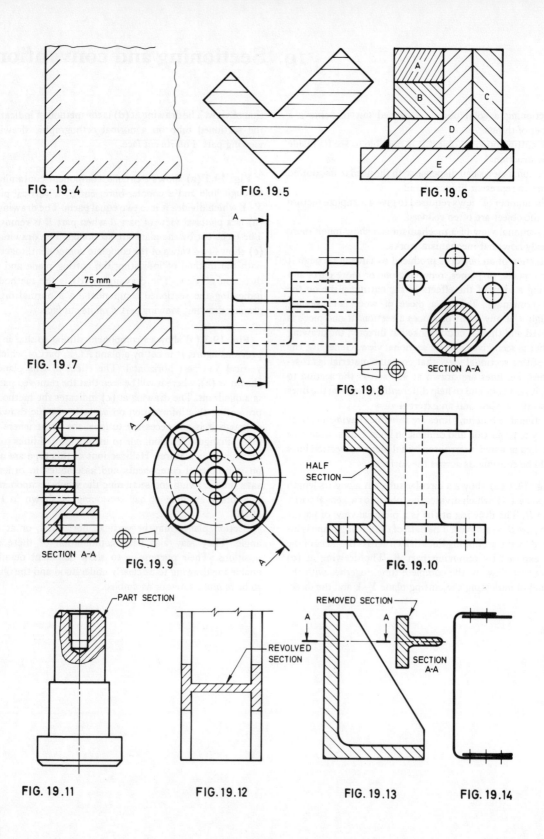

FIG. 19.4

FIG. 19.5

FIG. 19.6

75 mm

FIG. 19.7

A

A

SECTION A-A

FIG. 19.8

A

SECTION A-A

FIG. 19.9

HALF SECTION

FIG. 19.10

PART SECTION

FIG. 19.11

REVOLVED SECTION

FIG. 19.12

REMOVED SECTION

A   A

SECTION A-A

FIG. 19.13

FIG. 19.14

Fig. 19.4 shows the treatment of large areas in section which contain no features. The edges only need be cross-hatched.

The general rule for sectioning is that the lines should be at 45°. As with most rules, there are exceptions to this. One of the exceptional cases is shown in **Fig. 19.5**, where the object is lying at an angle of 45°. As hatching lines running parallel to the outline of an object can indicate materials other than metal, the lines are drawn horizontally. This retains the basic 45° angle to the sides of the section.

Some confusion can arise when a number of adjacent parts are to be sectioned. The hatching lines should be drawn alternately in different directions and, where necessary, with a varied spacing between the lines. An example of this is shown in **Fig. 19.6**. It will be noted that the closer spaced lines are reserved for the smaller sections. In some cases of grouped components it may not be possible to draw all the lines at 45°. In such a case another angle, such as 60° or 30°, may be used.

Where a sectioned area must contain a dimension or lettering, the section lines should be interrupted to ensure clarity. An example of this is shown in **Fig. 19.7**.

Fig. 19.8 shows two views of a casting. The elevation contains a section plane *AA* which is not on the centre line. The offset feature could not be shown clearly without drawing a sectional view of this type. Such a view also dispenses with the need to use dotted lines for hidden detail.

Fig. 19.9 shows a section taken in two planes. The object is circular and contains a number of through and blind holes. The section plane *AA* in the front elevation is staggered to pass through two pairs of holes. In the sectional view these holes are projected into the same vertical plane. In effect the two larger holes lying in the cutting plane are revolved into the vertical centre line and when they are projected in the sectional elevation there is no reduction in the outside diameter of the plate.

Fig. 19.10 shows a detail in half-section. This method of drawing can be adopted for assemblies as well as individual details which are symmetrical about a centre line. One half of the drawing shows the outside view and the other half shows the section. Dotted lines to show hidden detail behind the section are unnecessary, but hidden detail on the unsectioned part may be shown for clarity or for dimensioning purposes. Assembly drawings done in this way do not usually show hidden detail on the unsectioned side.

Fig. 19.11 shows an object which has been part-sectioned at one end to show clearly the threaded hole. This practice may be adopted at any convenient place to show otherwise hidden details. The boundary around a part section should be shown by a thin irregular line. The centre line in this object indicates that it is circular in cross-section. In general, circular sectioned parts should not be cross-hatched. Therefore part sections must be used where hidden details are required to be shown.

Fig. 19.12 shows an example of a revolved section. It shows the shape of the cross-section on the actual view, the cutting plane being revolved in position.

Fig. 19.13 shows the treatment of a ribbed object. Although the section plane passes through the centre of the rib, it is always shown blank so that there is a definition between angle thickness and rib. If the figure was sectioned completely across its area there would be no indication that a rib exists.

In addition to ribs and nuts, bolts and washers, all circular cross-sectioned items such as shafts, pins, rods, and rivets should be shown in full. Keys used to prevent rotation of bosses on circular shafts should be treated in similar way, even though they are usually rectangular in shape. Where a detailed explanation is required, part-sections should be used.

Fig. 19.14 shows the treatment of thin-walled parts such as sheet metal, gaskets, packing, etc. These parts can be shown solid as indicated, and where adjacent thin sections are involved a space should be left between the parts.

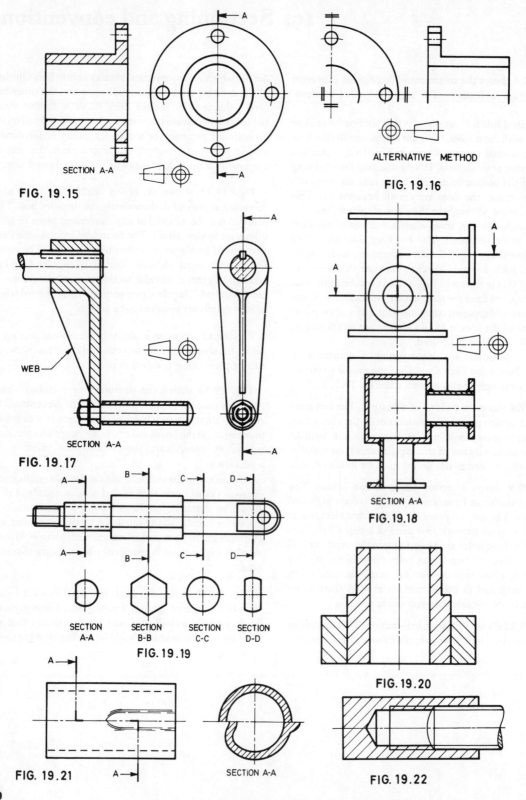

SECTION A-A

FIG. 19.15

ALTERNATIVE METHOD

FIG. 19.16

WEB

SECTION A-A

FIG. 19.17

A

SECTION A-A

FIG. 19.18

SECTION
A-A

SECTION
B-B

SECTION
C-C

SECTION
D-D

FIG. 19.19

FIG. 19.20

FIG. 19.21

SECTION A-A

FIG. 19.22

Fig. 19.15 shows two views in first angle projection of a flanged component. The longitudinal section on plane $A–A$ passes through two typical holes in the flange. An alternative method of drawing the same component is shown in **Fig. 19.16.** Owing to the symmetrical nature of the component, only slightly more than one quarter need be drawn. The lines of symmetry are indicated by the pairs of short thick parallel lines drawn near the ends of the centre lines and at right angles to them. The outline of the component and features it contains extend a short distance past the lines of symmetry. Although the sectioning plane passes along the axis of the component, sectioning lines can be omitted where there is no possibility of confusion in reading the drawing.

Fig. 19.17 shows two views in first angle projection of an assembly of parts making up an operating handle. In the interests of clarity certain of the features lying in the path of the sectioning plane $A–A$ are not sectioned. These features are: the main shaft, the key fixing the shaft and handle, the strengthening web, the main spindle for the handle and the nut and washer fixing the handle to the main casting. Items such as these should never be sectioned, otherwise misreading of the drawing could occur.

Fig. 19.18 shows two views in first angle projection of a piece of square pipe flanged at its ends and with circular flanged pipes protruding from it. The sectioning plane $A–A$ changes direction through 90° in two places indicated by the thickened lines. The plan view shows the interpretation of this method of sectioning.

Fig. 19.19 shows a shaft which changes section along its length. These sectional changes are located by four planes, with the shape of each section drawn immediately below each one. Sectioning lines across the areas cut by the planes are not necessary to the clarity of the drawing and have been omitted.

Fig. 19.20 shows two mating parts in section. The sectioning lines on each part are drawn in the same direction, those on one part sloping in one direction while those on the adjacent part slope in a direction at 90° to the first. When two components are joined together to make a single piece, the spacing of the section lines should be the same on both.

Fig. 19.21 shows a tubular part which changes section. The sectioning plane $A–A$ is, in effect, two parallel planes and this is shown in the sectional end elevation. The changes in section are indicated and the sectioning lines are similarly spaced for both planes but offset along the lines dividing the sections.

Fig. 19.22 shows a component containing a threaded hole and part of a bolt. The sectioning lines are extended into the spaces occupied by the screw thread when they are not covered by the bolt. If no bolt was present the sectioning lines would extend for the whole length of the screw thread.

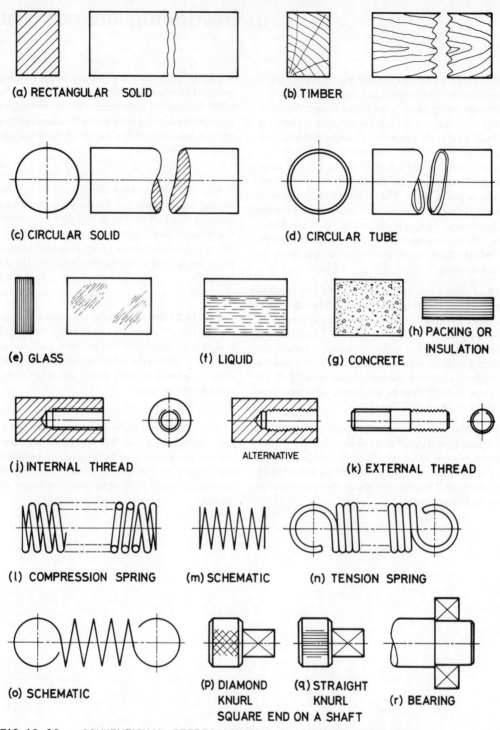

(a) RECTANGULAR SOLID

(b) TIMBER

(c) CIRCULAR SOLID

(d) CIRCULAR TUBE

(e) GLASS

(f) LIQUID

(g) CONCRETE

(h) PACKING OR INSULATION

(j) INTERNAL THREAD

ALTERNATIVE

(k) EXTERNAL THREAD

(l) COMPRESSION SPRING

(m) SCHEMATIC

(n) TENSION SPRING

(o) SCHEMATIC

(P) DIAMOND KNURL

(q) STRAIGHT KNURL

(r) BEARING

SQUARE END ON A SHAFT

FIG. 19.23   CONVENTIONAL REPRESENTATION OF COMMON FEATURES

Sectioning has been shown to be an aid to the production of easily understood drawings. Just as there are rules or conventions applied to the use of sectioning lines, so are there conventions to assist the draughtsman in portraying certain standard features. A spring, a housebrick, and a piece of glass all have their own conventions: a sort of shorthand which is universally understood. Many of the more common features of this kind are shown in the diagrams of **Fig. 19.12** some of which are combined with methods of sectioning.

Fig. 19.23 (a) indicates a section and a longitudinal view of a rectangular solid. The longitudinal break line is used when a solid has no feature to interrupt its surfaces or when the object is too long to be drawn on the page.

Diagram **(b)** shows a similar treatment with a rectangular piece of timber. Note that timber is sectioned differently from other solids.

Diagrams **(c)** and **(d)** indicate the method of drawing circular sectioned objects, a circular solid and a circular tube. Once again the longitudinal break is used where there is little point in drawing the complete object.

Glass in section and in full is shown at **(e)** while water in a container is indicated at **(f)**. Concrete is depicted in section at **(g)** where small irregular figures are interspersed with dots to represent the aggregate to be seen in a section of concrete.

Diagram **(h)** indicates the usual conventional representation of sectioning packing, such as gland material used in water and steam valves or insulation which may be used on hot or cold piping, etc.

An internal thread in section and in elevation is shown at **(j)** where an alternative longitudinal section is given. Note that external and internal threads in section are hatched on individual drawings and assemblies. Sections lines are drawn through the space representing the thread depth for internal threads, provided they are not covered by a bolt or screw, in which case only that portion of the thread not covered is sectioned. In the alternative drawing, the vee thread form is drawn in. It is sometimes necessary to show a thread in this way so that there is no confusion in the interpretation of the object. However, this convention is not recommended by BSI.

Diagram **(k)** shows a stud with alternative thread forms

at either end, together with the method of drawing the end elevation. It will be noted that the root diameter circle is a thin 'broken' line. This should be compared with the previous examples of an internal thread, where it will be seen that the outside diameter circle is a thin 'broken' line. The simulated thread form, although not recommended by BSI may be used for clarity.

A compression spring is shown in diagram **(l)**. Part of the spring is drawn in section. A compression spring has a gap between the coils and the ends are at right angles to the longitudinal axis so that an axial pressure can be applied which will act on the ends tending to move them towards one another. Another method of drawing a compression spring is indicated at **(m)**. This type of drawing is called *schematic* because the thinly drawn outline merely indicates the presence of a compression spring without giving its size.

Tension springs are similarly treated in diagrams **(n)** and **(0)**. A tension spring has hooked ends so that when it is assembled its movement will be such that the ends move apart as the spring stretches. The coils are wound touching one another. The method of sectioning is the same as that at **(l)**. It is not always necessary to draw the complete length of a spring. A few coils in outline or section at each end with chain-dotted lines to make up the centre part should be quite sufficient.

Diagram **(p)** shows diamond knurling and the method of indicating a flat surface. It is necessary to have a convention for square and rectangular flat surfaces, as indicated here, because when such a surface is machined on an otherwise circular object, the whole component could be interpreted as circular in section along its whole length. The diagonal lines across the flat surface are, therefore, invaluable to the correct interpretation of the drawing. Diagram **(q)** shows a representation of straight knurling.

Diamond and straight knurling are carried out on a lathe with special tools. The surface of the component is indented in a pattern so that it can be gripped with the fingers.

A ball or roller bearing mounted on a shaft is shown in diagram **(r)**. The outline shape of the bearing is shown and diagonals are drawn across the faces of squares or rectangles. There is often no need to show more detail than this on an assembly drawing.

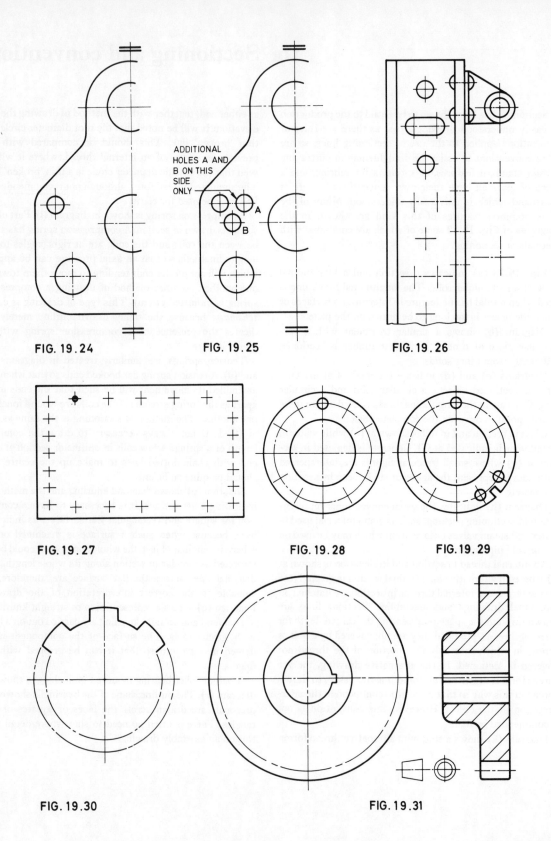

ADDITIONAL
HOLES A AND
B ON THIS
SIDE
ONLY

A

B

FIG. 19.24

FIG. 19.25

FIG. 19.26

FIG. 19.27

FIG. 19.28

FIG. 19.29

FIG. 19.30

FIG. 19.31

As previously mentioned when referring to Fig. 19.16, symmetrical parts need not always be drawn in full. **Fig. 19.24** shows slightly more than half of a shaped plate containing a series of holes. The short thick parallel lines close to the ends of the vertical centre line indicate that the right-hand half of the plate is identical to that shown. In some cases of asymmetry the conventional representation can still be used. This is shown in **Fig. 19.25**, where a plate similar to that in the previous figure contains additional holes on one side only. These features are drawn in position and the note explains their presence. The shape of the complete plate and the number and size of the holes to be drilled are now quite clear.

Fig. 19.26 shows a flanged component containing slots and holes in its web and a number of small brackets riveted to one of the flanges. In order to save time repeating these features, the centre lines only need be shown after one complete set has been drawn. Notes may be added to state the number of each of the features required.

Fig. 19.27 shows a rectangular plate containing a large number of small holes. Conventionally, one hole only need be drawn, provided all the holes are of the same size, after which centre lines are shown indicating the positions of the remaining holes. When holes of different diameters are required, they can be identified by drawing and/or labelling.

Fig. 19.28 shows a circular flange containing a number of equally spaced holes on a pitch circle diameter (PCD). Conventionally this is clearly indicated by drawing one hole and showing the positions of the other holes by centre lines. The size of the holes would be given in note form.

Fig. 19.29 shows a circular flange similar to that in the previous example, containing a notch in the periphery of the flange. The position of the notch relative to two of the equally spaced holes is indicated.

Fig. 19.30 shows a splined shaft. Three of the splines are drawn for identification and dimensional purposes, conventional representation and a suitable note would complete the drawing.

Fig. 19.31 shows two views in first angle projection of a gear wheel with a central boss. The boss is machined to accept a shaft and a keyway is provided to fix the gear wheel to the shaft.

Conventionally, the gear teeth are not sectioned so that the full tooth area can be clearly seen. On the front elevation, the outside diameter is shown in bold outline and the PCD is drawn as a centre line. Note the method of showing a keyway.

Figs 19.32 and **19.33** on the next two pages are examples of sectioning cast components. Fig. 19.32 shows a dimensioned drawing of the main frame of a bench-mounted punch, used for making holes in thin plate. Fig. 19.33 depicts a special pipe fitting and indicates the difference between a half-view and a half-section.

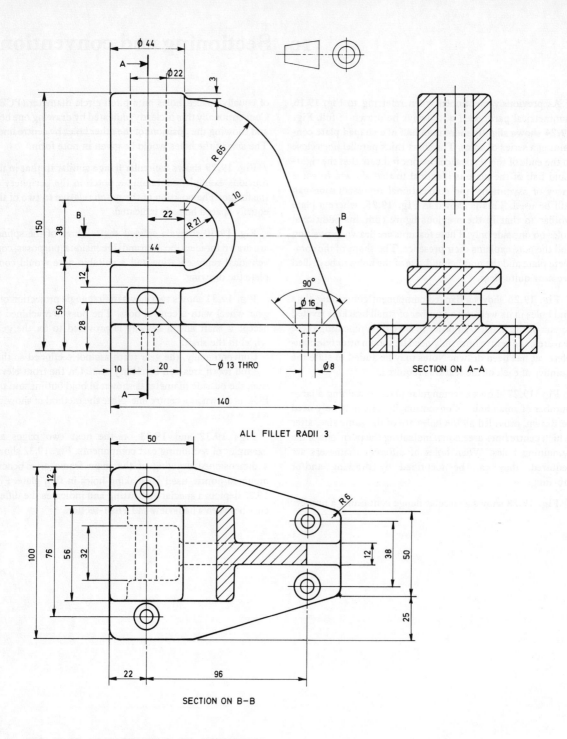

ALL FILLET RADII 3

SECTION ON A-A

SECTION ON B-B

FIG. 19.32   AN EXAMPLE OF SECTIONING

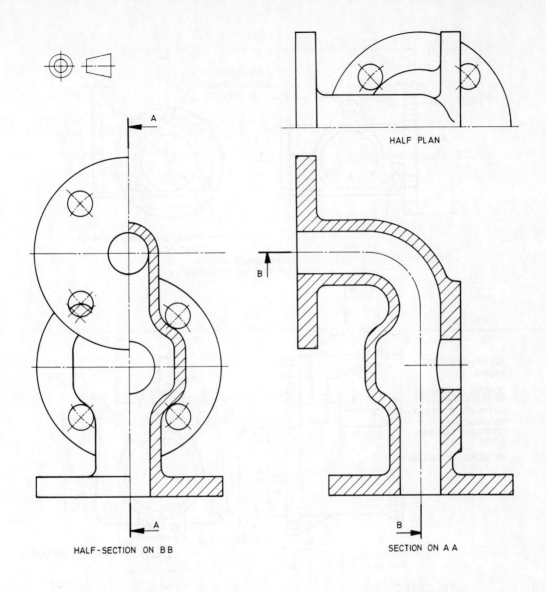

HALF PLAN

HALF-SECTION ON B B

SECTION ON A A

FIG. 19.33   AN EXAMPLE OF SECTIONING

137

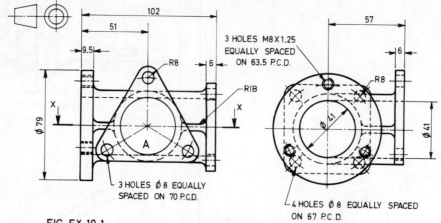

FIG. EX. 19.1

3 HOLES M8 X 1.25
EQUALLY SPACED
ON 63.5 P.C.D.

R8

3 HOLES ⌀ 8 EQUALLY
SPACED ON 70 P.C.D.

4 HOLES ⌀ 8 EQUALLY SPACED
ON 67 P.C.D.

ALL UNDIMENSIONED RADII 3
ALL WALL AND RIB THICKNESSES 5

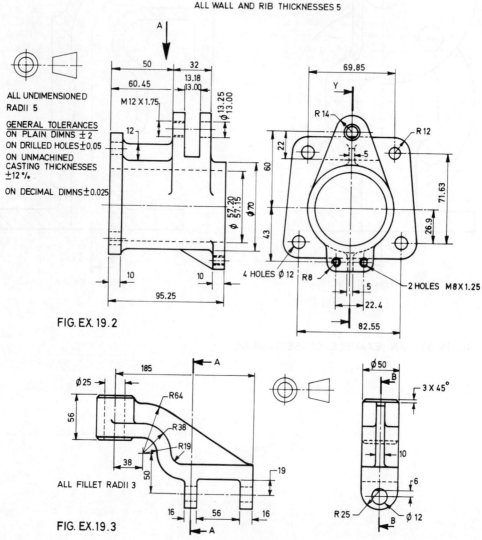

ALL UNDIMENSIONED
RADII 5

GENERAL TOLERANCES
ON PLAIN DIMNS ± 2
ON DRILLED HOLES ± 0.05
ON UNMACHINED
CASTING THICKNESSES
± 12 %.

ON DECIMAL DIMNS ± 0.025

FIG. EX. 19.2

4 HOLES ⌀ 12
2 HOLES M8 X 1.25

FIG. EX. 19.3

ALL FILLET RADII 3

3 X 45°

138

19. Sectioning and conventions

Exercises for Chapter 19

1. **Fig. Ex. 19.1** shows two views, in first angle projection, of a flanged pipe junction. Draw, full size, in first or third angle projection, the following views:
   (a) the given elevation marked A;
   (b) a half-sectional plan XX, the left-hand half to be in section and the right-hand half to be an outside view. Include a suitable shape for the ribs.
   Add a title and the scale to your drawing and a statement of the project angle. Fully dimension the triangular flange and the holes through it (no other dimensions are to be included) and show machining symbols on the other faces of all three flanges. (*CGLI*)

2. **Fig. Ex. 19.2** shows two views of a vertical support bracket in third angle projection. Draw the following views full size using third or first angle projection and British Standard conventions:

   (a) the given plan,
   (b) sectional elevation on the plane YY;
   (c) an elevation looking in the direction of arrow A without hidden detail.
   Add a title and scale, and the dimensions and notes necessary for drilling the four holes in the base.
   Show machining symbols on the upper and lower faces of the bracket and inside the 57 mm diameter bore.
   State which projection angle you have used. (*CGLI*)

3. **Fig. Ex. 19.3** shows two views, in third angle projection, of a cast-iron bracket. Draw the following views, full size, using first or third angle projection:
   (a) a sectional elevation on the plane BB,
   (b) a sectional end elevation on the plane AA,
   (c) a plan projected from the main elevation.
   State which projection angle has been used.

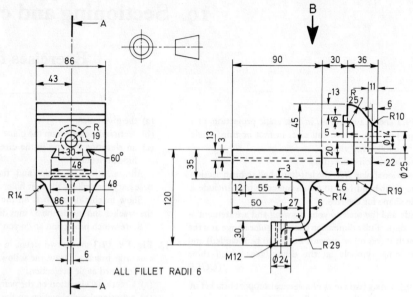

ALL FILLET RADII 6

FIG. EX. 19.4   BENCH VICE CASTING

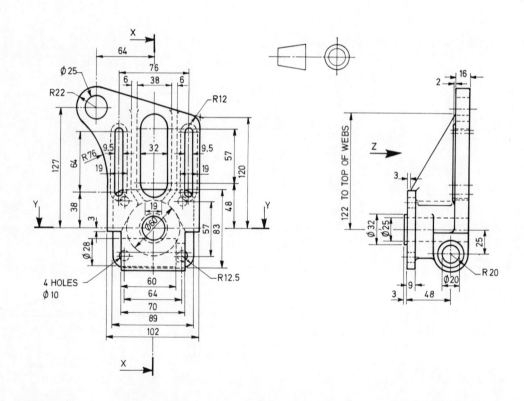

FIG. EX. 19.5   MACHINE TOOL CASTING

4. **Fig. Ex. 19.4** shows two dimensioned views of a bench vice casting in third angle projection.

   Draw, full size, in either first or third angle projection, the following views:
   (a) a sectional elevation on the plane *AA*,
   (b) a plan looking in the direction of the arrow *B*.

   Add a title to your drawing and, by indicating with the appropriate British Standard symbol, state which projection angle you have used.

5. **Fig. Ex. 19.5** shows two elevations in first angle projection of a special toolholder for a capstan lathe. Draw, full size, the following views:
   (a) an elevation in the direction indicated by the arrow *Z*;
   (b) a sectional end elevation, the section being taken on the centre line of the casting and looking in the direction indicated by the arrows *XX*; and

(c) a sectional plan, projected from view (a), the section being taken on the centre line of the 25 mm diameter bore and looking in the direction indicated by the arrows *YY*.

Hidden lines are not to be shown.

The following dimensions are to be shown on the drawing:
(i) the centres of the four 10 mm diameter holes in the rectangular flange, and
(ii) the important dimensions of the 32 mm slot in the main body.

Either first or third angle projection may be used, but the three views must be in a consistent system of projection.

In a title block 152 mm long and 76 mm high insert the title SPECIAL TOOLHOLDER in letters 8 mm high, and the scale and system of projection used in letters 5 mm high.

(AEB)

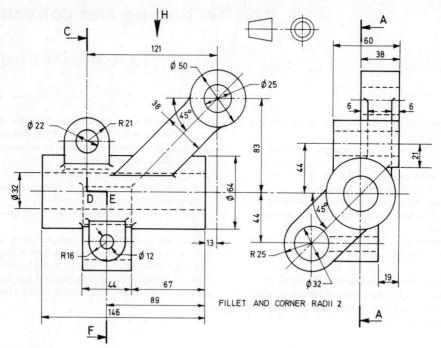

FILLET AND CORNER RADII 2

FIG. EX. 19.6

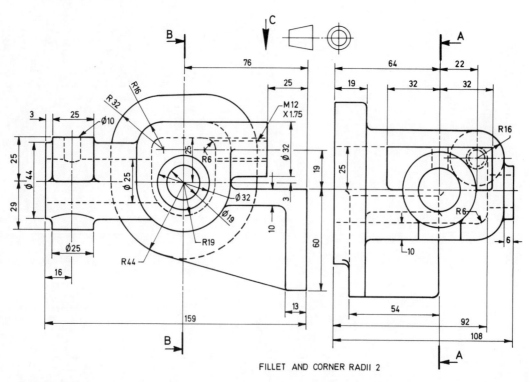

FILLET AND CORNER RADII 2

FIG. EX. 19.7

6. **Fig. Ex. 19.6** shows two views of a hinge arm drawn in first angle projection. Do not copy the given views but draw, full size, the following:
   (a) a sectional elevation, the plane of the section and the direction of the required view being indicated at *AA*;
   (b) a sectional elevation (a), the plane of the section and the direction of the required view being indicated at *CDEF*;
   (c) a complete plan as seen when viewed from the direction of arrow *H* and in projection with view (a).

   Hidden edges are not to be shown in any of the views. Give on each of the three views *two* important dimensions. In the lower right-hand corner of the drawing paper draw a title block 114 mm by 64 mm and insert relevant data.

   The views may be drawn in *either* first or third angle projection but the method used must be stated in the title block   (*Camb.*)

7. **Fig. Ex. 19.7** shows two views of a control valve body drawn in first angle projection. Do not copy the given views but draw,

full size, the following:
   (a) a sectional elevation, the plane of the section and direction of the required view being indicated at *AA*;
   (b) a sectional elevation in projection with view (a), the plane of the section and the direction of the required view being indicated at *BB*;
   (c) a complete plan as seen when viewed from the direction of arrow *C* and in projection with (a).

   Hidden edges are not to be shown in any of the views. Give on each of the three views *two* important dimensions. In the lower right-hand corner of the drawing paper draw a title block 114 mm by 64 mm and insert relevant data.

   The views may be drawn in *either* first *or* third angle projection but the method used must be stated in the title block.   (*Camb.*)

   There are more projection problems in the exercises at the end of Chapter 15 and in the later chapters.

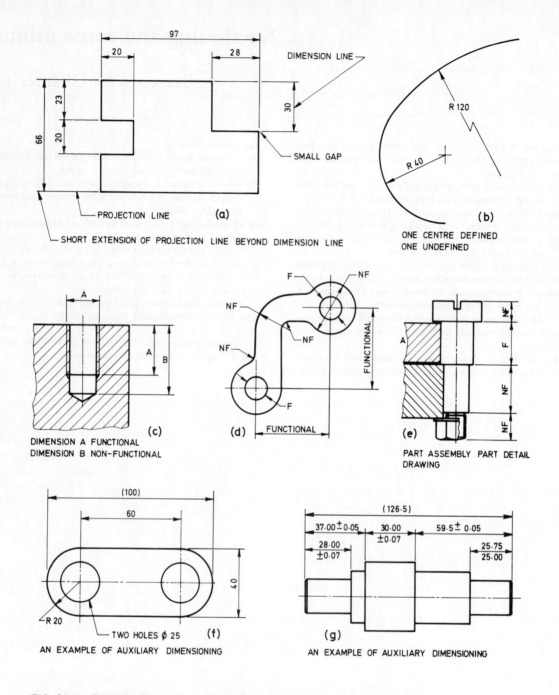

FIG. 20.1 EXAMPLES OF THE APPLICATION OF DIMENSIONING

20. Dimensioning

Dimensioning is one of the final actions of a draughtsman in the completion of a detailed drawing. It is also one of the most important because it must give all the necessary information to enable the component to be made in the workshop.

Dimensions should, as far as possible, give the reader a clear understanding of the size and shape of the component and assist him to appreciate the best methods of manufacture. To achieve this it is often necessary to add notes of explanation to the drawing and also in the title block beneath the drawing.

Correct dimensioning is an invaluable art which can be mastered with practice and by following a few general rules.

1. All dimensions on a drawing should be in the same units, e.g. millimetres. Where it is not possible to follow this rule any different units should be clearly indicated after the dimensions, e.g. 15 cm.

2. It should not be necessary to have to obtain an important dimension from other dimensions on the drawing.

3. It should not be necessary to have to use a ruler to obtain a dimension from a drawing.

4. Dimensions of a particular feature on a component should be placed on the view which gives the clearest details of that feature.

5. Projection and dimension lines should be thin continuous lines. Projection lines should extend beyond the dimension lines for a short distance and there should be a small gap between the ends of the lines and points to which they refer. These points are indicated in **Fig. 20.1 (a)**.

6. Projection and dimension lines should not cross other lines except where this is unavoidable.

7. The size of arrow heads at each end of a dimension line should bear a relationship to the thickness of the lines on the drawing.

8. One arrow head on the arc end of the dimension line is sufficient to dimension a radius **(Fig. 20.1 (b))**.

9. Dimensions must be large enough to ensure easy reading. They should have a size related to the size of the component.

10. Dimensions should preferably be placed at or about the middle of the dimension line. They should also be positioned above the dimension line and clear of it. In some cases where reading the dimension is improved, the dimension line may be interrupted and the dimension inserted in the space.

11. Dimensions should be placed so that they can be read from the bottom of the drawing or from the right-hand side.

12. Leader lines to dimensions or notes should have a dot at the end when they terminate within the outline of the component and an arrowhead when they terminate at the outline.

Many of these rules are explained in the diagrams on the facing page and throughout the rest of this chapter.

The most important dimensions on any drawing are those that directly affect the function, or correct working, of the product. These dimensions are called *functional dimensions*. Of secondary importance are the dimensions necessary for production purposes but which do not directly affect the function of the product. These are called *non-functional dimensions*. **Fig. 20.1 (c)** shows a threaded hole. The depth of full thread, dimension A, is a functional dimension, while the depth of penetration of the drill, dimension B, is non-functional. The link in **Fig. 20.1 (d)** shows the two types of dimension labelled F for functional and NF for non-functional.

In **Fig. 20.1 (e)** the only longitudinal bolt dimension that is functional is that immediately under the head. This dimension is important because it must allow for free movement of the part labelled A.

Auxiliary dimensions are given on drawings for information only. They are not used for production purposes nor are they functional. Their purpose is to provide information in the 'nice to know' category, e.g. the nominal overall dimension of a product whose intermediate dimensions are fully toleranced. These dimensions should be placed between single brackets, as indicated in **Figs 20.1 (f)** and **20.1 (g)**.

Toleranced dimensions are used to ensure complete interchangeability of parts and where definite classes of fit are required between mating parts. A tolerance may be defined as the dimensional difference between two limits of size. As will be seen later in this chapter, there are different ways of expressing toleranced dimensions on drawings. No matter which system is used, the end result is that a dimensional allowance is provided within which the craftsmen must work. It is not possible to produce numbers of similar parts to exact dimensions and a tolerancing system allows for small variations of size without impairing functional efficiency.

Examples of toleranced dimensions are shown in **Fig. 20.1 (g)**.

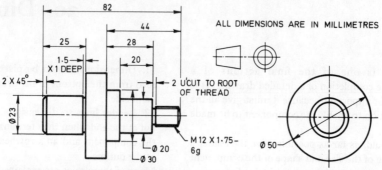

ALL DIMENSIONS ARE IN MILLIMETRES

FIG. 20.2   DIMENSIONING   A   COMPONENT

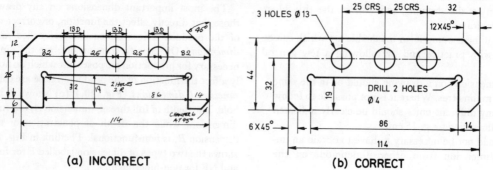

(a) INCORRECT

(b) CORRECT

FIG. 20.3   DIMENSIONING A GAUGE PLATE

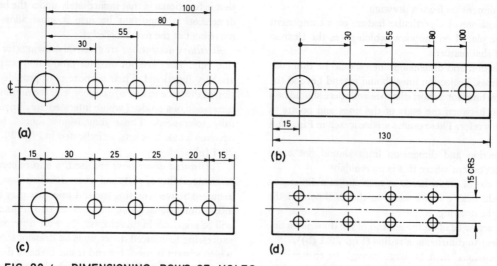

(a)

(b)

(c)

(d)

FIG. 20.4   DIMENSIONING ROWS OF HOLES

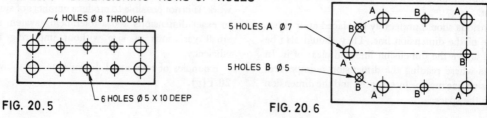

FIG. 20.5

FIG. 20.6

Fig. 20.2 shows the method of dimensioning a circular component having a screw thread at one end.

Notice on the component that the overall sizes are given so that bar material 50 mm in diameter and slightly more than 82 mm in length can be chosen. The width of the 50 mm diameter flange is omitted because it is considered the least important dimension. The 30 mm diameter could be expressed in the same way as the 20 mm diameter. In this way the dimension line would avoid crossing other lines.

In all cases the symbol for diameter, Ø, precedes the dimension. The note, 'U cut to root of thread', means that an undercut has been made equal to the depth of thread, so that a full thread can be formed up to the end of the threaded portion and also to allow space to withdraw the thread-cutting tool.

The designation of the thread, 'M12 × 1·75 — 6g', means that the thread is a metric one, 12 mm outside diameter and 1·75 pitch. The 6g is a code which denotes the accuracy of the thread, the small g indicating an external thread.

Note the method of showing a chamfer at 45° at one end of the component and the rounding of the thread end. Both of these features are to ensure that there are no rough or sharp edges.

Fig. 20.3 (a) and (b) show the incorrect and correct methods of dimensioning a gauge plate.

Some of the errors in diagram **(a)** are as follows.

1. Dimension lines are taken to axes of holes.

2. Dimensions are placed on the work where this could be avoided.

3. The holes in the corners of the jaws should not be given as a radius: holes are made by drills which have diameters, therefore diameter should be specified.

4. Dimension lines are too close to work.

5. Dimensions are incorrectly placed in relation to the dimension lines.

6. Arrowheads are missing or badly formed.

7. Chamfers are incorrectly dimensioned.

Drawing **(b)** is neater, and the dimensions do not obscure the drawing.

Fig. 20.4(a) shows the normal method of dimensioning a row of holes from a *datum*. The datum is the centre of the larger hole, and this indicates that the position of the smaller holes relative to the larger hole is important. The symbol ₵ indicates that the centre line of the row of holes lies on the centre of the plate.

Fig. 20.4 (b) is an alternative method of dimensioning the same row of holes. In this case the datum feature is denoted by a large dot. In both examples the dimensions are placed close to the appropriate arrowhead for the sake of clarity.

Fig. 20.4 (c) is an example of *chain-dimensioning* applied to the same plate as before. This method should only be chosen where the functional requirements of the part are in no way affected.

Fig. 20.4 (d) shows a plate containing two rows of holes. The dimension indicates the distance between centres of the rows, and the use of a centre line between the rows indicates that the rows are equally disposed about it.

Fig. 20.5 shows a plate with a number of holes of different sizes. The notes clearly imply that the four larger holes are drilled through the plate, while the smaller holes are 10 mm deep.

Fig. 20.6 shows a method of indicating the size of through holes of different diameters by labelling and notes.

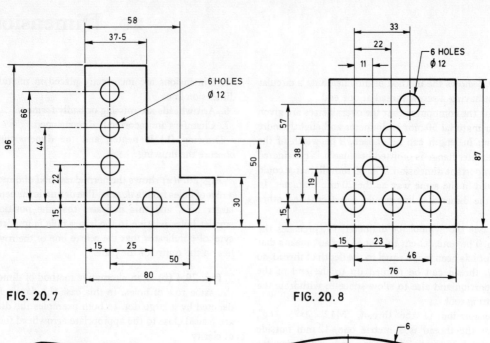

FIG. 20.7

FIG. 20.8

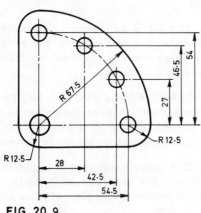

FIG. 20.9

FIG. 20.10
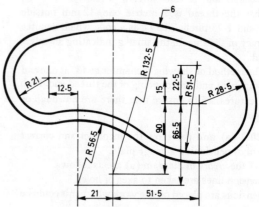

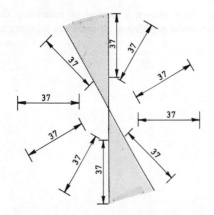

FIG. 20.11

FIG. 20.12
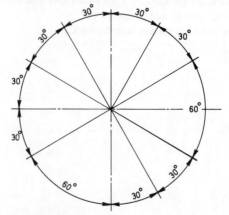

Fig. 20.7 indicates one method of dimensioning a series of holes in a plate. The horizontal position of the holes relative to one hole is important, therefore the centre line of this hole has been made a datum. The line may be labelled as a datum, especially when this will assist the reader of the drawing. In the vertical direction, position relative to the bottom row of holes is important and so the centre line of this row becomes a datum.

Notice that the dimensions have been positioned to avoid dimension and projection lines crossing one another. The plate is completely dimensioned except for its thickness. The layout is interesting because the dimensions of the plate have been positioned so that they in no way interfere with the dimensions of the holes.

Fig. 20.8 is another example of the datum-dimensioning of holes in a plate.

Fig. 20.9 shows a quadrant plate containing holes lying on a circle. The centres of the holes are dimensioned by *or-dinates*, the datum being the larger hole in the bottom left-hand corner of the plate. Where positional accuracy is required, this method of dimensioning is preferred to the use of angular dimensions and a specified pitch circle.

Fig. 20.10 indicates the method of dimensioning a series of tangential arcs. In some cases the centre of the arc is not shown in its true position in order to keep the drawing as compact as possible. Where this occurs the dimension line is cranked but the portion touching the arc is in line with the true centre. To indicate that the dimensions locating the arc centres are not to scale, they are heavily underlined.

Fig. 20.11 shows the method of dimensioning linear distances disposed at various angles 'around the clock'. The shaded areas should be avoided.

Fig. 20.12 is a similar example applied to angular dimensions. By adopting this procedure any angle in one revolution can be dimensioned without loss of clarity.

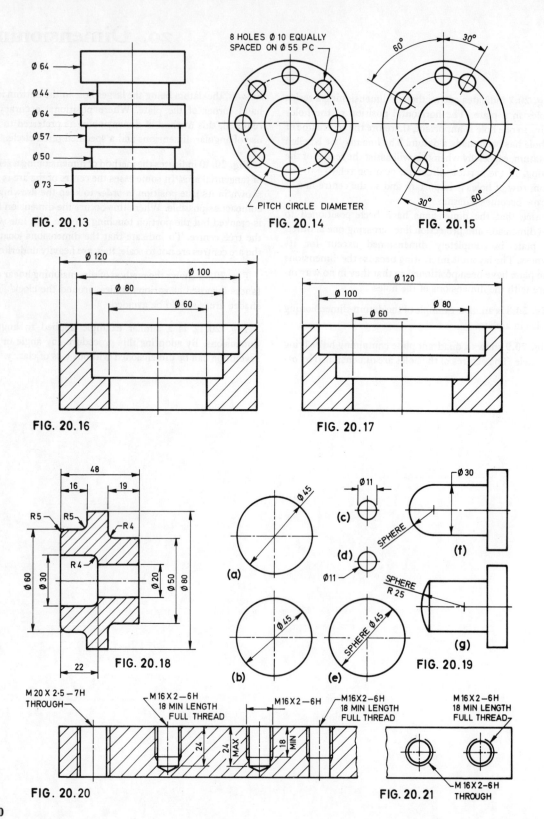

FIG. 20.13

8 HOLES Ø 10 EQUALLY
SPACED ON Ø 55 P C

PITCH CIRCLE DIAMETER

FIG. 20.14

FIG. 20.15

FIG. 20.16

FIG. 20.17

FIG. 20.18

FIG. 20.19

FIG. 20.20

FIG. 20.21

Some components that are circular in section and machined to different diameters, such as that shown in **Fig. 20.13**, are difficult to dimension without making the drawing appear cluttered when dimensioned in the conventional manner. There is also the problem of reading the drawing without confusing the features to which the projection lines refer. These problems are overcome by the method of dimensioning indicated in the figure. Each short dimension line is positioned approximately in the centre of the feature to which it refers and the diameter is placed adjacent to the end of the line as shown.

Dimensions indicating the length of the component would be positioned parallel to the axis in the normal way.

Fig. 20.14 indicates a method of dimensioning a series of holes equally spaced around a circle by means of a note. The circle containing the holes acts as a centre line and is called a pitch circle diameter. This can be abbreviated to PCD or Ø PC.

Fig. 20.15 shows holes unevenly spaced around a pitch circle diameter. The pitching of the holes is determined by angular dimensions, each referred to a datum which, in this case, is the vertical centre line of the flange and the single hole it contains.

Fig. 20.16 gives an example of the method of dimensioning a component that has a number of parallel dimension lines. The dimensions should be staggered as shown to avoid confusion when reading the drawing, especially when long dimension lines are employed.

Fig. 20.17 shows an alternative method of dimensioning the same component. Shortening the dimension lines saves space but does not detract from the clarity.

Fig. 20.18 is a fully dimensioned component requiring no second view. All the features are clearly defined and the method of indicating corner radii is of particular note.

Fig. 20.19 shows various ways in which circular features and spherical radii should be dimensioned. **Fig. 20.19 (a)** and **(b)** indicate two methods of dimensioning the same circle. **Fig. 20.19 (c)** and **(d)** show two methods of dimensioning a small circle. In **(d)** the leader should be drawn so that its continuation would pass through the centre of the circle.

Fig. 20.19 (e) shows the method of dimensioning a sphere.

Spherical radii are described in **Fig. 20.19 (f)** and **(g)**. In **(f)**, the diameter is defined and so there is no requirement for a dimension on the radius, merely an indication that the end of the component is spherical and of the same diameter as the given dimension. In **(g)** the spherical radius is required because it is different from the radius of the cylindrical portion.

Fig. 20.20 indicates various ways in which to dimension threaded holes. Commencing at the left-hand end of the plate, the first hole is of 20 mm diameter metric thread having a pitch of 2·5 mm. The class of fit is 7H and the hole goes through the plate. In the second case, the depth of the drilled hole is important and the minimum length of full thread is specified. The third hole shows an alternative treatment. The last hole is drilled through but threaded only for a short distance. It is noteworthy that the sectioning lines are drawn through the thread area in each case.

Fig. 20.21 shows two methods of indicating threaded holes when viewed in plan (or end elevation). The notes give full information.

Note that the outside diameter of the thread is 'broken' and the thickness of the line is less than the root diameter.

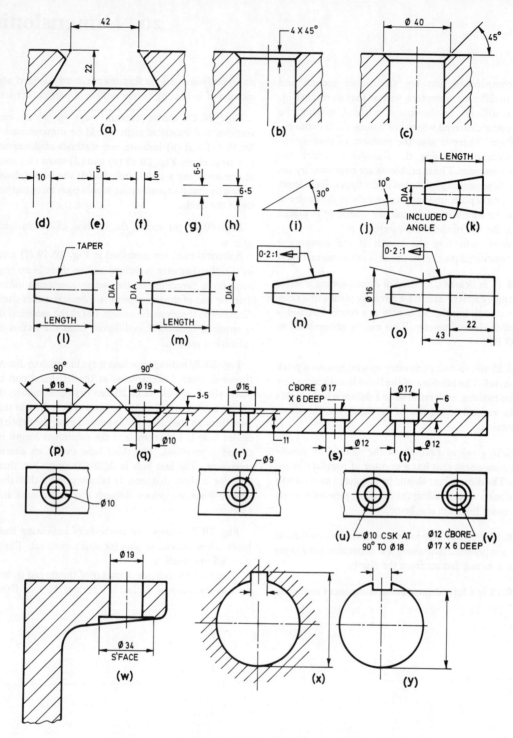

FIG. 20.22   DIMENSIONING   SOME   COMMON   FEATURES

Fig. 20.22 comprises of a whole page of features with approved methods of dimensioning those features.

At **(a)** is given the method of showing points of intersection. The dots are not mandatory but can be given for clarity of dimensioning.

At **(b)** and **(c)** are shown two methods of dimensioning internal chamfers. The former method is the most common.

At **(d)**, **(e)**, **(f)**, **(g)**, and **(h)** are shown the methods of dimensioning small features. In each case the dimension should be placed centrally or above one of the arrows.

At **(i)** and **(j)** are shown two methods of dimensioning small angles.

Diagrams **(k)**, **(l)**, **(m)**, **(n)**, and **(o)** indicate methods of showing tapered features. To define a taper the following dimensions may be used in various combinations:

(i)   the length of the taper,
(ii) the diameter at either end of the taper,
(iii) the included angle,
(iv) the rate of taper,
(v)   the diameter at a specified cross-sectional plane,
(vi) the dimension locating a cross-sectional plane.

At **(n)** is shown the method of indicating a taper. The arrow is the international symbol for a taper, whose direction indicates the direction of the taper. The cypher indicates the rate of taper on diameter. The rectangular frame signifies that any tolerance specified for the size of the tapered feature applies at any cross-sectional plane along its length. This method of dimensioning is called the *basic angle* or *basic taper* method and its use limits errors of form and size.

At **(p)** is shown the method of dimensioning a countersunk hole, and the plan view immediately beneath shows a method of dimensioning the hole itself.

At **(q)** is shown a countersunk hole that is also counterbored.

(r) depicts a counterbored hole, in which the length of the hole is important, while **(s)** and **(t)** are alternative ways of dimensioning the same counterbored hole.

(u) and **(v)** show alternative ways of dimensioning a countersunk hole and a counterbored hole respectively.

At **(w)** is shown a method of indicating a spotfaced hole in a casting, the object of which is to provide a flat face for a bolt head or nut.

Diagrams **(x)** and **(y)** show the correct method of dimensioning an internal feature with a keyway and a shaft with a keyway respectively.

153

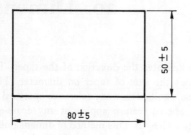

FIG. 20.23 DRAWING

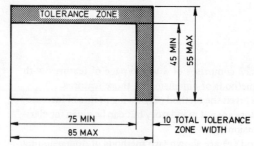

FIG. 20.24 INTERPRETATION

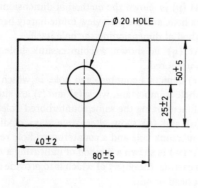

FIG. 20.25

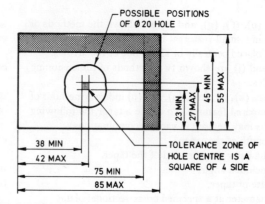

FIG. 20.26

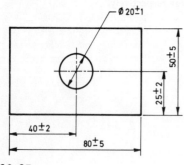

FIG. 20.27

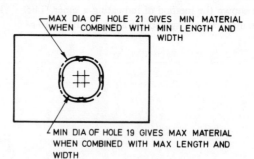

FIG. 20.28

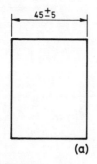

(a)

(b)

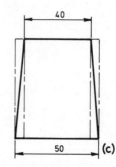

(c)

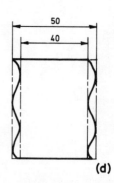

(d)

FIG. 20.29

Fig. 20.23 shows the drawing of a simple rectangular component, the dimensions on which are toleranced. The tolerance is applied where it is necessary to ensure that a dimensional band is not exceeded. Fig. 20.24 is the interpretation of the drawing and indicates that, if the tolerances are applied to two edges only, the component must not be less than the white area 75 × 45, nor more than the total area 85 × 55. The shaded area is, therefore, the working allowance for the craftsman. The total tolerance is the difference between the high limit and the low limit of the dimension. In this case the tolerance zone is 10 mm wide. A variation in size is necessary because it is not possible to manufacture components to exact sizes without using up a great deal of time and enormous sums of money. For general engineering purposes exact sizes are seldom called for and so tolerances are used to allow for interchangeability, inaccuracies in setting up for machining, inaccuracies in the machines themselves, and tool wear. For fine work of high precision tolerances will be less than 0·025 mm, while for work of a less precise nature the tolerances may be 10 mm or more. Tolerances should always be as wide as satisfactory functioning will permit and should be chosen with great care. Tolerances may be added to individual dimensions, or they may be given in note form to cover all, or specified, dimensions.

Fig. 20.25 shows the component previously described, but now containing a hole. When the dimensions governing the position of the hole are toleranced, the interpretation drawing takes on the appearance of Fig. 20.26. The

tolerance zone for the plate remains the same as before and the tolerance zone for the hole is a square of side 4 mm. The centre of the hole can be anywhere within this square.

Fig. 20.27 is a drawing of the same plate again but, in this instance, the hole is also toleranced. The effect of this is seen in Fig. 20.28, and superimposing this combination of hole sizes on Fig. 20.26 would give a picture of the tolerance diagram for the drawing in Fig. 20.27.

When a component is made to its maximum limits of size and any holes are drilled to their minimum limits of size, the component is said to be in its *maximum material condition* (MMC, symbol Ⓜ). Theoretically, when a component is everywhere at its maximum material limits of size, it is perfect in form.

Fig. 20.29 (a) shows a rectangular component with one edge carrying a toleranced dimension. Acceptable interpretations of this drawing are shown in the diagrams at (b), (c), and (d). At no point have the tolerances been exceeded. By placing Ⓜ after the dimension the vertical sides would have been parallel and the corners would have been square, making the component nearly perfect of form.

This simple example shows how important it is to choose tolerances carefully and now a simple subject can become complicated by adding tolerances. Careful dimensioning and the intelligent use of tolerances can improve functional efficiency and reduce costs but, in general, it must be borne in mind that the tighter the tolerances, the greater is the cost of a component.

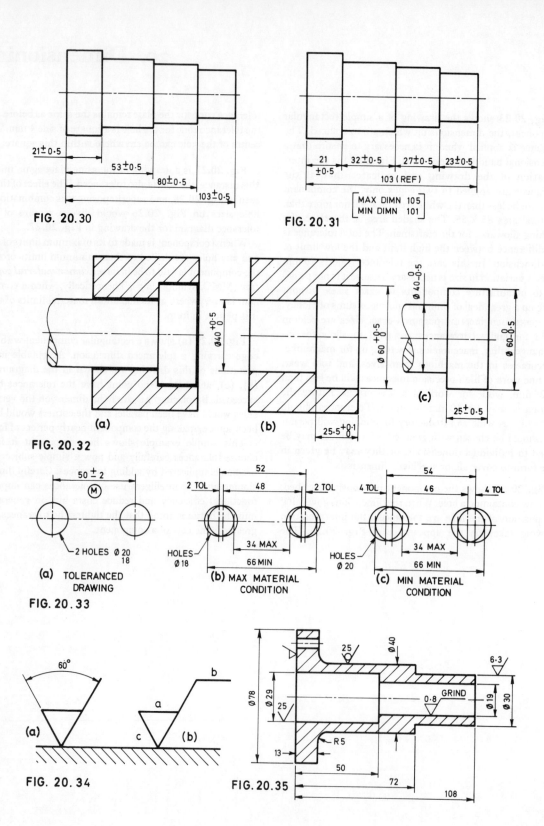

FIG. 20.30

FIG. 20.31

MAX DIMN 105
MIN DIMN 101

FIG. 20.32

(a)

(b)

(c)

FIG. 20.33

(a) TOLERANCED
DRAWING

(b) MAX MATERIAL
CONDITION

(c) MIN MATERIAL
CONDITION

FIG. 20.34

FIG. 20.35

20. Dimensioning

Fig. 20.30 shows a component, which consists of a series of stepped diameters, dimensioned longitudinally with the left-hand face as datum. By applying the same manufacturing tolerance to each length, i.e. ± 0.5 mm, the overall length of the component must lie within the dimensions 103·5 mm and 102·5 mm, a total allowance of 1 mm.

Fig. 20.31 shows the same component chain-dimensioned with each individual step carrying the same tolerance. Addition and subtraction of the tolerances now shows that the overall length must lie within the dimensions 105 mm and 101 mm, a total allowance of 4 mm. With such a vast difference between the two overall sizes, it is obvious that the choice of dimensioning method must be equated to (i) the correct functioning of the product and (ii) the economics involved in production.

Fig. 20.32 (a) depicts a simple assembly of a shaft with a circular head which must fit in a hole and counterbore. The head must not protrude from the counterbore and the shaft must be a reasonably close fit in the hole.

Diagram **(b)** illustrates one way of dimensioning the hole and counterbore while diagram **(c)** shows the dimensions necessary on the shaft and head. A close study of the dimensioning will show that the shaft and head will always fit snugly into the hole and its counterbore.

Fig. 20.33 (a) is a toleranced drawing of two holes basically 50 mm apart. The MMC symbol is applied to the distance between the centres of the holes.

The diagram at **(b)** is drawn for maximum material condition, i.e. with the smallest diameter of holes. Applying the tolerances to the centre distance of the holes gives a maximum centre distance of 52 mm and a minimum of 48 mm. These dimensions, in turn, give 66 mm minimum over the outside of the holes on 48 mm centres, and 34 mm maximum over the inside of the holes on 52 mm centres, and the tolerance between hole centres remains at a total of 4 mm.

Maintaining these maximum and minimum dimensions over the holes, and applying minimum material conditions gives the diagram at **(c)**. From this diagram it becomes apparent that the tolerance on hole centres doubles in size. This means that the limits on centre distance may be exceeded when the features are *not* on their maximum material limits of size. The symbol Ⓜ therefore also means that when features *are* on their maximum material limits of size the limits of centre distance must be observed. One ad-

vantage of this system is that a simple gauge can be used to check the centre distances instead of having to resort to time-consuming direct measurement.

Fig. 20.34 (a) and **(b)** show the use of a machining symbol. The symbol should only be used when the surface finish obtained by normal machining process is unacceptable. It should be placed normal to the face to which it refers or normal to the appropriate extension line.

Diagram **(a)** shows the general form of the symbol and diagram **(b)** is an extension of this symbol to give specific information. Letter *a* on the symbol refers to the position of the surface roughness value measured in micrometres (1 micrometre = 1 μm = 0·001 mm). Letter *b* refers to the position of an indication of the method of production or the surface treatment. Letter *c* refers to the position of the machining allowance.

Fig. 20.35 shows various derived symbols applied to a component. The open symbol containing the figure 25 indicates that a surface roughness of 25 μm is required but it is immaterial whether this is attained by machining or not.

The open symbol containing a circle and the figure 25 indicates that, for this feature, the surface roughness of 25 μm must be produced without machining.

BS 4500: 1969, ISO Limits and Fits is designed to give guidance and assistance to engineers in the choice of tolerances between mating parts, particularly holes and shafts. It gives suitable combinations of grades of tolerances to cover all possible requirements of interchangeable production techniques. The complete system covers all sizes up to 500 mm diameter, ranging from extreme clearance to extreme interference between the mating parts.

Tolerances for holes are denoted by capital letters followed by a number, and tolerances for shafts by small letters followed by a number, e.g. H7 hole, h6 shaft.

There are two main systems of tolerancing.
(i) The *unilateral system* in which the nominal size of hole or shaft becomes the low limit; i.e. the tolerance is in one direction only. This system, using the hole as the nominal part, is recommended by the British Standards Institution.
(ii) The *bilateral system* in which the tolerance is disposed above and below the nominal size of a product.

This chapter will deal with the unilateral system on a hole basis, covering a diameter range of 3 mm to 250 mm for H7, H8, H9, and H11 holes and a selection of their associated shafts.

FIG. 20.36 SELECTED HOLE-BASIS FITS

TYPE OF FIT		CLEARANCE						TRANSITION		INTERFERENCE	
SHAFT TOLERANCE		c11	d10	e9	f7	g6	h6	k6	n6	p6	s6
HOLE TOLERANCES	H7					▨	▨	▨	▨	▨	▨
	H8				▨						
	H9		▨	▨							
	H11	▨									

ES = UPPER DEVIATION FOR HOLES
EI = LOWER DEVIATION FOR HOLES
es&ei = UPPER AND LOWER DEVIATIONS FOR SHAFTS

FIG. 20.37 TOLERANCE LIMITS FOR HOLES

BASIC SIZES		TOLERANCE UNIT = 0.001mm							
		H7		H8		H9		H11	
OVER	UP TO AND INCL	ES +	EI	ES +	EI	ES +	EI	ES +	EI
mm	mm								
3	6	12	0	18	0	30	0	75	0
6	10	15	0	22	0	36	0	90	0
10	18	18	0	27	0	43	0	110	0
18	30	21	0	33	0	52	0	130	0
30	50	25	0	39	0	62	0	160	0
50	80	30	0	46	0	74	0	190	0
80	120	35	0	54	0	87	0	220	0
120	180	40	0	63	0	100	0	250	0
180	250	46	0	72	0	115	0	290	0

FIG. 20.38 TOLERANCE LIMITS FOR SHAFTS

TOLERANCE UNIT = 0.001 mm

BASIC SIZES		c11		d10		e9		f7		g6		h6		k6		n6		p6		s6	
OVER	UP TO AND INCL	es −	ei −	es −	ei −	es −	ei −	es −	ei −	es −	ei −	es −	ei −	es +	ei +	es +	ei +	es +	ei +	es +	ei +
mm	mm																				
3	6	70	145	30	78	20	50	10	22	4	12	0	8	9	1	16	8	20	12	27	19
6	10	80	170	40	98	25	61	13	28	5	14	0	9	10	1	19	10	24	15	32	23
10	18	95	205	50	120	32	75	16	34	6	17	0	11	12	1	23	12	29	18	39	28
18	30	110	240	65	149	40	92	20	41	7	20	0	13	15	2	28	15	35	22	48	35
30	40	120	280	80	180	50	112	25	50	9	25	0	16	18	2	33	17	42	26	59	43
40	50	130	290	80	180	50	112	25	50	9	25	0	16	18	2	33	17	42	26	59	43
50	65	140	330	100	220	60	134	30	60	10	29	0	19	21	2	39	20	51	32	72	53
65	80	150	340	100	220	60	134	30	60	10	29	0	19	21	2	39	20	51	32	78	59
80	100	170	390	120	260	72	159	36	71	12	34	0	22	25	3	45	23	59	37	93	71
100	120	180	400	120	260	72	159	36	71	12	34	0	22	25	3	45	23	59	37	101	79
120	140	200	450	145	305	85	185	43	83	14	39	0	25	28	3	52	27	68	43	117	92
140	160	210	460	145	305	85	185	43	83	14	39	0	25	28	3	52	27	68	43	125	100
160	180	230	480	145	305	85	185	43	83	14	39	0	25	28	3	52	27	68	43	133	108
180	200	240	530	170	355	100	215	50	96	15	44	0	29	33	4	60	31	79	50	151	122
200	225	260	550	170	355	100	215	50	96	15	44	0	29	33	4	60	31	79	50	159	130
225	250	280	570	170	355	100	215	50	96	15	44	0	29	33	4	60	31	79	50	169	140

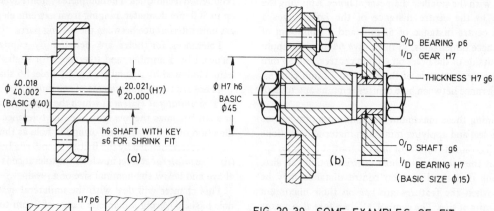

(a)

φ 40.018 / 40.002 (BASIC φ 40)

φ 20.021 / 20.000 (H7)

h6 SHAFT WITH KEY s6 FOR SHRINK FIT

(b)

φ H7 h6 BASIC φ45

O/D BEARING p6
I/D GEAR H7
THICKNESS H7 g6
O/D SHAFT g6
I/D BEARING H7 (BASIC SIZE φ 15)

(c)

H7 p6
H7 s6
H7 g6

FIG. 20.39 SOME EXAMPLES OF FIT SELECTION

At first sight the system may appear to be very complicated, but a close study will show that, for most purposes, a few only of the standard holes and shafts are needed to cover any eventuality.

The tolerance grades are labelled plus or minus to indicate whether they should be added to or subtracted from the basic size. In addition the letters ES and EI are used for holes and es and ei for shafts. These letters mean upper deviation and lower deviation respectively and are the initial letters of the French translation of these terms.

Fig. 20.36 indicates the selected shaft fits that should be used with holes H7, H8, H9, and H11. A clearance fit is one in which any combination of dimensions of hole and shaft will always produce a clearance between the parts. A transition fit is one which can provide for clearance or slight interference between the parts. An interference fit is one in which the shaft is always slightly larger than the hole. This system of fits and tolerances can be used for mating parts other than round holes and shafts, e.g. keys and keyways.

Fig. 20.37 gives, in tabular form, the upper and lower deviations of size for holes ranging from 3 mm to 250 mm. As the system is unilateral on a hole basis, the lower deviation in each case is zero.

Fig. 20.38 gives the deviations for the range of shafts given in **Fig. 20.36.**

Fig. 20.39 (a) shows a sectional elevation of one half of a rigid coupling. The spigot has a basic diameter of 40 mm and is designed to fit into a recess machined in the other half of the coupling. The toleranced diameter is 40·018 mm, 40·002 mm. This means that the upper and lower deviations are 0·018 mm and 0·002 mm respectively. The table in **Fig. 20.38** shows that the spigot corresponds to a k6 shaft.

Fig. 20.39 (b) is a sectional drawing of an idler gear assembly. The spigot location is of basic diameter 45 mm and the selected fits are H7 h6. The dimensions to be applied, taken from the tables, would be:
Hole: 45·025 mm, 45·000 mm diameter.
Shaft: 45·000 mm, 44·984 mm diameter.

Other fits are quoted on this drawing; these are left to students to translate into toleranced dimensions.

Fig. 20.39 (c) shows a dowel fixed in a plate, and a moving part fitted with a bush. The end fixing of the dowel and the outside diameter of the bush will both be interference fits with their mating parts. Assuming the basic diameter of the dowel to be 12 mm, the appropriate end dimensions would be:
Hole: 12·018 mm, 12·000 mm diameter.
Shaft: 12·039 mm, 12·028 mm diameter.
Other dimensions are left to the discretion of students.

A toleranced dimension can, to a certain degree, control the form or geometry of a part. **Fig. 20.29** illustrates that a tolerance alone will not impose a high degree of control.

Geometrical tolerances define the maximum permissible variation of form, or position, of the surface or axis of a component, or part of a component. It is a width or diameter of a tolerance zone within which the surface or axis of the feature must lie. Where a component with such a tolerance is tested or inspected with a dial indicator, the tolerance represents the full indicator movement.

Such tolerances should not be used unless the working requirements of the design dictate that they are necessary, or unless complete interchangeability would not be achieved without them.

Because greater care in design, manufacture, and inspection is required when such methods of dimensioning are employed, costs are also greatly increased.

It will be seen that a particular geometrical tolerance applied to a feature will also automatically limit other possible sources of geometrical error. Thus, a parallel tolerance applied to a surface limits errors of flatness, and concentricity tolerances ensure that the axis of a feature is straight.

In some cases, as will be shown later, it is possible to use 'position' to describe fully symmetry and concentricity tolerances. A positional tolerance may be used to limit errors of squareness of holes and parallelism with one another.

When geometrical tolerances are employed they take precedence over any other tolerancing system that may affect the geometry or form of the product.

159

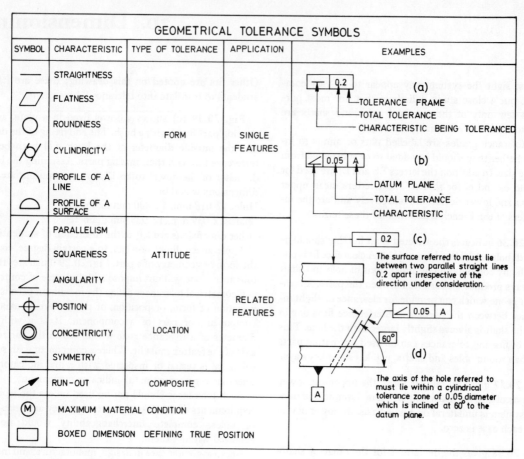

GEOMETRICAL TOLERANCE SYMBOLS

SYMBOL	CHARACTERISTIC	TYPE OF TOLERANCE	APPLICATION	EXAMPLES
—	STRAIGHTNESS	FORM	SINGLE FEATURES	(a) TOLERANCE FRAME / TOTAL TOLERANCE / CHARACTERISTIC BEING TOLERANCED
▱	FLATNESS			
○	ROUNDNESS			
⌭	CYLINDRICITY			
⌒	PROFILE OF A LINE			
⌓	PROFILE OF A SURFACE			(b) DATUM PLANE / TOTAL TOLERANCE / CHARACTERISTIC
//	PARALLELISM	ATTITUDE	RELATED FEATURES	(c)
⊥	SQUARENESS			The surface referred to must lie between two parallel straight lines 0.2 apart irrespective of the direction under consideration.
∠	ANGULARITY			
⊕	POSITION	LOCATION		(d) The axis of the hole referred to must lie within a cylindrical tolerance zone of 0.05 diameter which is inclined at 60° to the datum plane.
◎	CONCENTRICITY			
≡	SYMMETRY			
↗	RUN-OUT	COMPOSITE		
Ⓜ	MAXIMUM MATERIAL CONDITION			
▭	BOXED DIMENSION DEFINING TRUE POSITION			

FIG. 20.40

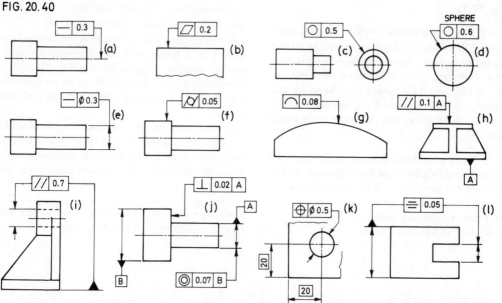

FIG. 20.41   SOME APPLICATIONS OF GEOMETRICAL TOLERANCES

160

Fig. 20.40 illustrates some of the symbols used in this method of dimensioning. The geometrical tolerance is displayed in a rectangular frame, which is divided into a number of compartments to suit the drawing requirements. In the left-hand compartment is placed the symbol for the characteristic being toleranced. In the next compartment is the total tolerance value. This is preceded by the sign $\emptyset$ when the tolerance zone is circular or cylindrical. In the third compartment from the left is placed the datum identification letter, or letters, when a datum system is used and the datum requires identification on the drawing.

A datum face or axis is indicated on a drawing by a solid, equilateral triangle, the base of which lies on the outline itself or an extension of the outline, on a dimension line or an axis. A leader line can be used to join the solid triangle to the tolerance frame, or a separate frame can be used. Some simple examples of the use of tolerance frames and geometrical tolerances are given in **Fig. 20.40 (a), (b), (c),** and **(d).**

Fig. 20.41 shows a number of examples of the use of geometrical tolerances.

At **(a)** is a drawing of a rod with the frame leading to the axis. The symbols indicate straightness of the axis of the rod within two parallel lines, 0·3 mm apart.

At **(b)** the surface indicated is required to lie between two parallel planes, 0·2 mm apart.

At **(c)** the periphery of the cylinder indicated is required to lie between two concentric circles, 0·5 mm apart, measured radially at any cross-section perpendicular to the axis.

At **(d)** the periphery of any section of maximum diameter must lie between two concentric circles, 0·6 mm apart, measured radially.

At **(e)** the axis of that portion of the part indicated must lie within a cylindrical zone 0·3 mm diameter.

At **(f)** the curved surface indicated must lie between two coaxial cylindrical surfaces, 0·05 mm apart.

At **(g)** the profile must lie between two lines which envelop a series of circles of diameter 0·08 mm whose centres lie on the theoretical profile.

At **(h)** the surface indicated is to lie between two planes, 0·1 mm apart, parallel to the datum surface *A*.

At **(i)** the axis of the hole is to lie between two planes, 0·7 mm apart, parallel to the datum surface.

At **(j)** the surface under the head is to lie between two planes, 0·02 mm apart, which are perpendicular to the axis of the cylindrical portion *A*. Also, the axis of the smaller cylindrical portion is required to be contained within a cylinder, 0·07 mm diameter, coaxial with the datum cylinder *B*.

At **(k)** the axis of the hole must be contained within a cylinder, 0·5 mm diameter, whose axis is in the specified true position of the axis of the hole.

At **(l)** the mean plane of the slot must lie between two parallel planes, 0·05 mm apart, which are symmetrically disposed about the mean plane, lying between the upper and lower faces of the part (i.e. the centre line).

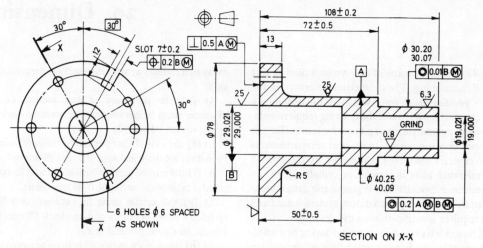

FIG. 20.42 DIMENSIONING A COMPONENT

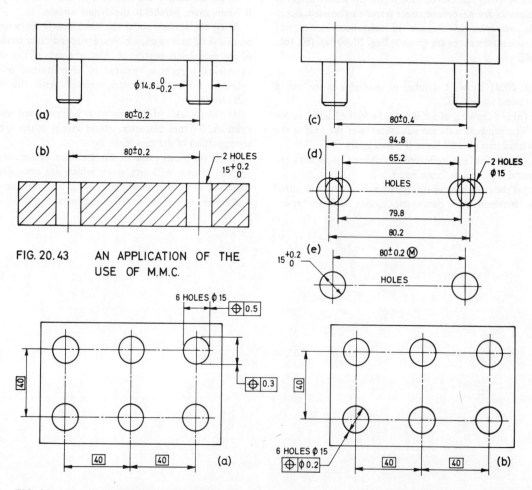

FIG. 20.43 AN APPLICATION OF THE
USE OF M.M.C.

FIG. 20.44 POSITIONAL TOLERANCES

20. Dimensioning

Fig. 20.42 shows a fully detailed drawing (single-part drawing) of the component previously seen in **Fig. 20.35**. The end elevation contains a slot which is to be controlled by a positional tolerance. This requires the median plane (plane on the centre line) of the slot to lie between two planes 0·2 mm apart equally disposed about the true position. The datum is the bore B, and the tolerance applies to maximum material condition. This means that, should the slot or the datum bore be finished away from their maximum material limits of size, an increase in the positional tolerance is permissible.

In the elevation, the end face of the flange must be square with datum diameter A (MMC); the small external diameter must be concentric with datum diameter B (MMC) and the small bore must be concentric with both datum diameters A and B (MMC).

Fig. 20.43 (a) and (b) show the application of linear tolerancing to the centre distances of mating pins and holes. The tolerances selected will ensure assembly under the worst conditions, assuming accuracy of form.

The diagram at (d) illustrates the maximum material condition for the plate, component (b). Assembly with the pins is possible provided that the dimension over the outside of the pins does not exceed 94·8 mm or that the dimen-

sion inside the pins is not less than 65·2 mm. This means that if the diameters of the pins are on their minimum material limits of size, the centre distance between them could vary, as follows:

$$98·8 - 14·4 = 80·4 \text{ mm,}$$
$$65·2 + 14·4 = 79·8 \text{ mm.}$$

This is equal to a centre distance for the pins of $80 \pm 0·4$ mm, and this dimension is applied to the pin centres in diagram (c) to show that the effect of applying MMC is to give greater freedom in manufacturing processes.

The tolerance diagram at (e) illustrates the method of specifying MMC to the hole centres in order to take advantage of this freedom.

Fig. 20.44 (a) and (b) show two methods of indicating true position on drawings. At (a), the positional tolerance states that the axes of the holes must lie within rectangles 0·5 mm long and 0·3 mm wide, and the rectangles must be in true geometrical position. There is no accumulation of errors of position and any variation of centre distance must be the same between any pair of holes. At (b), the message is the same except that the tolerance zones for the holes are cylinders of diameter 0·2 mm.

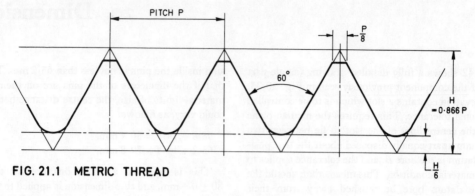

FIG. 21.1 METRIC THREAD

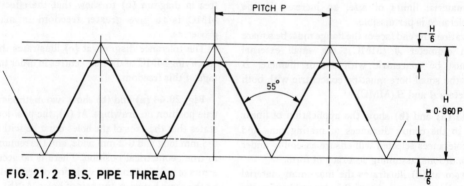

FIG. 21.2 B.S. PIPE THREAD

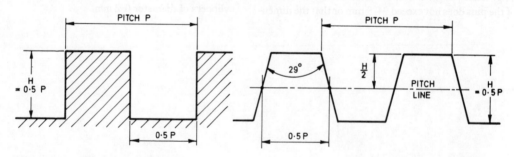

FIG. 21.3 SQUARE THREAD

FIG. 21.4 ACME THREAD

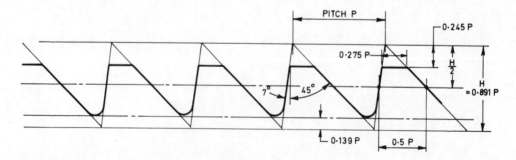

FIG. 21.5 BUTTRESS THREAD

Screw threads are *helices* generated either externally on a rod or internally on a circular hole.

Generally, threads fall into two groups: square section and vee section. The square-section threads are normally used for power transmission, while the vee threads are used for nuts and bolts and finer work.

Threads may be 'right-hand' or 'left-hand'. The nut on a right-hand thread moves away from its operator when rotated in a clockwise direction, whilst the nut on a left-hand thread moves towards its operator when similarly rotated.

The *pitch* of a thread is the distance between corresponding points on adjacent threads, measured parallel to the thread axis.

The *crest* of a thread, whether external or internal, is its most prominent feature.

The *flanks* are the straight sides joining the crest to the root.

The *major diameter* is the greatest diameter of the thread. This is also known as the outside diameter.

The *minor diameter* is the smallest diameter of the thread (sometimes called the core or root diameter).

The *effective diameter* is the diameter measured on the imaginary pitch line, the line on which the width of the threads equals the width of the spaces between the threads. The effective diameter and the thread angle are important because together they determine the quality of the fit between mating threads.

The *lead* of a thread is the axial distance a screw advances in one revolution. On single-start threads the pitch and the lead are the same. On two-start threads the lead is twice the pitch, and on three-start threads the lead is three times the pitch, etc. An increase in lead is effected by increasing the helix angle of the thread, the pitch remaining constant.

Fig. 21.1 shows the principal dimensions of a metric vee thread. The most significant feature is that the included angle of the thread is 60°.

Fig. 21.2 gives the principal dimensions of British Standard pipe threads. The threads are of Whitworth form, vee shaped, with an included angle of 55°.

Fig. 21.3 shows the drawing dimensions of a square thread. The actual dimensions would be slightly different from those given here to allow movement between mating threads. Square threads are used for power transmission.

The acme thread shown in **Fig. 21.4** is a modified form of square thread and is easier to produce. It is used for power transmission in screw jacks, lathe lead screws, fly presses, etc.

Another important thread is the buttress, shown in **Fig. 21.5**. This is also a modified square thread and is designed to transmit heavy forces in one direction only. An example of this is seen on quick-action vices.

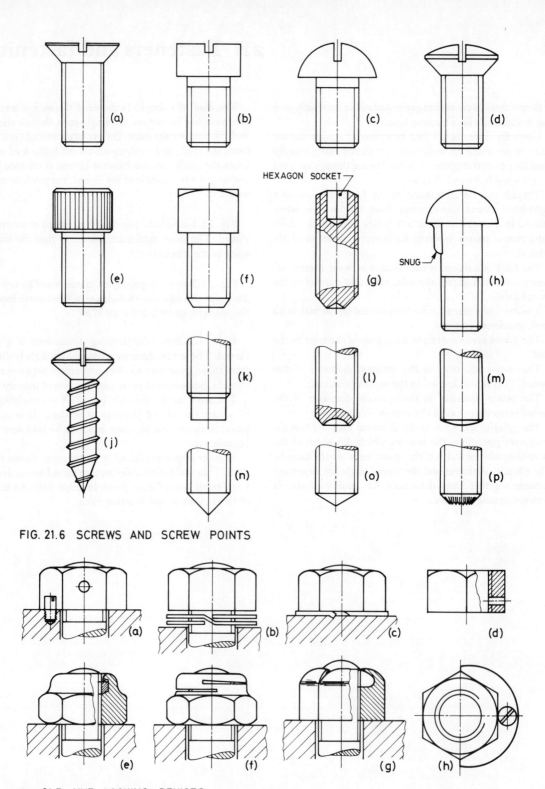

HEXAGON SOCKET

SNUG

FIG. 21.6 SCREWS AND SCREW POINTS

FIG. 21.7 NUT LOCKING DEVICES

Fig. 21.6 shows a selection of screws and the ends that may be machined on some of these screws.

Diagram **(a)** is a drawing of a screw having a countersunk head. This type of screw is used where the head is sunk below the level of the surface into which it is screwed.

Diagram **(b)** shows a screw with a cheese head. In use the underside of the head provides the contact face and the head protrudes above the face of contact. These screws are confined to relatively small sizes.

Diagram **(c)** is a round-headed screw. This type of screw is confined to relatively small sizes and is a protruding type.

Diagram **(d)** shows a raised countersunk screw. This small type of screw is used where only a part of the head can protrude. It is often plated to give a pleasing effect.

Diagram **(e)** is a drawing of a socket-head screw. The outside surface of the head is milled and a hexagonal hole is sunk into the centre of the head. These screws can be used either protruding or countersunk beneath the surface of contact. They are made from hardened steel and are black in colour.

Diagram **(f)** shows a square-headed set screw. Screws of this type are used to prevent rotation or movement of a shaft, for which purpose a flat is usually machined into the shaft to provide a contact area for the end of the screw.

Diagram **(g)** is a drawing of a hexagon-socket set screw. Such screws are used for a similar purpose to other set screws. Generally, these screws are used diametrically opposite keys to ensure that no axial movement occurs in a rotating shaft. The absence of a head means that no part of the screw need protrude, thus reducing the safety hazard.

Diagram **(h)** shows a round-headed screw that has no screwdriver slot. The small protrusion under the head, called a snug, fits into a suitable slot to ensure that the screw does not revolve when a nut is screwed on it.

Diagram **(j)** is a drawing of a self-tapping screw. Screws of this type are used with comparatively thin metal and form their own thread in a previously drilled hole. The motor car industry in particular uses large quantities of these screws.

Diagram **(k)** shows the end of a set screw. It is known as a *full dog* or *thimble* end and is used in conjunction with flat surfaces.

Diagram **(l)** shows an end similar to that drawn in diagram **(g)**. The object of these ends is that they should bite into a shaft to keep it firmly in place. They are, therefore, hardened so that they can penetrate the metal more easily.

Diagram **(m)** is the more usually seen rounded end used on bolts as well as screws. The radius of this end is about 1·25 times the outside diameter of the thread and provides a point contact with a shaft or other feature.

Diagram **(n)** shows an example of a cone point. This type of end is designed to penetrate other metal surfaces with which it comes into contact. The angle of the point is 90° and this angle is used, generally, when the length of the threaded portion of the screw is greater than its outside diameter.

Diagram **(o)** is another example of a cone point, the angle being 118°, equal to the angle made at the end of a drilled hole. This angle is used on screws having a threaded length less than the outside diameter.

Diagram **(p)** shows an example of a serrated cone point. This type of end is used almost to cut its way into the metal with which it is in contact. The end is always hardened to achieve this.

Fig. 21.7 shows a series of locking devices for nuts.

Diagram **(a)** is a drawing giving two such devices, a locking pin driven through both nut and bolt and a set screw situated close to one face of the hexagon to prevent rotation.

Diagram **(b)** shows a loosely assembled spring washer. When tightened, the spring steel from which the washer is made exerts a force against the underside of the nut keeping it tightly in engagement on the threads.

Diagram **(c)** shows a modified form of spring washer. In addition to being slightly coiled the ends of the washer are tabbed so that they bite into the contact surfaces.

Diagram **(d)** is a sketch of a nut which has a plastics plug inserted through one face of the hexagon. During assembly, the threads on the bolt cut into the plug and cause a tight fit to be made.

Diagram **(e)** shows a 'Simmonds' nut. This contains a plastics ring trapped in the upper, non-threaded portion of the nut. During the final phase of assembly the threads on the bolt cut into the plastics ring causing a tight fit to be made.

Diagram **(f)** shows a 'Philidas' nut which has two slots cut in the plain cylindrical portion and diametrically opposite one another. Once in position this type of nut has excellent resistance to vibration.

Diagram **(g)** is a drawing of an 'Oddie' nut which is made so that each of the six faces of the hexagon are formed into tongues at their outer face. These tongues grip the bolt thread and prevent it being loosened.

Diagram **(h)** is the plan view of a nut held in position by a fitting locking plate. The locking plate itself is attached to a component by means of a small screw or dowels.

Other methods of locking nuts include the use of wire threaded through holes drilled in the corners of nuts and having the ends twisted together, and tab washers which are washers with one or more tongues on them. Single tabbed washers are used in conjunction with slotted bolts and double tabbed washers are used where one tab can be turned up against a face of the nut while the other is turned down over the edge of a plate.

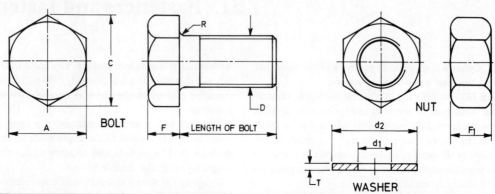

BOLT

LENGTH OF BOLT

NUT

WASHER

Nominal Size D	Pitch of Thread		Width Across Flats	Width Across Corners	Height of Bolt Head F	Thickness of Nut F_1	Radius R	Clearance Hole d_1		Diameter of Washer d_2		Thickness T
	Coarse	Fine	A max	C max	max	max	max	Bright	Black	Normal	Large	
M3	0.50		5.50	6.40	2.125	2.40	0.30	3.2		7.0		0.5
M4	0.70		7.00	8.10	2.925	3.20	0.35	4.3		9.0		0.8
M5	0.80		8.00	9.20	3.650	4.00	0.35	5.3	5.5	10.0		1.0
M6	1.00		10.00	11.50	4.150	5.00	0.40	6.4	6.6	12.5		1.5
M8	1.25	1.00	13.00	15.00	5.650	6.50	0.60	8.4	9.0	17.0	21.0	1.5
M10	1.50	1.25	17.00	19.60	7.180	8.00	0.60	10.5	11.0	21.0	24.0	2.0
M12	1.75	1.25	19.00	21.90	8.180	10.00	1.10	13.0	14.0	24.0	28.0	2.5
M16	2.00	1.50	24.00	27.70	10.180	13.00	1.10	17.0	18.0	30.0	34.0	3.0
M20	2.50	1.50	30.00	34.60	13.215	16.00	1.20	21.0	22.0	37.0	39.0	3.0
M24	3.00	2.00	36.00	41.60	15.215	19.00	1.20	25.0	26.0	44.0	50.0	4.0
M30	3.50	2.00	46.00	53.10	19.260	24.00	1.70	31.0	33.0	56.0	60.0	4.0
M36	4.00	3.00	55.00	63.50	23.260	29.00	1.70	37.0	39.0	66.0	72.0	5.0

FIG. 21.8   METRIC FASTENERS

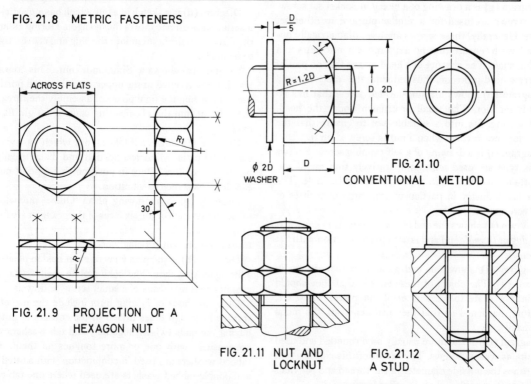

FIG. 21.9   PROJECTION OF A HEXAGON NUT

FIG. 21.10   CONVENTIONAL METHOD

FIG. 21.11   NUT AND LOCKNUT

FIG. 21.12   A STUD

Fig. 21.8 shows details of ISO metric hexagon bolts, nuts, screws, and washers conforming to *BS 3692: 1967* and *BS 4190: 1967*. The table of preferred sizes ranges from 3 mm to 36 mm diameter and covers both coarse threads and fine threads. The full range of sizes is given in the British Standards and extends from 1·6 mm diameter to 68 mm diameter. *BS 4190* deals with black hexagon bolts, screws, and nuts while *BS 3692* deals with precision bolts, screws, and nuts. Machine screws and machine screw nuts are covered in *BS 4183*.

The nominal length of bolts and screws with hexagon heads is measured from the underside of the head to the end of the threaded portion, including any chamfer or radius which may be applied to the thread end. Any such chamfer should be at 45° and a radiused end should have a radius of 1·25 times the diameter of the shank.

The difference between a bolt and a screw is usually indicated by the thread length. A bolt has a length of plain, unscrewed shank, while a screw has threads extending along the shank almost to the underside of the head. Also, bolts are always fitted with nuts while screws are used in tapped holes.

Both bolts and screws have chamfered heads, the chamfer angle being 30°.

Precision nuts are double chamfered whilst black nuts to *BS 4190: 1967* can be either double chamfered or chamfered on one face only.

The method of indicating a threaded fastener on a drawing, by means of a note, is to designate the metric size of the fastener followed by the thread pitch in millimetres and then the tolerance class symbol. Thus, for a 5 mm nut or other internally threaded hole, this may read : M5 × 0·8 − 6H.

A bolt, or other externally threaded bar, of nominal diameter 8 mm may be described as: M8 × 1·25 − 6g. It will be noted that the tolerance class symbol for nuts has a capital letter suffix while that for bolts has a lower case letter suffix.

Where two threaded mating parts are involved the relative fit between them is indicated as follows: M8 × 1·25 − 6H/6g. In some instances it is considered unnecessary to use the pitch measurement in the note and necessary to use the pitch measurement in the note and

where a threaded feature is described in this way it indicates that a coarse thread has been used. In all other cases the inclusion of the pitch measurement will determine whether the thread is coarse or fine.

Bolts and screws of 6 mm diameter and above are identified as ISO metric by having either 'ISO M' or 'M' on the top face of the ad.

Fig. 21.9 shows three orthographic views of a 30 mm diameter hexagon nut. The overall sizes are given and dimensions are provided to enable the radii to be drawn.

Note particularly the difference between the views across the corners and across the flats. In the latter view part of two faces of the hexagon are seen and the edges of the nut are square, whereas in the view across the corners one full face and two half-faces of the hexagon are seen and edges are chamfered.

Fig. 21.10 shows the conventional way of drawing a nut and washer, with approximate sizes. Drawing nuts and washers in this way means that both features will be larger than the true dimensions. This can be of assistance because if washers and nuts of this size can be accommodated in a given space, with enough space left for a spanner, then a true size assembly is sure to fit.

Fig. 21.11 shows a nut and locknut assembly. The thin nut is assembled first, followed by the plain nut. The thin nut should then be slackened back to ensure that the major forces are taken by the larger nut. This method of assembly prevents nuts from becoming loosened due to vibration.

A stud assembly is shown in Fig. 21.12 Studs are made in more than one form; that shown in the drawing being the most common. It is made from a piece of round bar threaded at both ends. The extremities of the bar can be either rounded or chamfered and there is no head.

The threaded portion that screws into the flange generally has a length of thread not less than the outside diameter of the thread. The plain or unthreaded portion of the stud, often called the land, is used as a means of location and also to assist in assembling the stud.

Studs are used where nuts or bolt heads cannot be accommodated, such as motor vehicle cylinder heads.

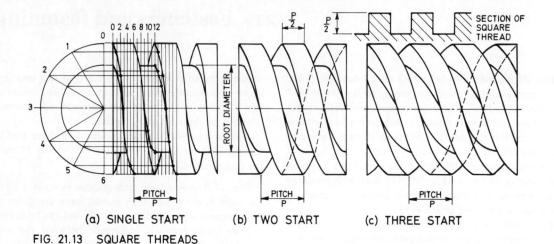

(a) SINGLE START **(b) TWO START** **(c) THREE START**

FIG. 21.13 SQUARE THREADS

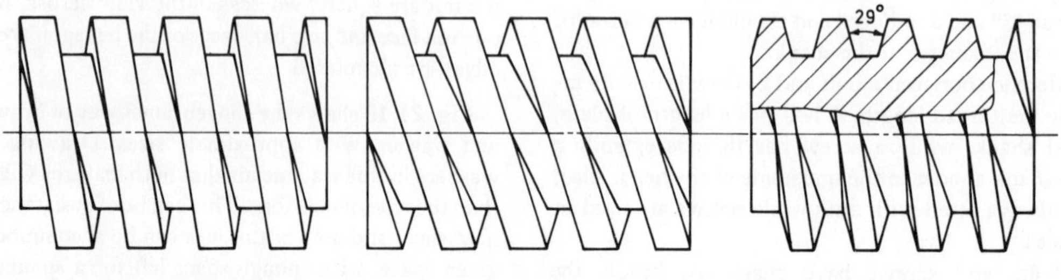

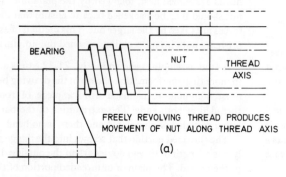

(a) SINGLE START **(b) TWO START** **(c) ACME THREAD**

FIG. 21.14 SQUARE THREAD FORMS

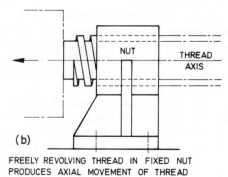

FREELY REVOLVING THREAD PRODUCES
MOVEMENT OF NUT ALONG THREAD AXIS

(a)

FREELY REVOLVING THREAD IN FIXED NUT
PRODUCES AXIAL MOVEMENT OF THREAD

(b)

FIG. 21.15 MACHINE MOVEMENTS

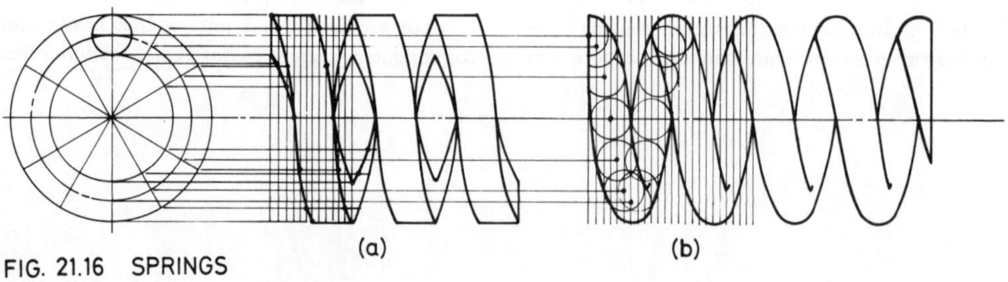

FIG. 21.16 SPRINGS   (a)   (b)

170

Fig. 21.13 (a) shows the construction of a square thread. Draw a rectangle representing the diameter and length of the thread required. Draw a half end elevation, showing the outside and core diameters and divide this into six equal parts, numbering as shown. Mark off the length of the rectangle into pitches and divide each pitch vertically into twelve equal parts.

The points of intersection of the projectors from points 1, 2, 3, 4, etc., with the corresponding vertical pitch divisions will give the helical curve of the flank of one thread, as indicated by the large dots.

Draw a similar curve, parallel with the first, half a pitch length away to complete the outside of one thread. As the helix twists around the core of the bar, the flanks of the thread are seen and the line of intersection of the two is plotted in similar fashion to the outside of the thread.

Project horizontally from points 0_1, 1_1, 2_1, etc., to intersect the verticals numbered 0, 1, 2, etc. It will be noticed that all the curves meet on the horizontal centre line.

Diagram (b) is a drawing of part of a two-start square thread. The general dimensions are the same as in the previous example, the main difference being an increase in the helix angle. To project this, divide longitudinally into pitches as before but move along two vertical divisions for each point plotted instead of one as before.

Diagram (c) is a drawing of part of a three-start square thread. The general dimensions are the same as before, but this time move along three vertical divisions for each point plotted.

A quicker method of showing square threads is indicated in Fig. 21.14 (a) and (b). The initial layout of the pitch and half-pitch distances is the same but, instead of plotting the true helical curve, the thread is shown made up of straight lines. On a small drawing this method is quite satisfactory and is, of course, much easier to produce.

An indication is given of single-start and two-start threads.

Also drawn in Fig. 21.14 (c) is an acme thread. This is a modified form of the square thread and is often chosen to transmit motion and power on such things as machine tools, presses, and screwjacks. It is easier to manufacture than the vertical sided square thread.

Although a vee thread is stronger than its equivalent square thread or acme thread, the latter have the advantage of offering less frictional resistance to motion, an important factor in power transmission.

Both the square thread and acme thread forms have similar relationships to their respective pitches.

Fig. 21.15 (a) shows a machine arrangement in which a square thread is free to rotate in a bearing housing at one end, the other end being driven. The nut, which is prevented from rotating, will travel backwards and forwards along the axis of the thread as it turns anticlockwise and clockwise.

At (b) is a sketch of a freely revolving thread passing through a fixed nut. As the thread revolves it travels through the nut and can be made to do work, e.g. a screw jack.

Fig. 21.16 (a) and (b) are drawings of a square-sectioned spring and a circular-sectioned spring. The method of projection is similar to that described for Fig. 21.13 (a). In the case of the circular-sectioned spring, it will be noted that the centre line of the spring wire is plotted and the outline is obtained by drawing tangentially to a series of faint circles, each of which is equal in diameter to the diameter of the wire.

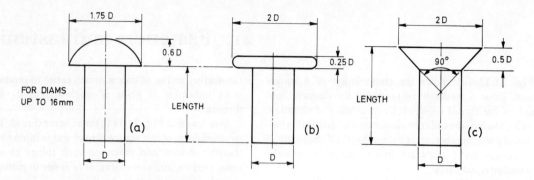

FIG. 21.17 RIVET PROPORTIONS

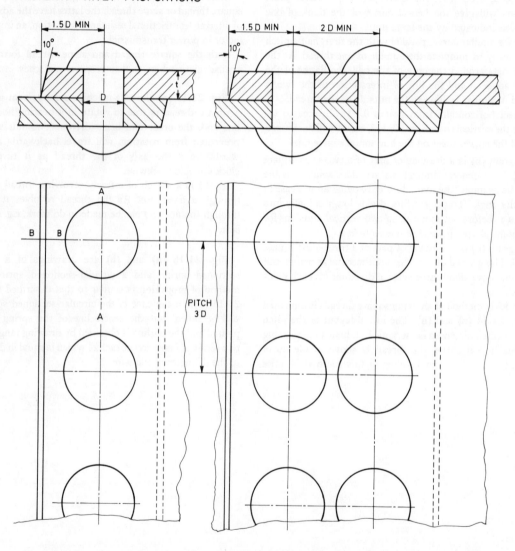

FIG. 21.18 SINGLE-RIVETED LAP JOINT   FIG. 21.19 DOUBLE-RIVETED LAP JOINT

21. Fasteners and fastenings

Rivets are used to provide a simple and effective means of joining structures and plates, giving a permanent and economical joint of great strength.

Rivets are made in machines which cut off lengths of heated bar, form a head under pressure, and eject the finished product at a rapid rate.

Holes slightly larger in diameter than the rivet are drilled in the parts to be joined, so that when the rivet is inserted and a pressure is applied to form the sealing head, the rivet will fill the hole completely.

Riveted joints may be made by hand or by machine. There are various types of riveting machines, which are either hydraulically or pneumatically operated. Perhaps the most commonly used machine is one in which the rivet is formed by a succession of rapid blows accompanied by rotation of the forming tool. Rivets may be cold-worked or hot-worked depending on the nature and size of the job.

Fig. 21.17 shows rivets which may be made from ferrous or non-ferrous metal. Certain special tests must be applied to the rivet material. A rivet shank must, for example, bend cold through 180° without cracking on the outside of the bend, and it must be possible to form a flat head while hot to $2\frac{1}{2}$ times the rivet diameter without cracking around the edge.

Rivet length in excess of plate thickness to form a satisfactory head is generally taken as three-quarters of the diameter ($0.75D$ for countersunk and $1.25D$ to $1.75D$ for ordinary rivets).

In designing a riveted joint consideration must be given to the correct choice of plates and the size and spacing of the rivets, so that the joint will give almost equal resistance to the five major causes of failure. Referring to **Fig. 21.18** these modes of failure are:

(1) tearing of the plate along the line of rivet holes AA;

(2) shearing of the rivets under the action of forces tending to pull the plates apart;

(3) crushing of rivet and plates due to bearing pressure (this is usually catered for by using Unwin's empirical formula for finding diameter, $D = 6.3 \sqrt{t}$, where t is the thickness of the plate);

(4) splitting of the plate in front of the rivet along the line BB;

(5) shearing of the strip of plate in front of the rivet.

Both causes of failure in (4) and (5) can be eliminated by making the minimum distance of rivet centre to edge of plate equal to $1.5D$.

In addition to the common rivet shapes shown in **Fig. 21.17**, there are many different types of patent rivets in common use, particularly in the aircraft industry, where great ingenuity has led to the development of lightweight but immensely strong rivets which are assembled at a rapid rate and give a very smooth, crinkle-free finish to the aircraft skin. Special tools have also been developed to achieve these efficient joints.

Where it is necessary to provide a water- or steam-tight joint, *caulking* and *fullering* tools are used.

These tools are like blunt-ended chisels and are struck with a hammer. Caulking tools are narrow at the working end and are used to peen the rivet head or plate. When the width of the tool used for plate equals the plate thickness the process is called *fullering*.

Three different types of rivet for general engineering purposes are shown in **Fig. 21.17**.

Diagram **(a)** is called a *snap head* rivet, diagram **(b)** shows a *flat head* rivet and diagram **(c)** a 90° *countersunk head* rivet.

Figs 21.18 and 21.19 show two different types of joint and the spacing dimensions of the rivets.

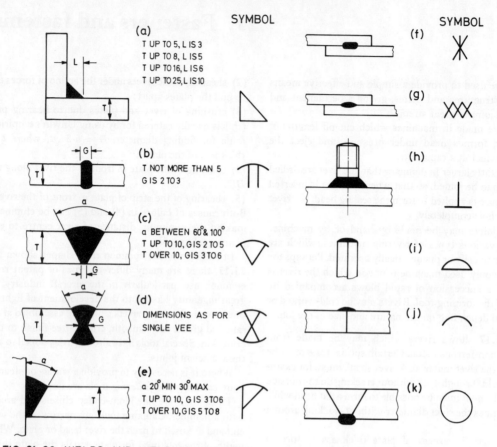

(a)
T UP TO 5, L IS 3
T UP TO 8, L IS 5
T UP TO 16, L IS 6
T UP TO 25, L IS 10

(b)
T NOT MORE THAN 5
G IS 2 TO 3

(c)
a BETWEEN 60° & 100°
T UP TO 10, G IS 2 TO 5
T OVER 10, G IS 3 TO 6

(d)
DIMENSIONS AS FOR
SINGLE VEE

(e)
a 20° MIN 30° MAX
T UP TO 10, G IS 3 TO 6
T OVER 10, G IS 5 TO 8

SYMBOL

(f)

(g)

(h)

(i)

(j)

(k)

FIG. 21.20 WELDS AND WELDING SYMBOLS

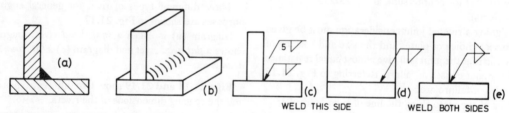

(a)

(b)

(c) WELD THIS SIDE

(d) WELD BOTH SIDES (e)

FIG. 21.21 CONVENTIONS FOR A FILLET WELD

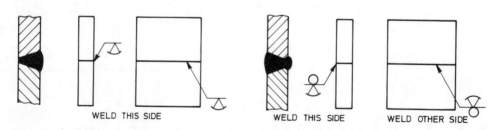

WELD THIS SIDE

FIG. 21.22 SINGLE-VEE BUTT

WELD THIS SIDE

WELD OTHER SIDE

FIG. 21.23 SINGLE-VEE BUTT WITH SEALING
RUN

Welding is a process whereby metals are locally united by fusing them together to form a permanent joint. Welding may be effected with or without the application of pressure, and filler metal may or may not be used.

The simplest method of *pressure welding* metals is to heat the pieces to be joined until they become plastic and then hammer them together, either by hand or in a machine. This is usually termed *forge welding*.

Resistance welding in its various forms is a more sophisticated pressure-welding technique in which components are butted together and an electric current is allowed to flow, either at or near the faces to be joined. This produces sufficient heat to cause the metal to become plastic. Under the influence of continual pressure, the interfaces deform, or are 'upset' and a weld is effected.

Spot welding is a method of resistance welding with pressure in which an electric current is passed through the workpiece via electrodes. The current develops heat, the workpiece becomes plastic, and the pressure of the electrodes forms the weld, which is of approximately the same area as the electrode tip **(Fig. 21.10(f))**.

Seam and stitch welding are variations of the spot-welding technique in which electrode wheels are employed **(Fig. 21.20 (g))**.

Stud welding is another example of resistance welding with pressure in which the stud is used as an electrode and an arc is struck between one end of the stud and the parent metal. This arc produces the necessary heat, and pressure is applied to complete the weld. It is usually necessary to retract the stud from the parent metal surface in order to initiate the arc. The amount of this retraction is known as 'lift' **(Fig. 21.10 (h))**.

Fusion welding is a process in which no pressure is applied to consolidate the weld. The metals are brought to a state of fusion by heat generated either by a gas flame or by an electric arc. Additional metal is often deposited as a part of these processes. With *gas* and *carbon-arc* welding this is often in the form of a rod or wire, whilst, with *metal-arc welding*, the rod or wire becomes the electrode, melting and filling the space between abutting metal faces as the weld progresses.

Bronze welding is a method of joining metals by depositing a weld metal consisting essentially of a mixture of copper and zinc. It is used to join brass and bronze components, but may also be usefully employed with steel, particularly steel pipes and tubes. To effect a good joint, fusion of the workpieces is not always necessary. Generally the filler metal has a melting-point above 850°C (1123 K).

Brazing is a process of joining metals by capillary attraction in which a molten copper base filler metal is used at a temperature above 500°C (773 K) and is drawn into the space between closely mating surfaces. It is sometimes referred to as hard soldering.

The process is used to join tungsten-carbide tips to mild steel shanks to form cutting tools.

Figs 21.20–21.23 show a series of welded joints together with their respective British Standard symbols and some notes relating to plate and weld proportions.

The welds would not, of course, be as clearly defined as drawn if taken in section because, during the fusion process, the side and edge faces of the parent metal would become plastic and would be penetrated by the weld metal. It must also be borne in mind that all the weld is not necessarily deposited at once. Quite often many passes, or runs, with varying electrode diameters, are essential to produce a good weld.

The simple fillet weld shown in **Fig. 21.10 (a)** is an external weld needing no plate preparation. In this type of joint the weld metal is deposited in the angle formed by the two plates and is the type of weld used in lap joints and tee joints. One of the major considerations must be distortion of the plates due to the high temperatures attained (up to 3000 °C or 3273 K for electric-arc welding). This may be relieved by securely clamping the workpieces or by suitable treatment after welding.

Thicker plates which have to be butted together may have to be pre-treated in the machine shop. The single-vee butt joint, shown in **Fig. 21.20 (c)**, for example, has the plate edges bevelled at an included angle of between 60° and 100°. The object of bevelling is to allow the welder to penetrate the plate thickness completely, so that the thicker the plate used the greater will be the included bevel angle. This pretreatment may take the form of a machining operation or it may be carried out in a guillotine. Somtimes a flame-cutter followed by a pneumatic hammer to upset the plate edge is used.

Fig. 21.21 (a)–(e) show the treatment of a fillet weld. The welded components are shown first in section, then pictorially, and finally as they may be depicted on a drawing. At **Fig. 21.21 (c)**, an end elevation corresponding to **Fig. 21.21 (a)** is shown. The arrow points to the joint and the horizontal leader carries the symbol in a position which indicates 'weld this side'. **Fig. 21.21 (d)** is a front elevation of **Fig. 21.21 (c)** looking at the joint, and the arrow again indicates 'weld this side'. **Fig. 21.21 (e)** is an alternative end elevation and the symbols indicate 'weld both sides'. The method of showing the proposed weld size is shown alternatively in Fig. 21.21 (c).

Fig. 21.22 shows a single-vee butt weld in section and two alternative ways of indicating 'weld this side'.

Fig. 21.23 shows a single-vee butt weld with a sealing run, first in section, and then a representation of the sectional view and the legend 'weld this side'. The final view is an elevation of the side away from the weld and the legend 'weld the other side'.

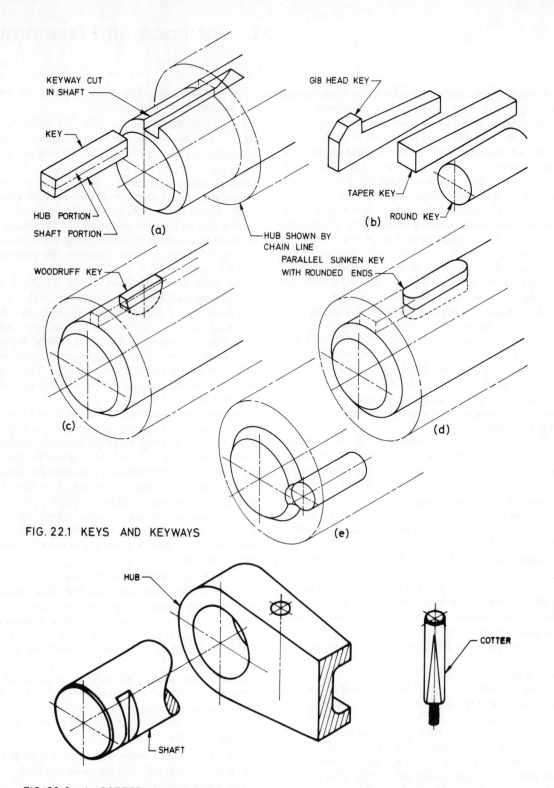

KEYWAY CUT
IN SHAFT

KEY

HUB PORTION
SHAFT PORTION

(a)

GIB HEAD KEY

TAPER KEY

ROUND KEY

(b)

WOODRUFF KEY

(c)

HUB SHOWN BY
CHAIN LINE

PARALLEL SUNKEN KEY
WITH ROUNDED ENDS

(d)

(e)

FIG. 22.1 KEYS AND KEYWAYS

HUB

COTTER

SHAFT

FIG. 22.2 A COTTER AND SHAFT

Rotating circular shafts are employed to drive machines and mechanical devices in the most efficient and positive of ways. This means that they must be fitted with components that not only transmit the driving forces but also prevent slip occurring between the shaft and its mating part. One way of achieving this is to machine a slot in the shaft and its mating part and insert a single piece of metal in the two slots so that both parts are rigidly held together. The machined slot is called a *keyway* and the metal insert is called a *key*.

Fig. 22.1 shows a number of different keys and some methods of positioning.

Diagram **(a)** is a key and keyway of the type described above and shows how a key locks together the shaft and hub by filling the spaces machined in each.

Diagram **(b)** shows three different types of key. From the left, the first one is called a gib-head key due to the shaped end which allows it to be knocked into place and also makes withdrawal easier. The key is rectangular in section and has parallel sides, the base is parallel to the axis of the shaft and the top face has a taper of 1 in 100.

The second key is of the plain rectangular taper variety. The shape is similar to the previous key but has no gib-head.

The third key is a piece of round steel bar. The hole to take this type of key is drilled with the two mating pieces clamped together to ensure a good fit. It would be almost impossible to drill half a hole in each component separately.

Diagram **(c)** shows the assembly of a Woodruff key. This is a sunken key, having flat parallel sides and of almost semicircular shape. It fits into a semicircular slot cut in the shaft, and the hub, which contains a continuous slot, is made to slide over the key. These keys are used only where light driving forces are experienced and usually on tapered drive shafts. For ease of assembly the key can be tilted slightly towards the hub which, on making contact with the

key, will rotate it into its correct position.

Diagram **(d)** in **Fig. 22.1** is another example of a sunken key. It is rectangular or square in section and has flat parallel sides. It is rounded at the ends and can sit in a milled groove in the shaft. The hub of the pulley or gear slides over the key before being locked in position.

Diagram **(e)** shows a round key in position locking together a hub and a shaft.

There are many different types of key, some of which allow sliding movements to take place while the mating pieces are revolving. Other keys and keyways are cut into the metal of the shaft and hub, there being no separate pieces at all. Such devices are called splines and are used where a great deal of power is to be transmitted.

There are occasions when shafts can be rigidly fixed to parts assembled on them. In such cases the design caters for no removal of the parts for maintenance or other purposes. When removal is called for in the design, cotters and taper pins are often used.

An everyday example of the use of cotter pins is the connection made between the pedal cranks and pedal shaft of a bicycle.

This is shown in **Fig. 22.2.** The shaft has a groove milled into the curved surface, and the crank has a hole drilled through it so that the cotter will fit snugly into both components and lock them together. The cotter is a piece of round bar having a tapered flat milled into it. This flat surface fits against the bottom of the groove in the shaft. Continued use can cause the cotter to work loose so it is provided with a screwed end on to which is assembled a washer and a nut. The advantage of this type of assembly is that it is relatively cheap to produce but is very effective. The cotter can be driven in with a hammer and removed by using a hammer and a softer piece of metal, such as brass, against the thread end. The softer metal is used so as not to damage the threads.

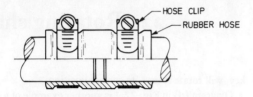

FIG. 22.3 SIMPLE FLEXIBLE COUPLING

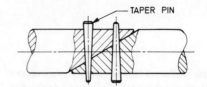

FIG. 22.4 SIMPLE RIGID COUPLING

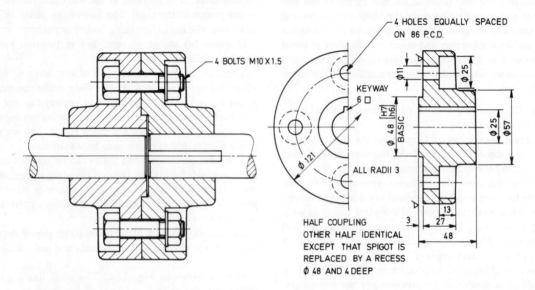

FIG. 22.5 ASSEMBLY AND DETAILS OF A RIGID COUPLING

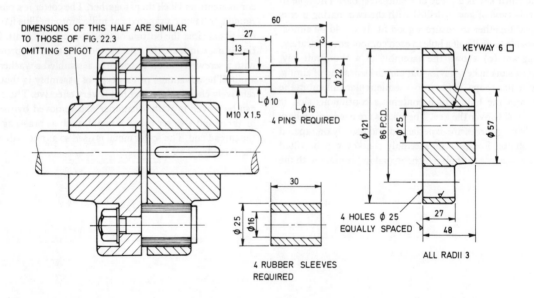

FIG. 22.6 ASSEMBLY AND DETAILS OF A FLEXIBLE COUPLING

178

For manufacturing and assembly reasons it is often necessary to join two shafts together so that they act as one continuous shaft in a machine. Sometimes it is necessary to provide a partially flexible joint between the shafts to take out large amounts of twisting or to cater for a small degree of misalignment. All of these conditions can be catered for by using a particular form of shaft *coupling* to suit the conditions of the rotating shaft.

Shaft couplings may be listed under four main headings: (1) rigid couplings, which keep shafts in rigid axial alignment; (2) flexible couplings, which allow a certain amount of axial misalignment; (3) universal joints, which allow large angular misalignment of shafts without loss of efficiency; (4) axially sliding couplings, or clutches, which enable the connection between shafts to be broken.

A simple form of flexible coupling is shown in **Fig. 22.3**. It consists of a piece of rubber hosepipe clamped on the shaft ends by means of standard hose clips. In such an arrangement, which should be used only on very light drives, all the driving forces are taken by the rubber hose between the shaft ends.

The rigid coupling shown in **Fig. 22.4** necessitates machining the shaft ends, fitting the ends together and then drilling and reaming to take the taper pins, each of which is assembled from different sides of the shaft. A sleeve or muff, locked in position by taper pins, could be used instead.

Fig. 22.5 shows details of a rigid flanged coupling. The flanges are attached to their respective shafts by square parallel keys and are spigot-located. The bolts and nuts are shrouded, for reasons of safety plus economy, the bolts being a good fit in their respective holes to reduce bending and shear stresses. Note that keys should be assembled at right angles to one another and not mounted in line or at 180°.

Fig. 22.6 shows a modification of the rigid coupling design to produce a certain flexibility, which not only takes care of minor misalignment of the shafts but also of slight power fluctuations. A natural rubber or fabric-reinforced rubber sleeve may be used.

The fixing bolts have been modified to accommodate the rubber sleeves and also to ensure that the clamping loads are not taken by metal-to-metal contact but by compression of the rubber axially between bolt heads and mating flange. The nuts, of course, should not be overtightened; care must be taken during assembly.

Bending stresses will now be evident on the pins, as all the driving loads are transmitted to them via the rubber sleeves. It is therefore essential that as much thread-free shank as possible is in fitted contact with the left-hand half of the coupling, to assist in reducing high stress values.

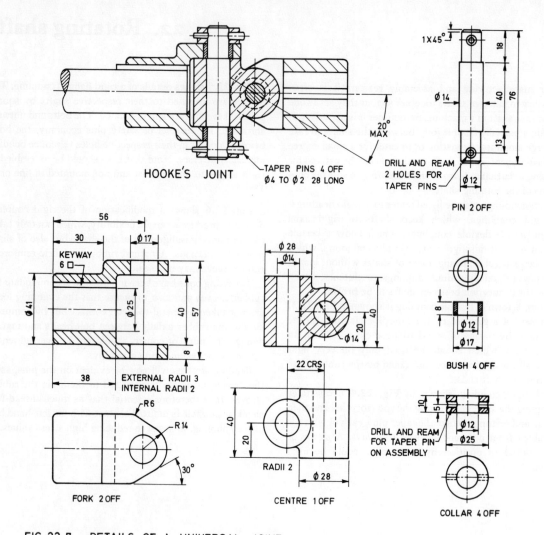

FIG. 22.7   DETAILS OF A UNIVERSAL JOINT

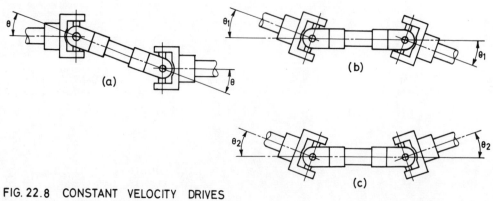

FIG. 22.8   CONSTANT VELOCITY DRIVES

22. Rotating shafts

Universal joints are used to couple shafts whose centre lines intersect. With the cross-type joint illustrated in **Fig. 22.7** the limiting angle of offset is usually 20°. The angle may be varied during rotation, but the limits imposed on this should be ascertained experimentally. By employing two such joints and an intermediate shaft, constant-velocity drives may be designed, provided that the angles between the main and intermediate shafts are equal. This is illustrated in **Fig. 22.8**.

The arrangement obviates one of the main faults of a straightforward Hookes' joint, which is that one half of the joint does not rotate at constant velocity when the two shafts are lying at an angle. If a driving shaft has constant velocity, the drive shaft speed will fluctuate, alternately faster and slower than the driving shaft, the magnitude depending on the angle of the shafts to one another.

There are many forms of universal joint on the market, both of the cross type shown and of the ring type, in which the two main members have forks which fit into bearing surfaces carried in an outer ring. Another type of ring joint takes the form of a central flexible disc to which spider connections are attached. The spiders usually consist of three equally spaced arms with provision for attachment to a shaft. The spider arms do not connect with each other but are interspaced to ensure that the flexible ring takes the driving loads.

Constant-velocity units are used in machine tools and motor vehicles, where drives to independently sprung wheels are of this type, due to the large angles of deflection involved.

Students are advised to assemble the parts shown in **Fig. 22.7** and to draw at least two views, together with an isometric view. A constant-velocity arrangement may also be attempted showing the disposition of the two joints and the intermediate shaft.

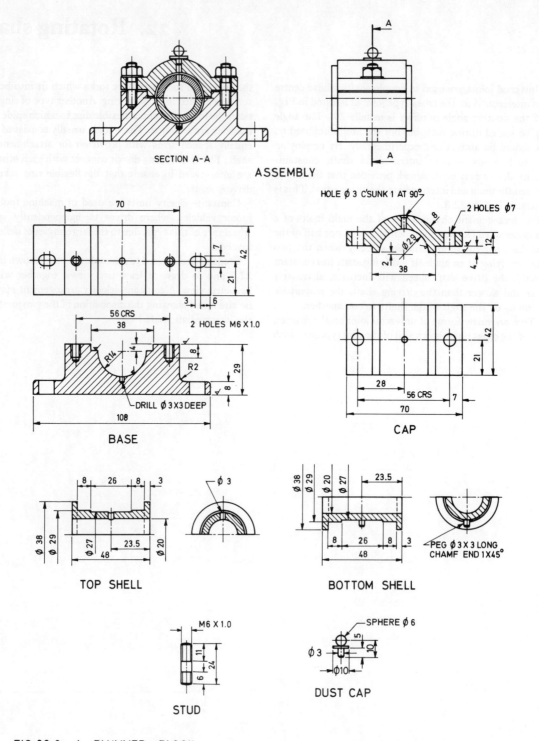

SECTION A-A

ASSEMBLY

HOLE Ø 3 C'SUNK 1 AT 90°

2 HOLES Ø 7

CAP

70

42

21

7

3   6

56 CRS

38

2 HOLES M6 X 1.0

R14

R2

4

8

8

29

8

DRILL Ø 3 X 3 DEEP

108

BASE

28

56 CRS

70

7

42

21

8

26

8

3

Ø 3

Ø 38

Ø 29

Ø 27

23.5

Ø 20

48

TOP SHELL

Ø 38

Ø 29

Ø 20

Ø 27

23.5

8

26

8

3

48

BOTTOM SHELL

PEG Ø 3 X 3 LONG
CHAMF END 1 X 45°

M6 X 1.0

11

24

6

STUD

SPHERE Ø 6

5

10

Ø 3

Ø 10

DUST CAP

FIG. 22.9   A   PLUMMER   BLOCK

182

Rotating shafts must be correctly aligned, and adequately supported axially, if they are to transmit power with the greatest possible efficiency. The supports or bearings, if accurately machined, will also provide the means of alignment. Bearings which carry loads acting perpendicular to the shaft, i.e. loads induced purely by aligned rotation of the shaft, are called 'journal' bearings and the part of the shaft within such a bearing is termed a journal.

A plain journal bearing is a sleeve of suitable material whose outside diameter is a press-fit in its housing and whose bore diameter is slightly larger than the shaft to allow for free rotation. Plain bearings of this type have a wide range of applications; some are lubricated, while others are self-lubricating.

The sleeve may be made from phosphor–bronze, lead–bronze, copper–lead, white metal, tin base alloys, or plastics materials such as nylon or PTFE.

Sintered metal bearings containing a reservoir of oil or plastics material in the pores between the metallic grains are often used in small mechanisms.

Usually the bearing and its housing are provided with some means of introducing oil or grease to the journal area because lubricants of some kind are necessary when a bearing system is subjected to heavy journal forces. The principle is that the film of lubricant between the shaft and the bearing supports the shaft, takes out the journal forces and helps to dissipate the heat. The bearing material is often made from an alloy of soft and hard metals, the soft ones pick up grit or other foreign matter and allow for some slight distortion under load, while the harder metals support the shaft and act as a bolster to the softer constituents.

Fig. 22.9 shows details of a plummer block, which is a self-contained bearing unit capable of being bolted in position to support lengths of 'open' shafting. This type of bearing is to be seen on overhead travelling cranes, line shafts, and other fabricated units, where alignment of built-in shaft supports would be difficult and expensive to fit. The bearing shell is made in two halves, the bottom section being radially located by hole and spigot. Axial movement is prevented by collars, which may also take thrust loads if required. The method of fitting the cap also allows for bearing wear. The type of bearing shells shown are often machined or scored on the journal face to form oil- or grease-ways.

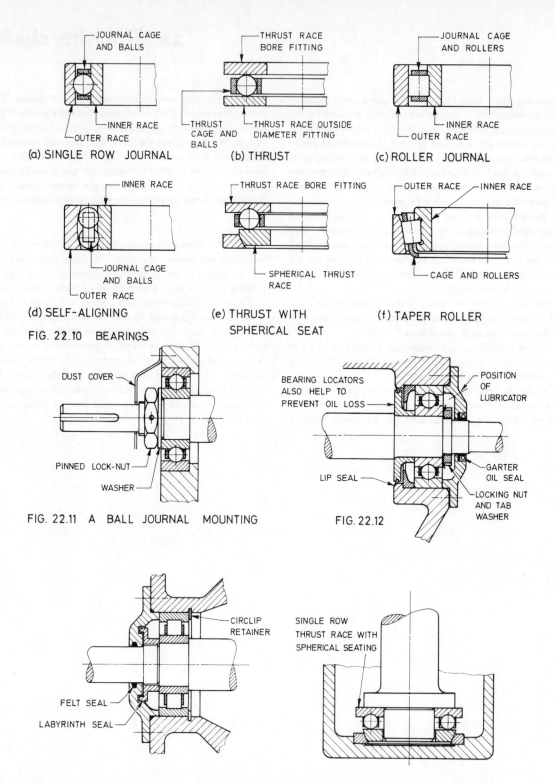

(a) SINGLE ROW JOURNAL

JOURNAL CAGE AND BALLS

INNER RACE
OUTER RACE

(b) THRUST

THRUST RACE BORE FITTING

THRUST CAGE AND BALLS

THRUST RACE OUTSIDE DIAMETER FITTING

(c) ROLLER JOURNAL

JOURNAL CAGE AND ROLLERS

INNER RACE
OUTER RACE

(d) SELF-ALIGNING

INNER RACE

JOURNAL CAGE AND BALLS

OUTER RACE

(e) THRUST WITH SPHERICAL SEAT

THRUST RACE BORE FITTING

SPHERICAL THRUST RACE

(f) TAPER ROLLER

OUTER RACE   INNER RACE

CAGE AND ROLLERS

FIG. 22.10   BEARINGS

FIG. 22.11   A BALL JOURNAL MOUNTING

DUST COVER

PINNED LOCK-NUT

WASHER

FIG. 22.12

BEARING LOCATORS ALSO HELP TO PREVENT OIL LOSS

LIP SEAL

POSITION OF LUBRICATOR

GARTER OIL SEAL

LOCKING NUT AND TAB WASHER

FIG. 22.13   A ROLLER JOURNAL MOUNTING

CIRCLIP RETAINER

FELT SEAL

LABYRINTH SEAL

FIG. 22.14   A THRUST RACE

SINGLE ROW THRUST RACE WITH SPHERICAL SEATING

184

Various types of ball and roller bearings are shown in **Figs 22.10–22.14** inclusive.

Generally, the revolving race should always be a press fit on or in its mating part, and the stationary race should be a transitional fit. In all cases, manufacturers' tables of recommended methods of mounting and the tolerances to be used on shafts and housings should be consulted.

Bearings should be accurately located and retained in position by machined shoulders, collars, spring clip retainers, nuts and washers, etc.

Ball and roller bearings offer less friction resistance than plain bearings, especially when starting from rest. This means that, for a more compact bearing system, less power is required. Theoretically they need no lubrication, but as the parts are made from hardened steel corrosion is a problem. To counteract this, and ensure smooth running under all conditions, it is usual to provide a continuous supply of lubricant.

Fig. 22.10 shows a series of ball and roller bearings. Diagram **(a)** is a typical single-row ball journal.

Ball journal bearings are formed of two rings, or races, with grooves provided for the balls. The races are made from case-hardened steel. The balls revolve in the race grooves and are spaced apart by a cage of phosphor–bronze or similar alloy. It is usual practice to leave one race free axially when purely radial loads are involved. Ball journals can take slight thrust loads.

Normal thrust bearings of the type shown in diagram **(b)** consist of disc-type races with or without ball grooves machined in their faces. The races and ball cage are free to part.

Diagram **(c)** shows a roller journal. Roller journal bearings can withstand heavier loads than ball journals, but cannot resist thrust loads, unless they are fitted in races both of which are grooved. If the races and rollers are tapered, however, as in diagram **(f)**, heavy end loads may be taken. Needle roller bearings have rollers whose length is several times greater than the roller diameter. The rollers are usually cageless.

The self-aligning bearing in diagram **(d)** has an outer race which is ground spherically inside, the radius centre lying on the shaft axis. This permits the outer race to be displaced relative to the inner race without loss of efficiency. Two rows of caged balls are used. Such bearings are positioned where shaft deflections are apparent, e.g. vehicle axles.

Diagram **(e)** shows a thrust race with spherical seat. This type of bearing will accept a small amount of misalignment. An example of its use is indicated in **Fig. 22.14**, where it is seen supporting a vertical shaft.

Fig. 22.11 shows a method of mounting a ball journal on a light drive shaft (e.g. an electric motor). Note the method of locating and clamping the bearing.

Fig. 22.12 is an application of a ball journal where oil seals are essential. Note the positive location and clamping of the bearing. Garter oil seals are leather or plastics rings which are held in place by wire springs. Lip seals rely on centrifugal force to throw to one side any liquid which comes into contact with them.

Fig. 22.13 shows a roller journal mounted on a shaft. The outer race is retained in the housing by a spring clip. The front end is provided with a labyrinth seal and a felt washer to prevent loss of lubricant.

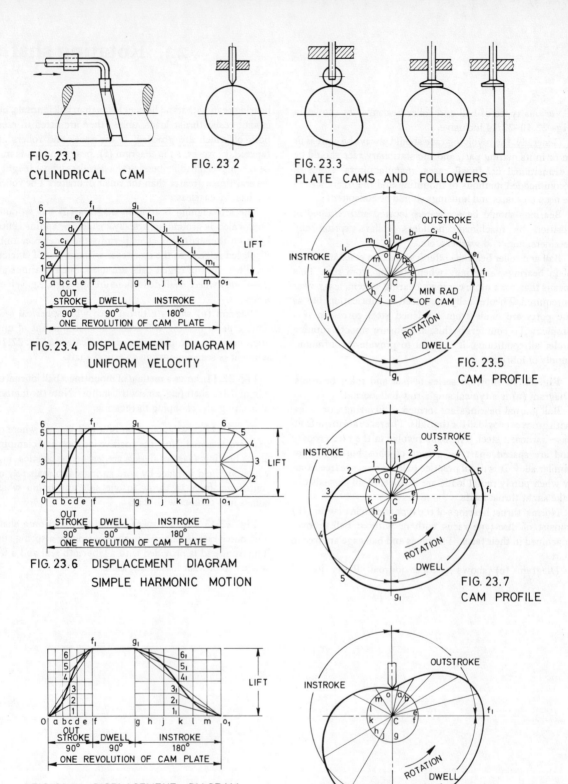

FIG. 23.1
CYLINDRICAL CAM

FIG. 23 2

FIG. 23.3
PLATE CAMS AND FOLLOWERS

FIG. 23.4 DISPLACEMENT DIAGRAM
UNIFORM VELOCITY

FIG. 23.5
CAM PROFILE

FIG. 23.6 DISPLACEMENT DIAGRAM
SIMPLE HARMONIC MOTION

FIG. 23.7
CAM PROFILE

FIG. 23.8 DISPLACEMENT DIAGRAM
UNIFORM ACCELERATION

FIG. 23.9
CAM PROFILE

23. Cams

A cam is a specially shaped body designed to impart motion to another body, called a follower, with which it is in contact. The shape of the cam will be decided by the motion required of the follower, the type of follower to be employed and by the motion of the cam itself.

The main types of cam are:

(1) cylindrical cams, as shown in **Fig. 23.1**, in which the motion imparted to the follower is in a plane parallel to the cam axis;

(2) radial or plate cams in which the motion imparted to the follower is in a plane at right angles to the cam axis, as shown in **Fig. 23.2**.

The knife-edge or point follower is capable of following complicated contours, but has the disadvantage of rapid wearing of the knife-edge, for which provision must be made in the design.

The roller follower, which reduces the problem of wear by reason of the rolling motion between the contact surfaces, imposes some limit on the cam contour in that any concave radius used must be at least equal to the radius of the follower.

The flat follower, being mounted off-centre, also reduces wear, since it tends to rotate about its own axis as the cam rotates, thus utilizing as much of its surface as possible.

The majority of the cams dealt with in this chapter will be plate cams and it will be assumed that they rotate at uniform speed.

The follower motion will vary, because it must start from rest and return to rest in one revolution and may rest, or dwell, during a part of the cam rotation.

Diagrams may be drawn to show the relationship between angular movement of the cam and the corresponding movement of the follower.

Fig. 23.4 shows the displacement diagram for a *uniform-velocity* knife-edge follower and **Fig. 23.5** shows the required cam profile. The follower is required to lift to its maximum in 90° of rotation, dwell for 90° and fall to rest in the remaining 180°. A specified minimum radius is given.

To construct the diagram, draw $0o_1$ any convenient length and mark off the required angular movements of the cam. Subdivide the outstroke and instroke into a number of equal parts (six in this case) and label them as shown. Set off the lift line from 0 and divide it into the same number of equal parts, numbering as shown. The intersections of the vertical and horizontal projections of these divisions will produce the required diagram. Note the method of showing the period of dwell.

To construct the cam profile, first draw a circle of radius equal to the minimum radius of the cam. Commencing at 0, set off the outstroke such that the angle $0Cf_1$ is 90°. Divide this into six equal parts and label them as shown. Mark off distances aa_1, bb_1, etc., from the displacement diagram. A smooth curve drawn from 0 to f_1 will give the cam outstroke. The period of dwell is the arc f_1g_1 concentric with the cam centre. From g_1, the follower is required to fall to rest uniformly. Divide g_1 to 0 into six equal parts, mark off the instroke in similar manner to the outstroke, and join g_1 to 0, by a smooth curve to complete the cam profile. It will be noted that the sharp changes of velocity at points 0, f_1, g_1, and 0_1 in the displacement diagram are smoothed out as curves in practice.

Figs 23.6 and 23.7 show the methods of constructing a diagram and cam along similar lines, except that the motion required is *simple harmonic*. The displacement diagram differs only in respect of the method of dividing the lift-line and is self-explanatory.

Figs 23.8 and 23.9 show the methods of construction to produce a follower motion which is of *uniform acceleration*. Again, the requirements and method of layout are similar to the previous example except for the displacement curve.

The outstroke and instroke are divided vertically and horizontally into six equal parts and labelled as shown. Join 0 to 3, 2, and 1 and join f_1 to 3, 4, and 5. The intersections of line 01 with vertical line a; 02 with vertical line b; 03 with vertical line c; $f_1 3$ with vertical line c; $f_1 4$ with vertical line d and $f_1 5$ with vertical line e, will give the outstroke curve.

Repeat this construction for the instroke and produce the cam profile as before.

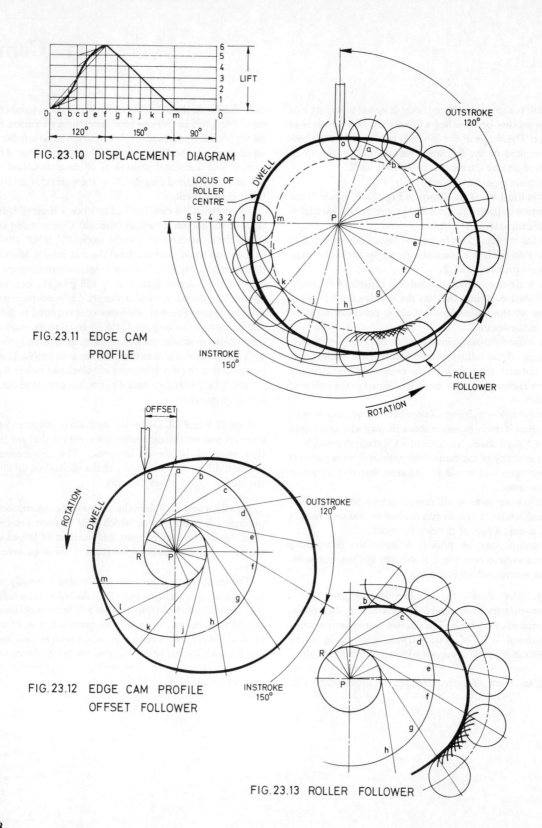

FIG. 23.10 DISPLACEMENT DIAGRAM

FIG. 23.11 EDGE CAM PROFILE

FIG. 23.12 EDGE CAM PROFILE OFFSET FOLLOWER

FIG. 23.13 ROLLER FOLLOWER

Figs 23.10 and 23.11 show the displacement diagram and cam profiles designed to satisfy the following conditions:

A cam rotating anticlockwise at a uniform speed is required to impart the motion set out below:
(1) to a knife-edge follower:
(2) to a roller follower of diameter 24 mm:
    (a) lift through 38 mm with uniform acceleration for 120° of cam rotation;
    (b) return to initial position with uniform velocity for 150° of cam rotation;
    (c) dwell for remainder.

The minimum radius of the cam is 50 mm and the stroke of the follower is coincident with the centre line of the cam.

The cam profile for the knife-edge follower is shown thick and that for the roller follower is shown dotted.

(1) Set out the displacement diagram as previously described, dividing the outstroke and instroke into six equal parts.

Draw the cam centre lines and from their intersection P, set off the minimum radius of the cam P0.

Mark off the 120° of outstroke and 150° of instroke and divide each into six equal parts, labelling as shown.

Using dividers or compasses, pick up increments of lift from the base of the displacement diagram to the curve, at points a, b, c, etc., and set off along the dividing arms from points a, b, c, etc., marked around the minimum radius circle.

Join the points thus obtained with a smooth curve, to give the cam profile for the knife-edge follower.

An alternative method of construction for the uniform velocity case is shown on the left-hand side of the cam. The instroke is divided into six equal parts and numbered 0, 1, 2, etc. These points are transferred as arcs struck from P, on to the appropriate dividing arms as shown.

(2) When the friction- and wear-reducing roller follower is fitted, the minimum radius of the cam now becomes the minimum distance of roller centre to cam centre and the follower displacement is determined by the displacement of its centre. It is therefore necessary to plot the path, or locus, of the roller centre, which in this example becomes the cam profile for the knife-edge follower.

With compasses set at 12 mm, the roller radius, draw a series of arcs or complete circles from the points of intersection of the dividing arms and the cam profile. Draw a smooth curve to touch the successive roller profiles.

It will be seen that the outline produced does not coincide with the intersection of the dividing arms and the roller perimeter, thus clearly demonstrating the main reason for plotting the locus of the roller centre. This is shown in **Fig. 23.13**.

The greater the number of divisions used, the greater will be the accuracy of the cam profile. This is demonstrated between points h and g, where a number of closely spaced arcs are drawn to give the cam shape.

Fig. 23.12 shows an edge cam profile to satisfy the same conditions of follower lift, but with the follower offset 19 mm from the cam centre.

As the cam is required to rotate anticlockwise, the follower will be offset to the left to increase smoothness in operation.

Draw a circle of radius PR equal to 19 mm, the amount of offset required. Divide this circle into the required angles of outstroke and instroke as before, and set off the dividing arms as tangents, such that for each angular division turned through as the cam rotates the dividing arms will successively take up the tangential position RO.

Mark off the amounts of lift from the displacement diagram as before and draw a smooth curve through the points obtained to produce the required profile.

Fig. 23.13 shows the treatment of the same cam for a roller follower, where again the original profile becomes the locus of the roller centre, from which the final cam shape may be obtained.

It will be seen that the use of an offset point follower imposes side loads on the follower guides and also bending of the follower itself, limiting the use of this mechanism.

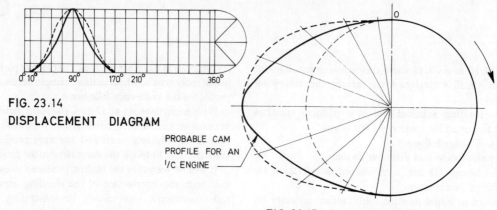

FIG. 23.14
DISPLACEMENT DIAGRAM

PROBABLE CAM
PROFILE FOR AN
I/C ENGINE

FIG. 23.15 CAM PROFILES

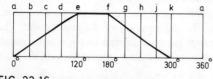

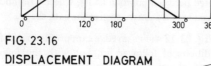

FIG. 23.16
DISPLACEMENT DIAGRAM

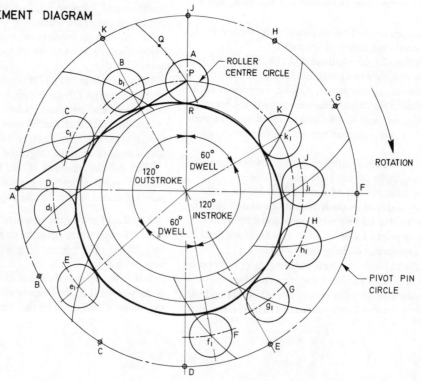

FIG. 23.17   CAM WITH OSCILLATING ROLLER FOLLOWER

The cams in internal-combustion engines are used to open and close the inlet and exhaust valves at predetermined times and in a smooth, controlled way. For this reason, the method of design is not to determine the shape of the cam from the motion of the follower, but to calculate the follower motion from a cam which consists of circular arcs and tangents.

The continuous thick outline in **Fig. 23.15** shows a probable internal-combustion engine cam made up of circular arcs. This has been divided into four equal parts for the outstroke and instroke and the displacement has been transferred to the diagram in **Fig. 23.14**, also in dark outline.

Superimposed on the diagram and on the cam layout in dotted line is shown the curve obtained when simple harmonic motion is employed. The amount of lift shown is greater than would normally be employed in an internal-combustion engine, but the cam profiles do give an idea of the difference between the more easily produced circular-arc cam and the geometrically plotted plate cam, which usually entails the manufacture by hand of a master template, from which other cams are made.

Fig. 23.17 shows a cam with an oscillating roller follower pivoted 100 mm from the axis of rotation, the pivot lying on the cam centre line.

It is required to lay out the cam profile to satisfy the following conditions:
(a) the cam is to rotate clockwise;
(b) the follower to lift through 12° for 120° of cam rotation;
(c) the follower to dwell for 60° of cam rotation;
(d) the follower to return to initial position for 120° of cam rotation;
(e) the follower to dwell for remaining 60° of cam rotation.

The minimum radius of the cam is 50 mm and the roller diameter is 25 mm. The roller centre is to lie on the vertical centre line of the cam.

The motion is to be uniform velocity for both the outstroke and instroke.

Draw the centre lines of the cam. With centre O, radius OA (100 mm), draw the chain-dotted circle to pass through the pivot-pin.

Draw the minimum radius of the cam (OR) and locate P, the centre of the roller follower. Draw a circle, centre O radius OP.

Although the oscillating arm remains fixed about A, the method of construction is to fix the cam plate and rotate the follower, together with its arm, for each plotted point.

Mark off the outstroke on the pivot-pin circle such that angle AOE is 120°. Divide this into any convenient number of equal parts (four in this case) and label as shown. Mark off the dwell angle of 60°, and then mark off and subdivide the instroke angle of 120°, labelling as shown.

With centre A, radius AP, draw an arc to pass through the roller centre circle.

Draw similar arcs through the other points obtained. The roller must lie along each of these arcs successively as the cam rotates.

Along the arc passing through point P and subtended from A, set off the total lift angle of 12°. This distance, PQ, should be used in setting out the displacement diagram, but the chord may be used, as the difference is so small that it will introduce very little error.

Construct the diagram, as shown in **Fig. 23.16**.

Along each of the follower arcs, the rise and fall of the roller centre may be traced measured outwards from the roller centre circle, as at bb_1, cc_1, dd_1, etc. Draw the roller follower for each point and from R connect with a smooth curve to give the required profile.

Note that the pivot-pin centre A is connected to roller A, centre B is connected to roller B, and centre C is connected to roller C, etc., and the roller centres themselves are denoted by b_1, c_1, d_1, etc.

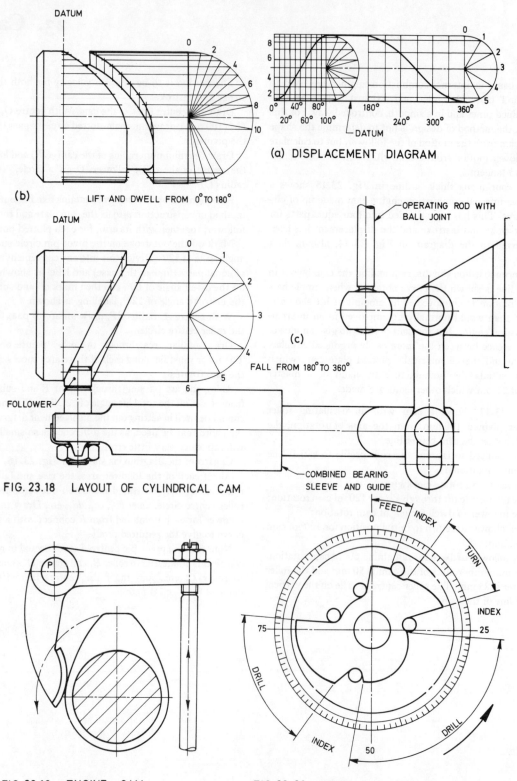

DATUM

0
2
4
6
8
10

(b)

LIFT AND DWELL FROM 0° TO 180°

(a) DISPLACEMENT DIAGRAM

DATUM

8
6
4
2
0° 40° 80° 180° 360°
20° 60° 100° 240° 300°
DATUM

0
1
2
3
4
5

DATUM

0
1
2
3
4
5
6

(c)

FALL FROM 180° TO 360°

FOLLOWER

OPERATING ROD WITH
BALL JOINT

COMBINED BEARING
SLEEVE AND GUIDE

FIG. 23.18   LAYOUT OF CYLINDRICAL CAM

P

FIG. 23.19   ENGINE CAM

FEED
INDEX
TURN
INDEX
DRILL
INDEX
DRILL
0
75
25
50

FIG. 23.20   LATHE CAM LAYOUT

192

Fig. 23.18 (b) and **(c)** show the layout of a cylindrical cam and at **(a)** the required displacement diagram for simple harmonic motion. The follower is required to travel from datum zero to a maximum value in 100° of cam rotation, dwell for 80° and return to datum zero in the remaining 180° of cam rotation. The method of dividing the displacement diagram and the production of the harmonic curve is as previously described.

Fig. 23.18 (b) is drawn to cater for the first 180° of cam rotation. A datum line, representing the base line of the displacement diagram, is drawn at a convenient point on the cam surface, and a half end elevation is produced, divided to suit the conditions of the initial 180° of rotation. These divisions, numbered 0, 2, 4, 6, 8, and 10, are projected horizontally along the surface of the cam cylinder to intersect with the datum line. The 'lift' and dwell distances are transferred from the displacement diagram to the appropriate angular divisions on the cam surface, measured from the datum in both cases. The points produced on the cam will, when joined, give the locus of the follower centre about which the follower diameter is drawn to produce the outer edges of the cam slot. When the depth and shape of the follower, or the required slot, are known, it is a straightforward task to draw the remainder of the cam slot. In the figure, the follower is assumed to be cylindrical and the depth of the slot is produced by dropping vertical lines from the intersections of the cam outer edges and angular displacement lines, equal in length to the slot depth. The dwell section is parallel to the datum line. A small part of the return section is also shown as the slot curves back towards the datum zero.

In **Fig. 23.18 (c)** the 180° return is shown projected. This view is not a direct plan view of **(b)**. The method of projection and the construction of the curves of the slot are as described above.

A probable follower assembly is also drawn to give an indication of the manner in which the rotation of the cam cylinder may be used to transmit movement. The follower itself is a freely rotating sleeve attached to the follower stem by a retaining screw passing through its centre. Such an arrangement may be used to operate a valve, or a function in an automatic machine.

A cam and follower suitable for a diesel engine are shown are **Fig. 23.19**. The follower is a lever pivoted about point *P* and in contact with the cam face at one end and a push-rod at the other.

Cams are important components in automatic production equipment, particularly lathes. They are used extensively to rotate the turret carrying the tools, via a geneva-wheel mechanism, and to operate the front, rear, and cut-off slides. The cams used are of both the plate and cylindrical types.

When a component is to be manufactured on an automatic a cam design sheet is drawn up, showing the various machining operations to be carried out, the periods of dwell and the time and shaft revolutions required to complete the machining and also index the turet. When all this is done the work required of each cam is determined and the cam design is put in hand. All the cams are usually drawn together on one diagram as a second stage preceding detailed design. The single cam shown in **Fig. 23.20** is an example of this second-stage layout. The diagram shows the various aspects of the cam plate and the position of the follower for the operations required of the particular part of the machine controlled by the cam. The drawing is superimposed on a diagram which is divided into hundredths of cam surface, to give an immediate idea of the amount of cam rotation required for each operation. Periods of rise, fall, and dwell of the follower are clearly shown.

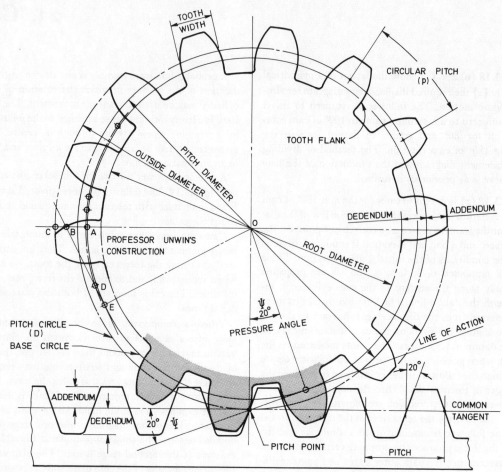

FIG. 24.1 INVOLUTE RACK AND PINION WITH 20° PRESSURE ANGLE

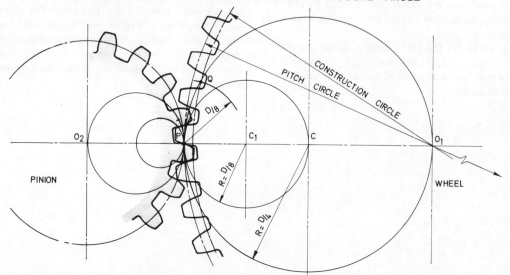

FIG. 24.2 INVOLUTE WHEEL AND PINION

Toothed gearing is a positive means of transmitting high-torque loads from one shaft to another at a constant velocity ratio.

Fig. 24.1 shows an incomplete spur gear in mesh with a rack (which may be defined as a wheel having an infinite pitch circle diameter).

Definitions of gearing terms for a wheel

Pitch diameter (D) is the diameter passing through the point of contact of mating wheels, and is found by multiplying the number of teeth by the module (m) (D = Tm).

Addendum (A) is the distance from the pitch diameter to the tip of a tooth, and is equal to the module.

Dedendum (B) is the distance from the pitch diameter to the root of a tooth space and is given by the module plus clearance (B = m + P/20). It is also addendum plus tooth tip clearance.

Circular pitch (p) is the distance between a point on a tooth and a corresponding point on an adjacent tooth, measured along the circumference of the pitch circle. It is given by

$$p = \frac{\pi \times D}{T} \quad \text{or } \pi m.$$

Module (m) is given by the pitch diameter divided by the number of teeth (m = D/T).

Number of teeth (T) may be found from D/m or $\pi \times D/p$. Tooth-fillet radius is usually taken as $\frac{1}{7}$ of space width at tooth tip.

Root diameter (Dr) is the diameter formed by the bottom of the tooth spaces.

Pressure angle (Ψ (psi)) is the angle formed by the line of action and the common tangent passing through the pitch point.

Base circle is the circle from which the involute curve is generated. Its radius from the centre of the wheel is given by the point of intersection of the pressure angle, subtended from the centre of the wheel, and the line of action. Its diameter is given by $D \times \cos \Psi$.

To draw a gear wheel using Professor Unwin's approximate construction, first draw circles to represent pitch diameter, addendum, and dedendum. Construct the base circle appropriate to the pressure angle. Along the line OC mark off BC equal to $\frac{1}{3} AC$. Draw BE tangential to the base circle such that angle OEB is a right angle. Mark off BD equal to $\frac{3}{4} BE$. Then D is the centre of the tooth arc passing through B. Mark off the number of teeth on the wheel, either by trial and error, using compasses, or by angular divisions. 360° divided by the number of teeth will give the angular pitch spaces (circular pitch), and dividing this angle by two will give the tooth width. (Always use the pitch diameter as datum). This need only be done for one tooth; the remainder may be marked off using the compasses.

To construct the rack in mesh draw the common tangent, the pitch line of the rack teeth, and mark off the tooth widths p/2. Draw lines to represent the addendum and dedendum. The sides of the teeth may now be drawn at 20° (Ψ) to the vertical, the tips being eased by a radius.

Fig. 24.2 shows a gear wheel and pinion in mesh. The teeth on the wheels meet at the pitch point P, where the pitch circles of the wheels are tangential. The diagram illustrates an approximate gear wheel construction that is satisfactory for sixteen or more teeth.

With centres O_1 and O_2 draw the pitch circles of the two gear wheels intersecting at P. With the same centres draw the addendum and dedendum circles.

Consider the construction of the wheel. Bisect O_1P at C and, with C as centre, draw a circle of radius D/4, where D is the pitch circle diameter. Bisect CP at C_1 and, with C_1 as centre, draw a circle of radius D/8. All of these circles pass through the pitch point P. With P as centre, radius D/8, draw an arc to intersect the circle of radius D/4 at Q. With O_1 as centre, radius O_1Q, draw a circle which, for the purposes of this construction, acts as a base circle. With centre Q, radius QP, draw an arc through P to represent the flank of one tooth. From P mark off successively tooth widths and tooth spaces around the pitch diameter. With compasses set at a radius of D/8, and using points on the construction circle as centres, draw a series of arcs to represent the flanks of the teeth. Complete the wheel by drawing the root radii and the tips and roots of the teeth.

The mating pinion can be constructed in similar fashion.

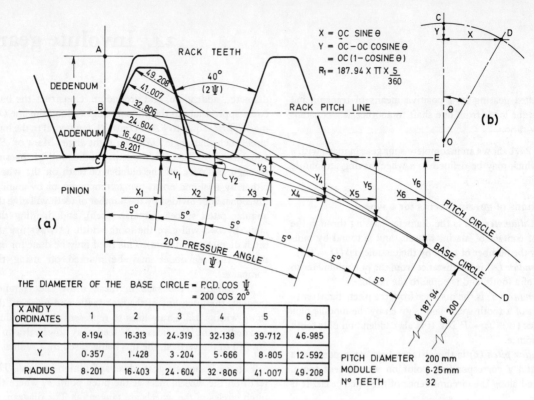

FIG. 24.3 CONSTRUCTION OF GEAR TOOTH PROFILES

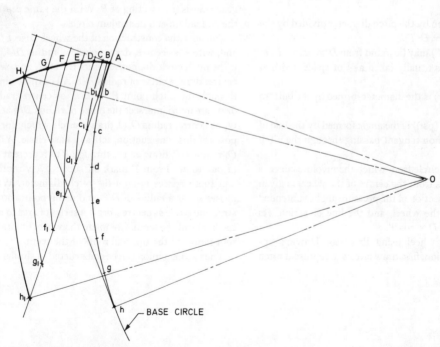

FIG. 24.4 CONSTRUCTION OF AN INVOLUTE

A method of constructing gear teeth from calculated dimensions is shown in **Fig. 24.3 (a)** and **(b)**. This is particularly useful for the large-scale layout of teeth, to give accurate profiles.

In the example given the pitch circle is 200 mm in diameter, the module 6·25 mm and the pressure angle is 20°. The calculated diameter of the base circle is given by $D \cos \Psi = 200 \cos 20° = 187·94$ mm.

This is shown by the arc CD in **Fig. 24.3 (a)** and **(b)**. In the latter figure the arc subtends an angle θ and the method of calculating the required ordinates X and Y is given. OC is the radius of base circle.

Draw up a table of ordinates for angular increments of 5°, as shown.

Draw the vertical line ABC produced and the horizontal line CE, which is tangential to point C, a point lying on the base circle. Point B lies on the pitch circle and distance AB is the rack-tooth dedendum.

At C the involute radius is 0 and to the right of C the involute radius increases by an amount given by

$$\frac{5°}{360°} \times \pi D_b = \frac{5 \times 187·94\pi}{360} = 8·2014 \text{ mm},$$

where D_b is the diameter of the base circle.

Draw the 5° increments to intersect with the base circle. The points obtained should coincide with the calculated ordinates Y. From each point, draw tangents equal in length to the calculated radii, until the limit of the tooth height is reached.

The wheel addendum and dedendum must be calculated from the data previously given in this chapter.

Straight spur gears may be produced by a milling operation in which the 'formed' cutter is the shape of the tooth space. There are a number of disadvantages with this method of production, the main ones being discontinuous cutting action with consequent high cost, fixed dimensions for addendum and dedendum making further operations necessary for smooth tooth engagement, and that different cutters are required for variations in pitch and number of teeth.

Spur and bevel teeth may be cut by a planing process in which the cutting action of the tool is 'controlled' by a follower tracing the outline of a tooth form. When this method is used for machining bevel gears the tool reciprocates along a straight line which terminates at the apex of the front pitch cone. The process is very slow, as only one face of a tooth is machined at a time.

The more modern approach to the problem is to *generate* the teeth on the gear blanks rather than to form them.

Essentially, the generating cutter becomes a rack or pinion of the same pitch as the required gear, the machine tool giving a relative motion to blank and cutter equal to that of a finished pair of mating gears.

The main advantage of using a rack type of cutter lies in the fact that being straight sided the rack teeth may be very accurately formed. A disadvantage is the intermittent cutting action, coupled with the necessity to index the blank when the tool has traversed its cutting path. This path is tangential to the gear blank pitch circle, to give the correct rolling action that would be obtained with a pair of finished gears.

The equivalent cutter for generating bevel gears becomes the bevel 'rack' or crown wheel. The machine tool rotates the spindles of the gear blank and cutter to provide the correct rolling action of pitch surfaces.

The cutter is, in effect, a tooth split in two halves which reciprocates along a straight line passing through the apex of the front cone. Straight and curved spiral bevels are produced by varying the path of the cutting tool. In generating curved teeth, the cutter is made to rotate continuously with the blank.

Hobbing is a continuous generating process in which the tool is shaped like a worm. The hob and the blank are geared to rotate together to give the required rolling action. The cutting edges of the hob are formed by gashing the worm thread axially at a number of equally spaced points. The resultant teeth are then relieved to improve the cutting and wear characteristics.

The hob is usually fed into the gear blank at an angle, such that the cutting thread is parallel to the axis of the blank. This method of gear production gives the greatest accuracy of tooth form and, due to its continuous cutting action, is the most economical, being used widely in automobile engineering.

Gear materials range from plastics impregnated fabric to nickel chrome steel.

For large gear wheels operating under no-shock conditions, cast iron may be used due to its low cost of production, but where serious casting difficulties would be experienced it is not uncommon to use a cast-iron framework on which a steel rim has been shrunk. The teeth are then cut into the steel.

Where a large wheel is meshing with a small one, it is good practice to make the pinion of a harder material, to even out the wear. This is seen to advantage with worm-and-wheel assemblies, where the wheel is often made from phosphor-bronze and the worm is made from case-hardened steel. Case-hardened carbon steel is commonly used for

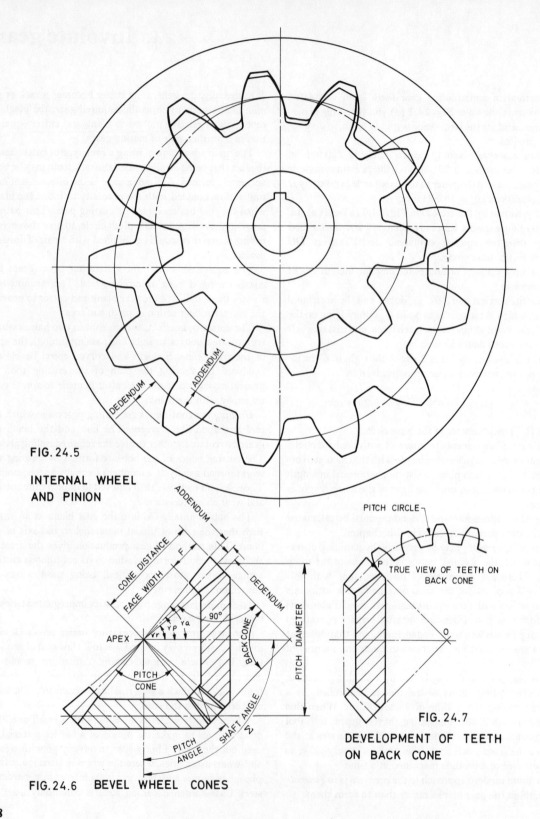

FIG. 24.5

INTERNAL WHEEL
AND PINION

ADDENDUM

DEDENDUM

FIG. 24.6 BEVEL WHEEL CONES

CONE DISTANCE

FACE WIDTH F

90°

APEX γr γp γa

PITCH
CONE

DEDENDUM

BACK CONE

ADDENDUM

PITCH DIAMETER

PITCH
ANGLE

SHAFT ANGLE

Σ

PITCH CIRCLE

P

TRUE VIEW OF TEETH ON
BACK CONE

O

FIG. 24.7

DEVELOPMENT OF TEETH
ON BACK CONE

spur and helical gears; a typical steel containing 0·4% carbon would have a minimum tensile strength of $540 \times 10^6 N/m^2$.

The method of producing an involute from a given base circle is shown in **Fig. 24.4**. Through point A on the base circle draw a tangent Ah_1, and along its length mark off a number of equal divisions, given by b_1, c_1, d_1, etc. Mark off similar equal divisions around the circumference of the base circle, at b, c, d, etc.

With O as centre, draw an arc through h_1 and with h as centre, radius Ah_1, draw another arc to intersect the first arc at H, a point on the required involute.

For strength purposes, gear teeth are considered as cantilevers and it is usual practice to assume that all the load is taken by one tooth at its pitch diameter. With a pressure angle of 20°, the tooth root is thick and the tooth form is at its most efficient, with less possibility of undercutting of the teeth and of interference between large and small gear wheels. The face width of the teeth usually lies between $2p$ and $5p$.

The disadvantage with hardened steels is that the hardening processes must take place after cutting, which results in some distortion and inaccuracy of tooth shape, although this can be obviated to a large extent by gear shaving or gear grinding to correct the tooth form.

It will be noted with the internal gear arrangement that not only do the two gears rotate in the same direction but there is a considerable saving of space. These two facts are used to considerable advantage in motor-vehicle technology. The method of constructing the teeth of the internal gear is as previously described, except that the cutter used forms the shape of the teeth and the addendum and dedendum change places relative to the pitch-circle diameter. This is shown in **Fig. 24.5**.

Fig. 24.6 shows two bevel gears in mesh and indicates the method of showing teeth on a sectioned drawing.

It will be seen that the pitch surfaces of bevel wheels may be considered as portions of cone surfaces in contact along a common line or generator meeting at a common apex, the point of intersection of the shaft axes.

The pitch angle is the angle formed by the shaft axis and the pitch cone generator. It is given as γp (gamma p). The corresponding addendum and root angles are γa and γr respectively.

The back cone (or normal cone) generators lie at 90° to the pitch cone for all bevel wheels.

The principal dimensions required in setting out the wheels are shown in the figure, which is based on a shaft angle of 90°, and it will be noted that the main linear dimensions are related to the back faces of the wheels, the points thus obtained being joined to the pitch-cone apices.

The true view, or development, of teeth on the back cone shows that the involute profile is similar to that of a spur gear of the same circular pitch. The addendum and dedendum are measured along the back cone generator, displaced about the pitch diameter in the normal way. This construction is shown in **Fig. 24.7**.

With centre O (the apex of the back cone) and radius OP, draw the developed pitch circle. The teeth may now be constructed in the same way as for spur gears.

The pitch diameter is founded by $T \times p/\pi = Tm$, and the outside diameter or overall diameter of the wheel is given by $D +$ (twice addendum $\times \cos \gamma p$).

The face width (F) of bevel wheels should not exceed one-third of the cone distance or 3 times the circular pitch.

When the pitch angle of a bevel wheel is 90° the pitch cone becomes a plane surface. Such a gear is termed a 'crown wheel' and is to the bevel wheel what a rack is to a spur gear. As such, the teeth may be straight-sided.

When two different-sized gears are in mesh, the larger is termed the 'wheel' and the smaller is termed the 'pinion'. This applies to spur and bevel gears.

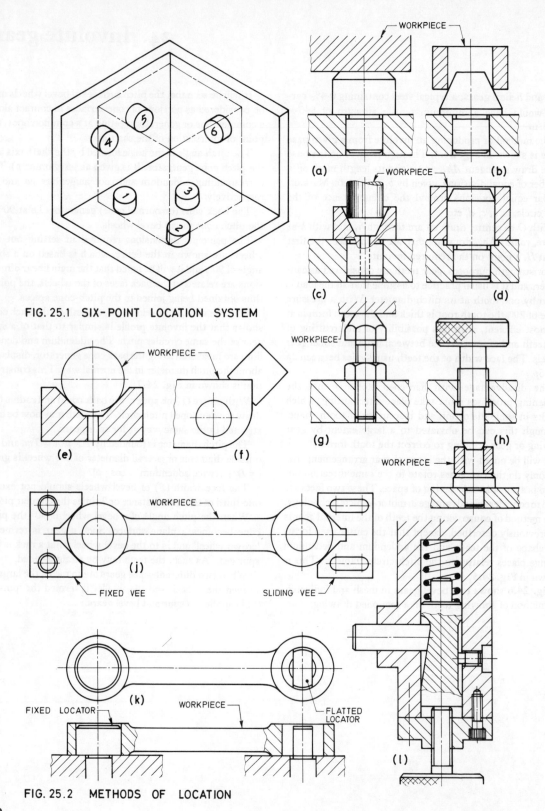

FIG. 25.1 SIX-POINT LOCATION SYSTEM

FIG. 25.2 METHODS OF LOCATION

Location devices

A workpiece, or component, must be firmly clamped and accurately located to ensure that there is no movement during machining and the cutting tools do their work quickly and efficiently.

In jig design, location of the workpiece within its planes of freedom is very important, because it is usually considered to require six degrees of restraint.

This is known as the six-point system of location.

Fig. 25.1 shows the three planes in which an unrestrained workpiece (shown chain-dotted) may move. Considering the lower plane first: the smallest number of points on which the component will effectively seat is three, therefore the pads numbered 1, 2, and 3 are placed in this plane. The pads should be spaced in such a way that each takes one-third of the clamping forces.

As it is a rule that clamping friction alone must not be relied upon to restrain the workpiece against cutting forces, there are two planes of freedom remaining.

Considering the left-hand vertical plane: if one location pad is placed in this plane, the workpiece could oscillate about it, thus two pads are provided to give complete restraint.

Finally, in the third plane, one location point only is required, because there is only one direction remaining in which the workpiece may move.

With suitable clamps opposite the location faces the workpiece is now held in the ideal conditions for machining operations.

Various methods of locating a workpiece are shown in **Fig. 25.2 (a)–(l).**

A conventional external location pad is shown at **(a)**, while **(b)** depicts a conical locator for circular holes. **(c)** shows a female coned locator and **(d)** shows a short location post of full form. At **(e)** and **(f)** two uses of a vee block are described, the former to seat a round bar and the latter to locate a shaped workpiece.

Adjustable methods of location are often employed such as that shown at **(g)**, where the shaped hexagon head is capable of being raised and lowered to the desired position and clamped by the locking nut. The design at **(h)** is a combined locator and clamp.

The use of fixed sliding vees is depicted at **(j)**, where a link is firmly located externally. Another method of locating such workpieces is shown at **(k)**, where a full-form and a flatted locator are employed. It is not possible to use two full-form locators because of the extreme precision required. When the workpiece is firmly located on the full-form post, the only movement is a rotational one about the centre of the post. All that is necessary for complete restraint is a locator to oppose this tendency to rotation; hence the flatted locator which locates over a small area only of the bored hole and lying in the direction of possible rotation.

At **(l)** may be seen an adjustable locator which utilizes the wedge principle of applying a force, and hence movement, to the horizontal peg. Rotation of the screw produces linear movement of the piston, which is prevented from rotating by the grub-screw key. The forward movement of the piston forces the pin outwards and also compresses the spring, which acts as a return device when the peg is retracted.

This design is best suited to operate at 90° to the position shown, so that the weight of the peg assists in the retraction process.

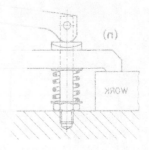

FIG. 25.3
METHODS OF CLAMPING

201

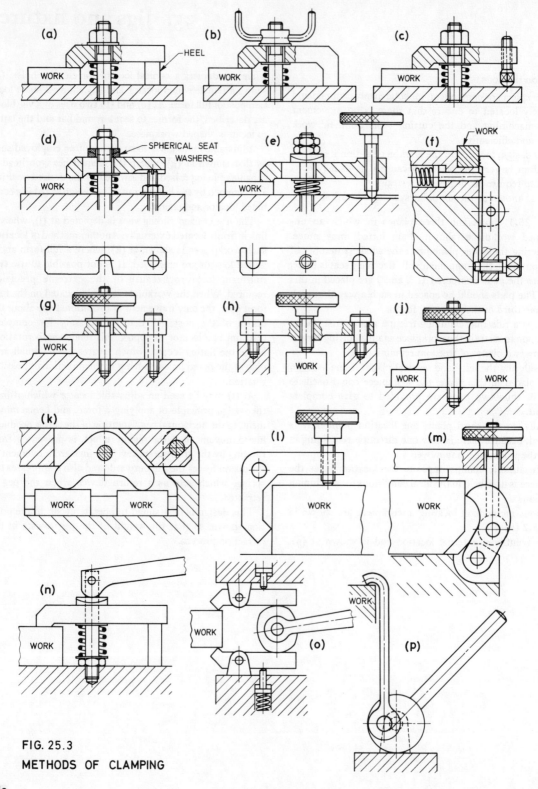

FIG. 25.3

METHODS OF CLAMPING

Fig. 25.3 (a)–(p) show a series of small clamps designed to hold workpieces firmly against their locators and to dissipate the forces imposed by the cutting tools.

The essential features in the design and positioning of clamps are that there should be no distortion of the workpiece, or the clamp, either due directly to the clamping forces themselves or to the loads imposed by the cutting tools. The clamps must, therefore, be robust and at the same time quick and easy to operate.

The method of creating the clamping pressure must be chosen carefully to accord with the requirements of the machining involved and also with speed and economy of operation. For milling and turning operations it is usual to provide clamps with hexagon nuts, while drilling and reaming operations may employ hand-operated nuts, due to the smaller cutting forces involved. Where possible, the use of 'loose' tools such as spanners should be avoided.

Fig. 25.3 (a) shows a solid clamp with a separate heel, making provision for height adjustment. It will be noted that a compression spring and washer are provided to support the clamp when the pressure is released, and that the stud is positioned closer to the clamp toe than the heel to ensure that the workpiece receives the major share of the clamping force, and to minimize bending of the clamp.

The design at (b) is a modified form of (a) with a combined heel. The nut is a form of wing nut. To prevent rotation when the clamping forces are applied, these clamps are often provided with a heel pin which fits into a suitable hole.

At (c), an adjustable heel is provided. This is designed to accommodate readily workpieces which may vary in height due to rough surfaces or wide tolerances.

At (d) and (e) are two clamping systems which allow the clamp to slide away from the workpiece for release. Both have adjustable heel pins with provision for the prevention of rotation. Spherical washers are also fitted to allow a degree of tilt of the clamps. The use of these washers is more clearly shown at (j).

A side clamp, operated by the heel screw, is shown at (f), return being effected by the spring-loaded pin close to the clamp toe.

Button, or swing clamps are depicted at (g) and (h), the operation of which is self-explanatory.

An equalizing clamp is shown at (j) combined with spherical washers. The finger nut pressure is transmitted equally to workpieces via a solid clamp. At (k) is another form of equalizing clamp attached to a swinging leaf. The clamping force is applied at the leaf fixture point. The clamp swings freely about its fulcrum pin and hence finds its own level when brought into contact with the workpieces.

The design shown at (l) is a two-way clamp in which two faces of the workpiece are gripped by the action of one clamp screw.

A dual clamping arrangement is shown at (m), where the leaf clamping force is utilized to produce a side force on the workpiece by means of a clamping link.

The figure (n) is a solid clamp acutated by a cam handle exerting a force on spherical washers. This is a refinement of (a).

A cam-actuated clamp operating two clamps is shown at (o). A pair of spring-loaded pins are used to pivot the clamps away from the workpiece.

A further application of a cam or eccentric is given at (p), where a hook clamp is forced downwards on to the workpiece by the rotation of the eccentrically mounted spindle.

These are a few common methods of clamping; some others will be seen incorporated in either a jig or fixture design later in this chapter. It is essential to understand fully the principles of design and operation of clamping devices and it is therefore suggested that sketching the components listed here and also modifications of these designs will prove to be invaluable.

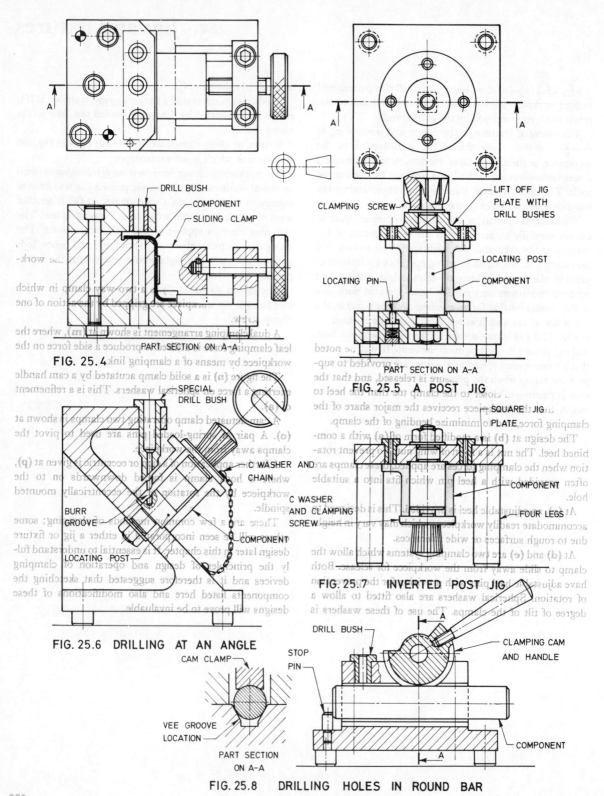

DRILL BUSH
COMPONENT
SLIDING CLAMP

PART SECTION ON A-A

FIG. 25.4

SPECIAL
DRILL BUSH

BURR
GROOVE

LOCATING POST

FIG. 25.6 DRILLING AT AN ANGLE

CLAMPING SCREW

LIFT OFF JIG
PLATE WITH
DRILL BUSHES

LOCATING POST

COMPONENT

LOCATING PIN

PART SECTION ON A-A

FIG. 25.5 A POST JIG

SQUARE JIG
PLATE

C WASHER AND
CHAIN

C WASHER
AND CLAMPING
SCREW

COMPONENT

FOUR LEGS

FIG. 25.7 INVERTED POST JIG

CAM CLAMP

DRILL BUSH

STOP
PIN

CLAMPING CAM
AND HANDLE

COMPONENT

VEE GROOVE
LOCATION

PART SECTION
ON A-A

FIG. 25.8 DRILLING HOLES IN ROUND BAR

25. Jigs and fixtures

Jigs

A jig is a structure which positively locates and clamps a component and incorporates a device for guiding the cutting tools. The jigs considered here are of the type most suited to drilling and reaming operations only, although designs are produced to enable tapping operations to be carried out. In many cases assembly jigs have to be built so that components may be assembled in correct relationship to one another; and inspection jigs, to remove the tedium of checking each dimension of a finished component.

Fig. 25.4 is a jig design for drilling three holes in a thin-gauge component. The drill bushes are pressed into a separate top plate which is dowelled and screwed to the jig body and base plate, which is also fitted with four feet. Note the clamp design, in which the rod end is held captive by the dowel pin, but is able to rotate freely.

A cylindrical component with circular flanges is shown in a simple post jig in **Fig. 25.5**. The location post is held firmly in the jig base, which is fitted with four feet. The lift-off jig plate, containing four drill bushes, is positioned by the square machined on the post and located by the post itself. Clamping is achieved by the finger nut. Before the second flange is drilled the component is removed and reversed on the post. The previously drilled holes are located by the spring-loaded location pin in the jig base. This enables the holes to be drilled in line.

A similar component is shown in **Fig. 25.6** mounted on an angled location post. The design enables a hole to be drilled at an angle to the vertical centre line of the compo-

nent. A special drill bush is provided to take the drill as close to the component as possible.

The location post is partly machined away to form a burr groove. If the post were full-form the burr resulting from the breakthrough of the drill could lock the component or damage the post on removal. A 'C' washer and finger nut forms the clamping device. The 'C' washer has a large outside diameter and a slot which slips over the location-post threads. To remove the component, the finger nut is slackened, the washer slipped from the post, and the component is removed by passing it over the finger nut. The washer is chained to the base to prevent its loss.

An inverted post jig to drill a number of holes in a flanged component is shown in **Fig. 25.7**. Support on the worktable is provided by four legs which are pressed into the jig plate. The component is clamped by a 'C' washer and finger nut as before.

A method of drilling accurately placed holes in a round-bar workpiece is depicted in **Fig. 25.8**. The bar rests in a vee-block base which is fitted with four feet and a stop pin which provides longitudinal location of the component. The top plate, which is dowelled and screwed to the base, carries the drilling bush and the shaft for the cam-operated clamp. A part section shows how the component is firmly clamped in the vee base. The clamp is shaped somewhat like a pulley with an eccentric inner radius.

Should it be necessary to drill a hole in one end of the bar relative to the hole in the other end, some form of location pin would be essential. This would require a modification to the design, which students may care to carry out for themselves.

205

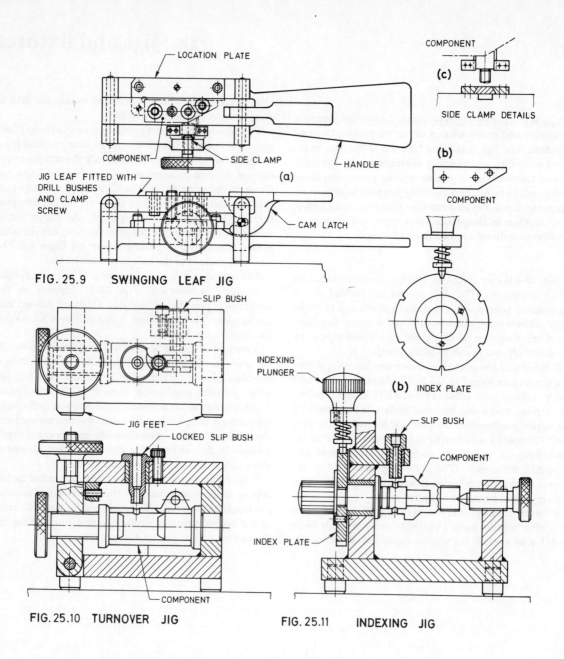

LOCATION PLATE

COMPONENT

JIG LEAF FITTED WITH
DRILL BUSHES
AND CLAMP
SCREW

SIDE CLAMP

HANDLE

(a)

CAM LATCH

FIG. 25.9   SWINGING LEAF JIG

COMPONENT

(c)

SIDE CLAMP DETAILS

(b)

COMPONENT

(b) INDEX PLATE

SLIP BUSH

JIG FEET

LOCKED SLIP BUSH

COMPONENT

FIG. 25.10 TURNOVER JIG

INDEXING
PLUNGER

SLIP BUSH

COMPONENT

INDEX PLATE

FIG. 25.11   INDEXING JIG

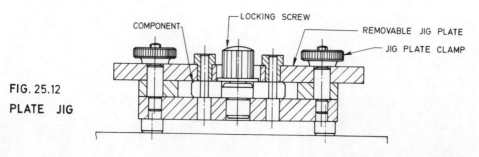

COMPONENT

LOCKING SCREW

REMOVABLE JIG PLATE

JIG PLATE CLAMP

FIG. 25.12
PLATE JIG

The jig design shown in **Fig. 25.9 (a)** is a special leaf jig for drilling three holes in the workpiece drawn alongside at **(b).** To load the workpiece for drilling, the cam latch is released and the latch and leaf are swung away, pivoting about the leaf hinge. The component is seated against the hardened and ground location plate and is clamped in position. The side clamp, shown at **(c),** is a dovetail sliding in two small shaped plates which control the direction of movement. The clamp plate is shaped to fit the machined edge of the component and is operated by the finger screw.

The lower portion of the jig is a casting machined locally to clear the cam latch. The handle and four feet are cast integrally with the base, and holes are drilled beneath the position of the holes in the workpiece to allow the drills to penetrate and the swarf to fall freely to the worktable.

Fig. 25.10 shows another form of swing-leaf jig for drilling holes in a cylindrical workpiece. This jig is of the turnover type and is made from steel plates welded together with four press-fit feet in the base. The component has two lugs cast into it at one end with a slot machined between the lugs. This slot is used to assist in the location of the workpiece by providing a fitting key attached to a press-fit location peg.

With the leaf swung away, the component is located on the peg. The leaf is closed and clamped and the movable locator is screwed into position. An adjustable leaf stop is provided to ensure correct alignment of the movable locator.

A slip bush and liner bush are provided, the intention being to remove the slip bush after drilling to allow the hole to be reamed or tapped.

Following this operation the jig is turned on to its side and the holes in the lugs are also drilled and reamed. A welded plate locates the drill bush and liner.

To unload the component the movable locator is wound back, the leaf clamp is released and the leaf is swung clear. The slip bushes are removed and the workpiece is taken from the jig.

A previously machined component is seen located in an indexing jig in **Fig. 25.11 (a).** It is required to drill six equally spaced holes around the periphery of the bored cylinder. The main location post, which is fitted into a hardened steel bush, is pegged to the indexing plate through the screwed indexing handle flange. The free end of the component is located by a hardened, movable centre. The indexing device consists of a spring-loaded plunger and handle, the plunger engaging one of six slots machined in the index plate as shown at **(b).**

Raising the indexing handle removes the plunger from its groove and allows the index plate and component to be indexed to the next slot, clamping being effected partly by the tight fit of the parts and also by the movable centre.

Fig. 25.12 shows a plate jig, the main plate holding the drill bushes being removable. The component is located on a centre post and clamped. The jig plate is fitted over the smaller location post and clamped. Drilling may now take place.

A separate plate may be used for any subsequent operations, such as reaming or tapping, without disturbing the workpiece. This ensures accurate alignment of the cutting tools.

It will be noted that in order to help students differentiate between jig parts and workpieces, the latter have not been sectioned. In practice it is advisable to show the outline of the workpiece in coloured pencil, preferably red.

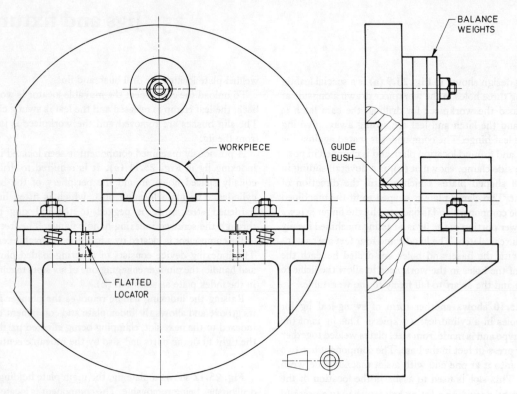

WORKPIECE

BALANCE WEIGHTS

GUIDE BUSH

FLATTED LOCATOR

FIG. 25.13 TURNING FIXTURE FOR A PLUMMER BLOCK

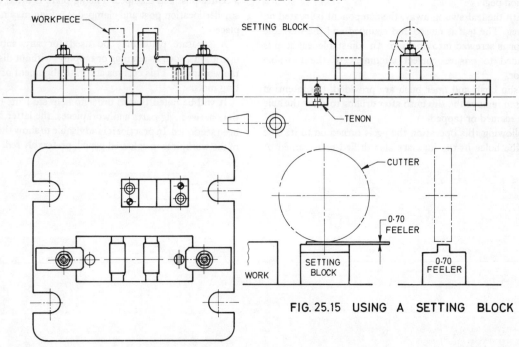

WORKPIECE

SETTING BLOCK

TENON

CUTTER

0·70 FEELER

WORK

SETTING BLOCK

0·70 FEELER

FIG. 25.15 USING A SETTING BLOCK

FIG. 25.14 MILLING FIXTURE FOR A BEARING BRACKET

25. Jigs and fixtures

Fixtures

A fixture is a structure, fixed to the machine worktable, which positively locates and clamps a workpiece for machining operations, but which does not guide the cutting tools.

Lathe fixtures may consist of specialized components designed to replace the normal chuck, or they may be modified forms of existing chucks and chuck jaws. The various types of collets and mandrels, either of standard design or purpose-built, may also be considered as lathe fixtures.

Turning fixtures may be held in the chuck jaws or clamped to the faceplates of centre lathes or turret lathes. Special considerations are given to long production runs on automatics when it is usually an economic proposition to design special adaptors for the machines, or even new parts for the machines themselves, in order to achieve the desired effect in the machining of a component.

Other standard machine-tool equipment such as angle brackets and angle plates may be adapted to serve as fixtures or parts of fixtures. These are then clamped to the lathe faceplate in the normal way.

Welded structures are often used as fixtures, the choice between the various methods of manufacture being mainly that of economics.

The fixture shown in **Fig. 25.13** is provided with an angled shelf for mounting the workpiece which, in this case, is a plummer block.

The method of location is to use a full-form and a flatted locator in two previously drilled holes in the plummer-block base. Standard solid clamps are employed to hold the workpiece firmly against the mounting plate, and a guide bush is provided for the boring bar.

In this set-up the plummer block and cap are to be turned together to ensure accuracy of the mating parts.

This type of fixture could be of welded construction instead of a casting as shown.

In addition to their uses on the lathe, fixtures are used in conjunction with grinding machines, boring machines, broaching machines, and milling machines. As many of the aspects of the design of the fixtures for these various machines are common to them all, some features of the layout of milling-machine fixtures will be considered.

A simple milling-fixture design is depicted in **Fig. 25.14**, where the workpiece is a bearing bracket.

The fixture consists of a base plate provided with slots to allow tee bolts to be used to anchor the complete assembly to the machine table, and tenons are located in milled grooves and are secured in place by socket-headed cap screws.

A full-form and a flatted locator, firmly fitted into the base plate, are used to locate the workpiece from two previously machined holes, and clamping is by two solid clamps.

It has already been stated that fixtures do not guide the cutting tools, so that when the workpiece is firmly located and clamped to the fixture base it is not necessarily in correct relation to the cutter or cutters. To achieve correct alignment and hence accuracy of machining, a tool-setting gauge, or *setting block*, is used. This is shown in heavy outline on the fixture, superimposed on the chain-dotted outline of the workpiece.

Fig. 25.15 shows an example of the use of the setting block in conjunction with a feeler gauge. The setting faces of the block are positioned away from the work piece faces to be machined, by a pre-determined amount. This will allow the cutters to traverse backwards and forwards across the worktable without fouling the block, and also allow the cutters to clear the block when the worktable is wound into a position to remove the fixture.

The feeler gauge is laid against the appropriate setting face and the cutter is brought to this position to set it for height, to give a correct depth of cut, or to set it laterally for facing operations. The thickness of feeler gauge to be used should be stamped on the setting block in some suitably prominent position.

The block is made from steel and is hardened and ground to give the dimensions required. It is sometimes machined from an integral part of the fixture itself, but more often is a separate item firmly located to the fixture base by dowels and set screws.

It is not always necessary to provide a setting block. For one-off components, or where economics dictate, the correct relationship between workpiece and cutter can be obtained by a 'trial and error' adjustment of the worktable. Slip blocks and slip gauges can also be used for this type of setting.

Cast iron is most frequently used for the main part of a fixture because of its ability to absorb the vibrations set up by the action of the cutting tools. Welded, and other steel constructions, are also used for various specialized purposes.

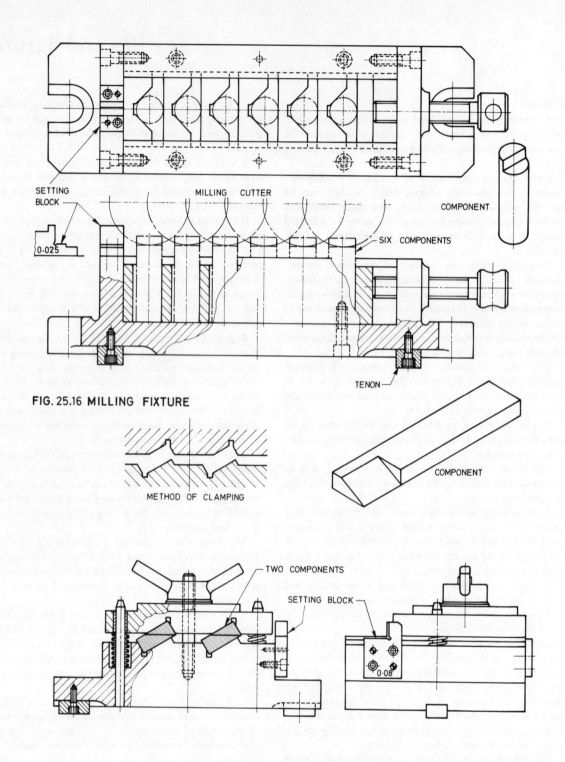

SETTING BLOCK

0·025

MILLING CUTTER

SIX COMPONENTS

COMPONENT

TENON

COMPONENT

METHOD OF CLAMPING

FIG. 25.16 MILLING FIXTURE

TWO COMPONENTS

SETTING BLOCK

0·08

FIG. 25.17 MILLING FIXTURE

25. Jigs and fixtures

Vices

Machine vices are frequently used to hold workpieces relative to milling cutters and thus take the place of the more specialized fixture. Jaws of various designs are often made and fitted to the machine vices to suit the components being machined. In this way the expense of providing a special fixture is avoided. Sometimes, however, a fixture is required which has the characteristics of a vice, the conditions for which cannot be met by the standard article. Such a fixture is shown in **Fig. 25.16.**

In this design the main base and end plates are a single casting, with separate side plates machined to hold the small sliding vee blocks. The side plates are dowel-located and screwed into position after assembly of the vees. The fixture is designed to machine away one half of the ends of six cylindrical workpieces as shown by the isometric sketch.

The path of the cutter and the position and method of location of the setting block is clearly shown. The setting block is designed for use with a feeler gauge of 0·025 mm thickness, as indicated.

Slots are provided in the base of the fixture to ensure firm clamping to the worktable and tenons are secured in fitting slots in the fixture to give location. The method of loading and unloading the components should be self-explanatory.

With this type of fixture, it is essential to ensure that, when the components are unloaded, all the swarf is removed, otherwise it is possible that all the components subsequently loaded into the fixture will not seat correctly.

Fig. 25.17 shows a workpiece and fixture of a more specialized nature. Two components are to be machined together and are located and clamped by a machined block and holding plate. The relative positions and the necessary dimensions of the location and clamping system are shown

separately above the front elevation.

The holding plate is positioned by the two spring-loaded dowels and the centre fixing stud. The dowels fit into hardened steel bushes which are pressed into the holding plate.

A setting block is dowelled and screwed to the fixture end; this is clearly shown in the end elevation. It is designed for use with a feeler gauge of 0·08 mm thickness as indicated.

Endwise location of the workpieces is obtained by loading them into the lower body of the fixture until they make contact with a location plate, which is dowelled and screwed to the back face of the fixture.

Tenons are provided in the base of the fixture, and flange faces are machined in the main casting to provide clamping surfaces.

Milling fixtures are used for all types of milling operations. These include simple vertical milling using one cutter and vertical gang milling, where more than one cutter is used on the same arbor to produce different shapes in the workpiece, or to produce more than one component per cycle. The disadvantage with this set-up is that the arbor is unsupported at its free end, and therefore only light cuts must be taken.

Gang milling is more effectively used on the horizontal milling machine, where the arbor is supported at both ends. This enables a relatively large number of cutters to be used together.

Duplex milling machines having horizontally opposed spindles are also widely used. These machines enable workpieces to be machined from both sides at once, to give either parallel faces or faces machined square to one another, depending upon the machine setting and the cutters used.

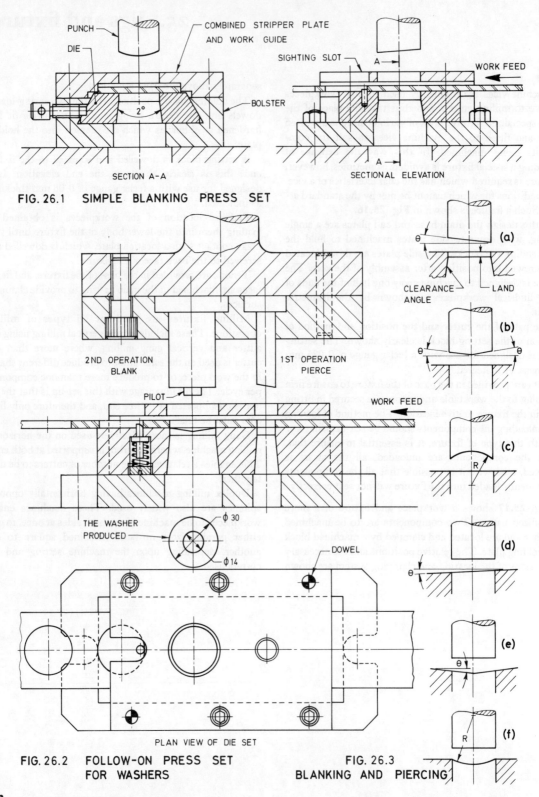

PUNCH

DIE

COMBINED STRIPPER PLATE
AND WORK GUIDE

BOLSTER

2°

SECTION A-A

FIG. 26.1   SIMPLE BLANKING PRESS SET

SIGHTING SLOT

A

WORK FEED

A

SECTIONAL ELEVATION

2ND OPERATION
BLANK

1ST OPERATION
PIERCE

PILOT

WORK FEED

THE WASHER
PRODUCED

φ 30

φ 14

DOWEL

PLAN VIEW OF DIE SET

FIG. 26.2   FOLLOW-ON PRESS SET
FOR WASHERS

(a)

θ

CLEARANCE
ANGLE

LAND

(b)

θ   θ

(c)

R

(d)

θ

(e)

θ

(f)

R

FIG. 26.3
BLANKING AND PIERCING

212

26. Press tools

Press tools are mainly used to produce, in quantity, parts made from thin-gauge metal, although it is possible to use a tool set and press to mass produce small components which are normally made on capstan and automatic lathes.

Blanking is a method of cutting finished components from a strip of material using a punch and a die. The material remaining is scrap. Two views of a simple blanking press set are shown in **Fig. 26.1**.

The die, which may be made from an expensive metal and will be accurately machined and heat treated, is located and firmly secured in a bolster, which may be made from a cheaper material such as cast iron. Above the bolster, dowel located and firmly attached to it by socket-headed set screws, is the combined stripper plate and work guide. This locates the material, or stock, longitudinally and also strips the remaining material from the punch on its return stroke. A stop-pin locator is fitted in the die to position the stock beneath the punch after the first and subsequent holes have been made. A suitable sighting slot is often provided to enable the press operator to see that the material is correctly aligned.

The punch would be made from a good-quality metal, probably a nickel-bearing alloy steel. It will be noted that the punch is designed to shear the stock gradually by providing it with a sheared edge. This causes a certain amount of side thrust, which on very thin-gauge metal will create no harmful effects, but it does assist in reducing the loads on the press. The punch is held captive in the top plate in a manner similar to that shown in **Fig. 26.2**.

Shearing pressures can be readily found once the shear strength of the stock is known. For circular blanks, the circumference of the circle multiplied by the thickness of the material will give the area under shear, neglecting a shaped edge on the punch. Thus, if A is the area under shear, d is the diameter of the blank, t is the thickness of the material, and σ is its shear strength,

$$\text{Shear area, } A = \pi dt \text{ mm}^2,$$
$$\text{Shear pressure, or press capacity, } P_s = A\sigma \text{ N.}$$

When several punches are used together to perforate, blank and strip components at a rapid rate, the cutting edges are arranged at varying height, so that they do not all operate at the same time, thus reducing the total press loading.

The press set shown in **Fig. 26.2** is of the follow-on type and is designed to produce the washer detailed. The two punches are fixed in the top plate lying in line, location being effected by means of dowels, and the whole assembly is secured by socket-headed set screws.

The stock is fed on to the die bed beneath the piercing punch. The punch assembly descends and a hole is pierced; the stock lifts with the punch on its return stroke and is stripped off by the stripper plate. The material is advanced along the die bed and the pierced hole is placed beneath the blanking punch. The pilot on this punch will locate in the pierced hole and the outer diameter will shear the blank. At the same time the piercing punch will have made a second hole in the stock. The material is stripped off the punches on the return stroke and further advanced until the perimeter of the blanked hole is located against the stop pin. The above processes may now occur continuously.

Fig. 26.3 shows a variety of punch and die shapes for various operations.

At **(a)** is a punch with a sheared edge. Such a punch would produce a clean hole and a deformed blank. The 'land' area is provided so that the die edge may be sharpened without causing an increase of the clearance between punch and die.

A clearance angle is important, ensuring that the blanks fall freely through the base of the die without becoming wedged.

The shear angle is a function of the amount of penetration required to shear the blank and the length of the perimeter of the blank.

In **Fig. 26.3 (b)** a punch is shown with a double-sheared edge which should be used in preference to single shear because it cancels out the side-thrust tendencies.

At **(c)** is a cupped punch.

At **(d)**, **(e)**, and **(f)** the die is 'sheared' and the punch is flat. This will give an accurate blank.

It will be noted that the blanking die on the follow-on set is double sheared.

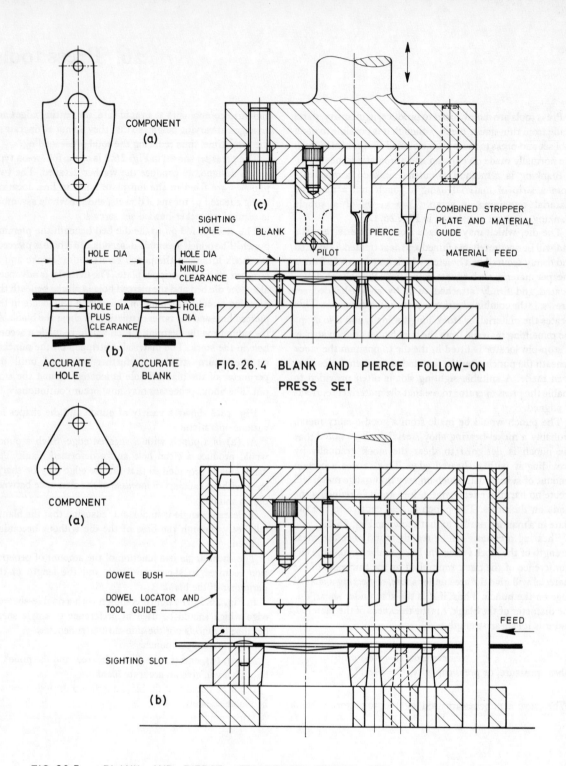

COMPONENT
(a)

HOLE DIA

HOLE DIA
MINUS
CLEARANCE

HOLE DIA
PLUS
CLEARANCE

HOLE
DIA

(b)

ACCURATE
HOLE

ACCURATE
BLANK

SIGHTING
HOLE

BLANK

(c)

PILOT

COMBINED STRIPPER
PLATE AND MATERIAL
GUIDE

PIERCE

MATERIAL FEED

FIG. 26.4 BLANK AND PIERCE FOLLOW-ON
PRESS SET

COMPONENT
(a)

DOWEL BUSH

DOWEL LOCATOR AND
TOOL GUIDE

SIGHTING SLOT

FEED

(b)

FIG. 26.5   BLANK AND PIERCE FOLLOW-ON PRESS SET

A blank-and-pierce follow-on press set is shown in detail in **Fig. 26.4 (c)**. The three punch stations are used to produce the brass keyhole component or escutcheon plate shown at **(a)**. The brass stock is 1·5 mm thick.

At the first station two piercing punches, mounted one behind the other in the top plate, descend to make the two 3 mm diameter rivet holes. At the next station the keyhole shape is pierced and finally the component blank is sheared from the stock.

With this type of press set, the punches are usually fixed at different heights to decrease the press loading. In this case it would be advantageous to allow the blanking punch to descend in advance of the piercing punches, because the more robust punch causes considerable vibration when contacting the stock.

The slender piercing punches, some short distance behind the blanking punch, are thus isolated from the harmful effects of the shock loading set up by the vibration.

The importance of the shape of the punch and die is indicated in **Fig. 26.4 (b)**, where the relative clearances between the two parts are also shown. For an accurate hole the punch is hole size, the required clearance being given in the die. For an accurate blank the die is hole size, the required clearance being given on the punch. The actual clearances will vary with the thickness and type of material used, but for soft steel, brass and other soft materials a figure of 10 per cent of stock thickness is usual. As this is the clearance between the punch and the die, the actual dimensions on diameter will be twice the clearance.

It is also worthy of note that the punches do not need to penetrate completely the stock in order to shear it. This fact is dependent upon a number of factors, such as type of material, punch design, and type of press to be used, but experience has shown that 25 per cent penetration is sufficient to sever completely a blank from 25 mm thick stock. A greater percentage penetration is required for thinner-gauge material, reaching about 70 per cent for material of 1·5 mm thickness and under.

Another follow-on press set is shown in **Fig. 26.5 (b)** with the component produced detailed at **(a)**.

The basic design concept is as previously described, but it will be noted that the press set is provided with two guide pillars. This is common practice on most press sets, because accurate location by the movement of the press cannot be relied upon. The guides are usually positioned at the back of the set, that is away from the operator and, as shown here, are often provided with press-fitted bush liners.

The type of stop pin chosen for the stock is a one-piece machined component. It is more likely to be of the spring-loaded variety, because should the stock 'jump' the stop and rest on top of it the blanking punch would cause serious damage to the tool. The spring-loaded designs allow for this contingency by being able to depress into the die body. Students should note this point and design such components for both the tool sets shown opposite. A further useful exercise is to redesign the methods of location and fixture of the punches in the top plate.

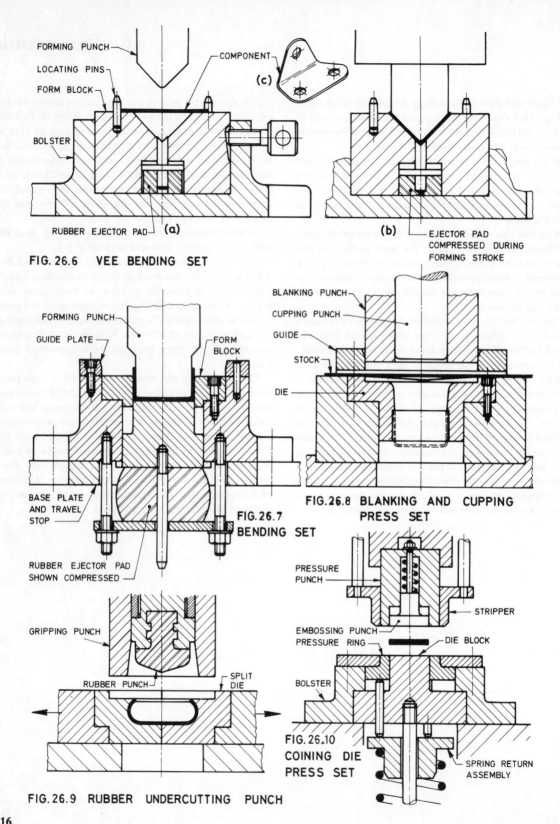

FORMING PUNCH

LOCATING PINS

FORM BLOCK

BOLSTER

COMPONENT

(c)

RUBBER EJECTOR PAD (a)

EJECTOR PAD COMPRESSED DURING FORMING STROKE

(b)

FIG. 26.6   VEE BENDING SET

FORMING PUNCH

GUIDE PLATE

FORM BLOCK

BASE PLATE AND TRAVEL STOP

RUBBER EJECTOR PAD SHOWN COMPRESSED

FIG. 26.7 BENDING SET

BLANKING PUNCH

CUPPING PUNCH

GUIDE

STOCK

DIE

FIG. 26.8 BLANKING AND CUPPING PRESS SET

GRIPPING PUNCH

RUBBER PUNCH

SPLIT DIE

FIG. 26.9 RUBBER UNDERCUTTING PUNCH

PRESSURE PUNCH

STRIPPER

EMBOSSING PUNCH

PRESSURE RING

DIE BLOCK

BOLSTER

FIG. 26.10 COINING DIE PRESS SET

SPRING RETURN ASSEMBLY

The vee-bending press set shown in **Fig. 26.6 (a)** is designed to bend through 90° the component given at **(c)**.

As in the case of the pierce-and-blank sets, the bending sets are usually of composite construction; the most costly, heat-treated, die steel is surrounded by a cheaper, easily worked material such as good-quality cast iron or cast steel. Also, where accuracy is required, the two halves of the set would probably be brought together by guide pins running in bushes, rather than placing reliance on the accuracy of the press itself.

The main drawing shows the component located between pins, lying on the form block in a position to receive the forming blow from the punch. As indicated at **(b)**, the punch will not only form the component, it will also depress the ejector pin and compress the rubber ejector pad. As the punch ascends the energy stored in the rubber pad will be released, the ejector pin will rise and the component will be lifted from the form block. A compression spring could take the place of the rubber pad.

A set for bending channel sections of short length in thin-gauge metal is shown in **Fig. 26.7**. The stock is located between the guide plates with the piston-like centre portion of the form block in the raised position. When the punch descends the piston is forced downwards, the metal is formed into the desired shape within the form block and the rubber pad is compressed. Travel of the piston is limited by the combined base plate and stop. As the punch is raised by the press, the ejector raises the piston which lifts the component free from the form block.

Fig. 26.8 shows a combined tool set designed to blank and cup stock fed through a combined guide and stripper.

The action of the tool is much the same as for previously described sets. The blanking punch descends and cuts out the required, carefully calculated, cup blank. It will not hold the stock at a pre-determined pressure as the cupping punch descends and forms the cup within the die block.

The holding pressure of the blanking punch prevents wrinkles forming in the material, thus giving a good finish to the final product.

When the cupping punch has passed through the die block with the cup attached, the material will tend to spring outwards. On the return stroke the lip machined in the die block will arrest the cup and strip it from the punch. This position is shown chain-dotted.

A rubber forming punch is the main feature of the design given in **Fig. 26.9**.

The prepared blank is located in the machined cavity in the split die block. As the punch assembly descends, the outer punch exerts a holding pressure on the blank and the forming punch forces the material into the die cavity. At the end of the press stroke the rubber punch is compressed, the curved edges are forced outwards and the component is formed with a distinct undercut. Removal of the punch coincides with parting of the die and the component falls through the base of the press set into a waiting container.

A coining or medal-forming press set is shown in **Fig. 26.10**. The lower portion consists of a die-block and pressure-ring assembly held within a bolster and incorporating a spring-loaded return device for the pressure ring.

The upper assembly consists of an embossed punch, a pressure punch and a stripper.

The material to be worked is placed on top of the die block, the punch assembly descends and a blank is formed by the action of the pressure punch. The pressure ring descends under this action, compressing the spring return device. The embossed punch makes contact with the blank and the design on its face and on the die block is reproduced. The blank cannot flatten out, because it is held within the pressure punch cavity. As the punch assembly returns, the embossed punch rejects the coin or medal and the pressure ring returns to its original position under the action of the spring return assembly.

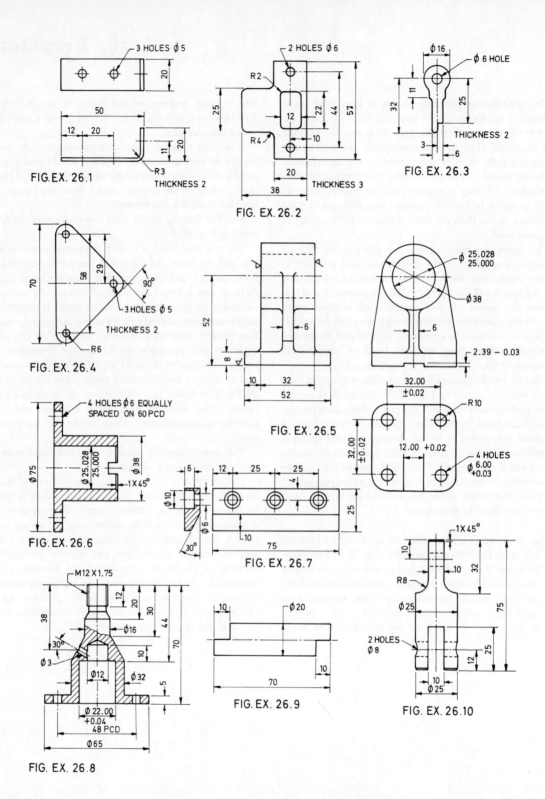

FIG. EX. 26.1

FIG. EX. 26.2

FIG. EX. 26.3

FIG. EX. 26.4

FIG. EX. 26.5

FIG. EX. 26.6

FIG. EX. 26.7

FIG. EX. 26.8

FIG. EX. 26.9

FIG. EX. 26.10

26. Press tools

Exercises for Chapters 25 and 26

1. **Fig. Ex. 26.1** shows a thin-gauge bracket made from mild steel. Design a punch-and-die set to produce the three holes from strip stock and a bending set to make the bracket.
2. **Fig. Ex. 26.2** shows a door-catch plate made from brass. Design a follow-on press set to produce this component from strip stock.
3. A small key blank is shown in **Fig. Ex. 26.3.** Design a follow-on punch-and-die set to produce it.
4. Design a punch-and-die set to produce the pierced plate shown in **Fig. Ex. 26.4.**
5. A bearing bracket is shown in **Fig. Ex. 26.5.** Design a lathe fixture suitable for boring the toleranced hole. All other machining, apart from the base slot, has been carried out. The lathe spindle nose is of flanged form, 165 mm diameter, 22 mm thick and with six fixing holes for 16 mm diameter bolts equally spaced on 133 mm PCD.
6. Design a milling fixture to mill the slot in the bearing bracket shown in **Fig. Ex. 26.5.** All other machining has been carried out.
7. Design a milling fixture to produce the 6 mm wide 6 mm deep slot shown in **Fig. Ex. 26.6.** Assume that all other machining has been carried out.
8. Design a drilling jig to produce the four holes in the base flange of the component shown in **Fig. Ex. 26.6.**
9. Design a turning fixture to bore the nominal 25 mm hole in the bearing sleeve, **(Fig. Ex. 26.6).** The lathe spindle details are as given in question 5.
10. Design a milling fixture and a drilling jig to produce the component shown in **Fig. Ex. 26.7.**
11. Design a drilling jig, or jigs, to produce the inclined hole and the four 5 mm diameter equally spaced base flange holes in the component shown in **Fig. Ex. 26.8.**
12. Design a string-milling fixture to produce simultaneously six components as indicated in **Fig. Ex. 26.9.** (Two operations may be employed.)
13. Design milling fixtures and a drilling jig to produce the small quill shaft shown in **Fig. Ex. 26.10.**
14. Design an indexing jig suitable for producing four equally spaced inclined holes shown in **Fig. Ex. 26.8.**
15. Design a drilling jig to produce the four holes in the base of the bearing bracket shown in **Fig. Ex. 26.5**, assuming all other machining has been carried out.
16. Design a bending press set to form a channel section 250 mm long from 2 mm thickness mild steel strip 75 mm wide. The web of the channel is to be 38 mm and flanges 20 mm each.
17. Using **Fig. 26.10** as a guide, design a coining set to produce a medallion 38 mm diameter and 3 mm thick. The process is to be continuous.

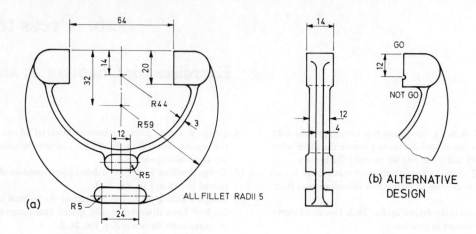

FIG. 27.1 SOLID GAP GAUGE

(a)

ALL FILLET RADII 5

(b) ALTERNATIVE DESIGN

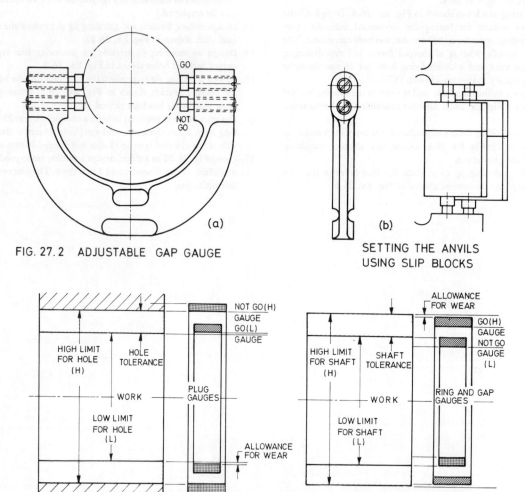

FIG. 27.2 ADJUSTABLE GAP GAUGE

SETTING THE ANVILS USING SLIP BLOCKS

FIG. 27.3 WORK AND GAUGE TOLERANCE ZONES

27. Gauges and gauge tolerances

Dimensions translated from a drawing and built or made into an engineering product may require specialized methods of measurement by the craftsman and inspector to ensure conformity with the designer's requirements.

Micrometers, vernier gauges, and slip blocks (extremely accurately made blocks of steel of varying thicknesses), may be used to check each individual feature of a product where small batch work or one-off jobs are involved. For quantity production, however, gauges of either standard or special construction are used. These gauges are highly accurate, quick and easy to use, and obviate the need to read and interpret the fine divisions of a measuring instrument.

All gauges must be plainly marked with the minimum amount of information consistent with quick recognition of the important details of the gauge. Usually, these markings consist of the gauge size, that is, the limiting dimension which it is intended to control; the words GO or NOT GO, or the letters H or L which represent the high or low limit of the work; the words GENERAL (or GEN) or REFERENCE (or REF), as appropriate, and the manufacturer's name or trade mark and serial number.

On solid-plug gauges this information is stamped on a flat surface machined on the handle, the remainder of the handle being knurled. It is also usual to provide plug gauges of all types with an air vent to ensure ease of entry and withdrawal of the gauging member.

Gauges are usually made from hardened forged steel and are ground to the required limits.

Gauges for shafts and external screw threads may take the form of a simple 'ring' which completely encompasses the shaft, or they may be gap gauges which slip over the shaft diameter in the same manner as a pair of callipers. Ring gauges are generally not adjustable, requiring separate rings for GO and NOT GO, but they can be designed as progressive gauges.

Gap gauges may be adjustable or they may be made in a form which combines the GO and NOT GO gauging members. Because of these features, such gauges are more commonly used than plain ring gauges.

The gauges are sometimes made from flat steel sheet and plate for all sizes up to 250 mm, but many are also supplied as steel forgings. The latter type is shown in **Fig. 27.1.** Such gauges are usually obtained as blanks in the softened condition and are hardened and ground to suit the requirements of the work.

With the solid non-adjustable type, separate gauges may be used for GO and NOT GO, or a progressive type of gauging member, to include both limits, may be used; this can be seen in **Fig. 27.1 (b).**

Adjustable anvils of the type shown in **Fig. 27.2 (a)** may be incorporated in a gap gauge. The anvils are not only adjustable individually but they may also be reground should wear take place. The adjustment is usually 6 mm on sizes up to 38 mm and 12 mm for the larger sizes, and is effected by turning a fine screw at the back of the anvil, which is locked in the required position by a clamping screw. This type of gauge is often preferred for economic reasons, since the frame (aged and stress relieved) is expensive.

The method of setting the anvils, using slip blocks, is shown in **Fig. 27.2 (b).**

The disposition of work and gauge tolerance zones for plug, ring, and gap gauges is shown in **Fig. 27.3.**

For plug gauges, the GO plug is machined to lie within the work tolerance, the low limit of the gauge being, basically, the low limit of the hole. As indicated in the figure, a margin for wear is allowed when the work tolerance exceeds 0·09 mm.

The NOT GO gauge should never enter the work.

For ring and gap gauges, the high limit of the GO gauge is, basically, the high limit of the shaft tolerance.

The high limit of the NOT GO gauge lies on the low limit of the shaft, thus ensuring that the shaft will not be accepted by the anvils.

A SELECTION OF TOLERANCES FOR PLUG RING AND GAP GAUGES IN MILLIMETRES

(a) PLUG GAUGE — WORK / HOLE TOL — HIGH(H) LIMIT FOR HOLE — LOW(L) LIMIT FOR HOLE — NOT GO (H) GAUGE — DIRECTION OF WEAR — GO(L) GAUGE — MARGIN FOR WEAR — T A

(b) RING AND GAP GAUGE — HIGH(H) LIMIT FOR SHAFT — SHAFT TOL — LOW(L) LIMIT FOR SHAFT — WORK — MARGIN FOR WEAR — T A — GO(H) GAUGE — DIRECTION OF WEAR — NOT GO (L) GAUGE

WORK TOLERANCE DIFFERENCE BETWEEN HIGH(H) LIMIT AND LOW(L) LIMIT		GAUGE TOL T	GO PLUG		NOT GO PLUG		GO RING & GAP		NO GO RING & GAP	
ABOVE	UP TO & INCL		H LIMIT OF GAUGE TOL FROM L LIMIT OF WORK	L LIMIT OF GAUGE TOL FROM L LIMIT OF WORK (A)	H LIMIT OF GAUGE TOL FROM H LIMIT OF WORK	L LIMIT OF GAUGE TOL FROM H LIMIT OF WORK	H LIMIT OF GAUGE TOL FROM H LIMIT OF WORK (A)	L LIMIT OF GAUGE TOL FROM H LIMIT OF WORK	H LIMIT OF GAUGE TOL FROM L LIMIT OF WORK	L LIMIT OF GAUGE TOL FROM L LIMIT OF WORK
0.030	0.045	0.0035	+0.0035	0	+0.0035	0	0	−0.0035	0	−0.0035
0.045	0.065	0.0050	+0.0050	0	+0.0050	0	0	−0.0050	0	−0.0050
0.065	0.090	0.0075	+0.0075	0	+0.0075	0	0	−0.0075	0	−0.0075
0.090	0.130	0.0100	+0.0125	+0.0025	+0.0100	0	−0.0025	−0.0125	0	−0.0100
0.130	0.170	0.0125	+0.0175	+0.0050	+0.0125	0	−0.0050	−0.0175	0	−0.0125
0.170	0.230	0.0150	+0.0225	+0.0075	+0.0150	0	−0.0075	−0.0225	0	−0.0150
0.230	0.300	0.0175	+0.0275	+0.0100	+0.0175	0	−0.0100	−0.0275	0	−0.0175
0.300	0.400	0.0200	+0.0325	+0.0125	+0.0200	0	−0.0125	−0.0325	0	−0.0200
0.400	0.500	0.0250	+0.0400	+0.0150	+0.0250	0	−0.0150	−0.0400	0	−0.0250
0.500	0.600	0.0300	+0.0450	+0.0150	+0.0300	0	−0.0150	−0.0450	0	−0.0300
0.600	0.750	0.0400	+0.0600	+0.0200	+0.0400	0	−0.0200	−0.0600	0	−0.0400

SOME RECOMMENDED MINIMUM GAUGE TOLERANCES	PLUG BAR AND ROD GAUGES			RING AND GAP GAUGES		
	SIZE OF GAUGE mm ABOVE	UP TO & INCL	MINIMUM TOL ON GAUGE	SIZE OF GAUGE mm ABOVE	UP TO & INCL	MINIMUM TOL ON GAUGE
CYLINDRICAL PLUG GAUGE	13	25	0.0015	15	25	0.0025
	25	30	0.0025	25	50	0.0035
	50	100	0.0035	50	75	0.0050
	100	150	0.0050	75	125	0.0075
	150	200	0.0075	125	175	0.0100
CYLINDRICALLY ENDED BAR	100	175	0.0075	175	250	0.0125
	175	250	0.0100	250	325	0.0150
	250	375	0.0125	325	400	0.0175

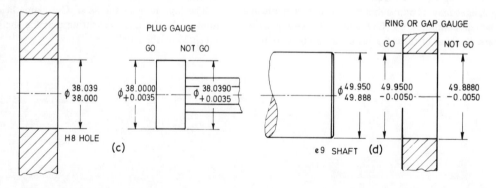

(c) $\phi\dfrac{38.039}{38.000}$ H8 HOLE — PLUG GAUGE GO $\phi\dfrac{38.0000}{+0.0035}$ NOT GO $\phi\dfrac{38.0390}{+0.0035}$

(d) $\phi\dfrac{49.950}{49.888}$ e9 SHAFT — RING OR GAP GAUGE GO $\dfrac{49.9500}{-0.0050}$ NOT GO $\dfrac{49.8880}{-0.0050}$

FIG. 27.4 GAUGE TOLERANCES

27. Gauges and gauge tolerances

Fig. 27.4 gives a selection of tolerances appropriate to the type and size of the gauge concerned. The dimensional units used are millimetres.

Fig. 27.4 (a) and **(b)** show, in diagram form, the dispositions of work and gauge tolerances for plug gauges and ring and gap gauges respectively. They are smaller editions of **Fig. 27.3** and give the same information about the requirements of gauging dimensions.

Fig. 27.4 (c) and **(d)** show examples of dimensional selection for plug gauges and ring or gap gauges.

In the first example, it is required to dimension the GO and NOT GO plug gauging features for a hole of basic diameter 38 mm, toleranced H8. The actual dimensions of the hole, from **Fig. 20.38**, are: H 38·039 mm, L 38·000 mm. The work tolerance is, therefore, 0·039 mm, which is found in the first line of the large table, lying between 0·030 and 0·045, and the gauge tolerance (T) is given as 0·0035 mm.

The high (H) and low (L) limits of the gauge tolerance from the low (L) limit of the work are +0·0035 mm and 0 mm. As the L limit of the work is 38·000 mm, the limits for the GO gauging member will be: ∅ H 38·0035 mm, L 38·0000 mm. These limits should be shown on the drawing as a low limit with a plus tolerance.

For the NOT GO gauging member, the H and L limits of the gauge tolerance from the H limit of the work are +0·0035 mm and 0 mm. As the H limit of the work is 38·039 mm, the limits for the gauging member will be: ∅ H 38·0429 mm, L 38·0390 mm. These dimensions should be shown on the drawing as a L limit with a plus tolerance.

In the second example it is required to dimension the GO and NOT GO gauging features of a ring gauge suitable for a shaft of basic diameter 50 mm, toleranced e9. The actual dimensions of the shaft are: H 49·950 mm, L 49·888 mm. The work tolerance is, therefore, 0·062 mm, which is found in the second line in the large table, lying between 0·045 mm and 0·065 mm, and the gauge tolerance T is given as 0·0050 mm.

For the GO ring gauge, the H and L limits of the gauge tolerance from the H limit of the work are 0 mm and −0·0050 mm. As the H limit of the work is 49·950 mm, the limits for the GO gauging member will be: ∅ H 49·950, L 49·945 mm. These limits should be shown on the drawing as a high limit with a minus tolerance.

For the NOT GO ring gauge, the H and L limits of the gauge tolerance from the L limit of the work are 0 mm and −·00050 mm. As the L limit of the work is 49·888 mm, the gauging limits will be: ∅ H 49·888 mm, L 49·883 mm. These limits should be given on the drawing as a high limit with a minus tolerance.

The recommended minimum gauge tolerance tables must always be consulted to ensure that the chosen gauge tolerance is not less than that recommended. The basic size of the gauging member is important in this respect. It will be seen that in the two examples given above the gauge tolerances are greater than the recommended minimum.

Suppose a hole is required which has dimensions, ∅ 115·003–0 mm. The work tolerance is 0·003 mm, but the appropriate minimum gauge tolerance for the size of the gauge is 0·005 mm. In such cases either the dimensions of the hole should be re-analysed to see if it is possible to conform to the minimum requirements, or some other method of gauging, such as a direct comparator must be used. On the two following pages various designs of gauges to measure holes are shown.

Fig. 27.5 shows a tapered plug gauge for measuring tapered holes. The machined flat at the larger end of the taper acts as the GO—NOT GO indicator by the inspector observing the distance of entry of the plug; full depth of entry being NOT GO. This feature is labelled *gauge plane* on the drawing.

Fig. 27.6 shows the detailed parts of a plain plug-gauge design. The sizes range from diameter 38 mm to diameter 203 mm.

Fig. 27.7 shows details of a cylinder gauge for use in holes above diameter 114 mm and up to diameter 134 mm.

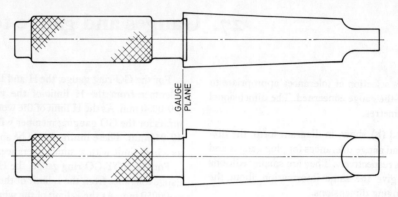

FIG. 27.5 TAPERED PLUG GAUGE

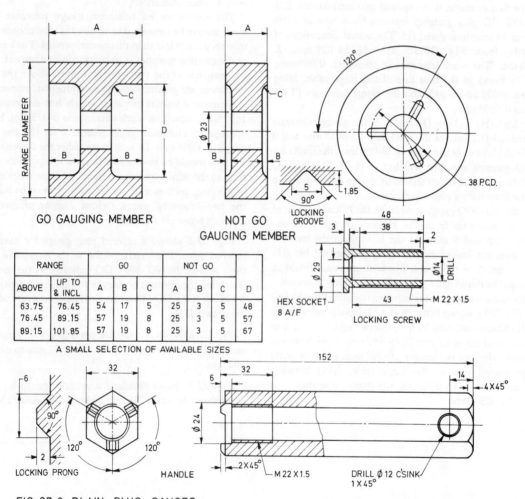

GO GAUGING MEMBER

NOT GO
GAUGING MEMBER

RANGE		GO			NOT GO			
ABOVE	UP TO & INCL	A	B	C	A	B	C	D
63.75	76.45	54	17	5	25	3	5	48
76.45	89.15	57	19	8	25	3	5	57
89.15	101.85	57	19	8	25	3	5	67

A SMALL SELECTION OF AVAILABLE SIZES

LOCKING PRONG

HANDLE

FIG. 27.6 PLAIN PLUG GAUGES

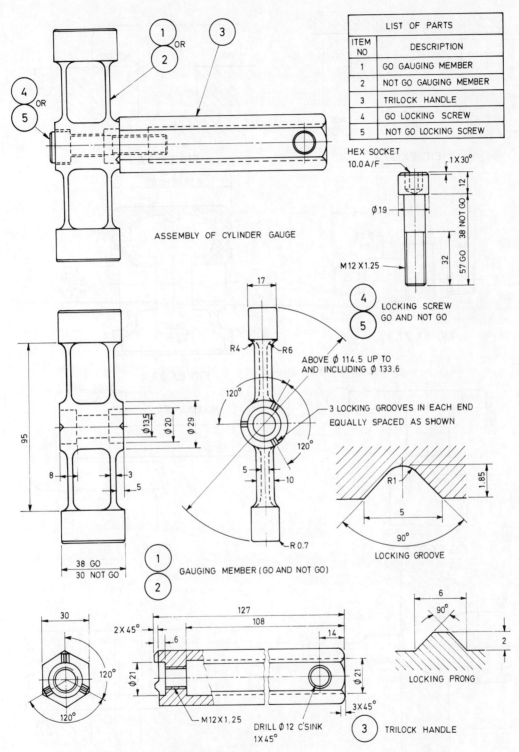

LIST OF PARTS		
ITEM NO	DESCRIPTION	
1	GO GAUGING MEMBER	
2	NOT GO GAUGING MEMBER	
3	TRILOCK HANDLE	
4	GO LOCKING SCREW	
5	NOT GO LOCKING SCREW	

ASSEMBLY OF CYLINDER GAUGE

HEX SOCKET
10.0 A/F

1 X 30°
12
Ø 19
38 NOT GO
32
57 GO
M12 X 1.25

④ LOCKING SCREW
⑤ GO AND NOT GO

17
R4   R6
ABOVE Ø 114.5 UP TO
AND INCLUDING Ø 133.6

120°
Ø 13.5
Ø 20
Ø 29
95

3 LOCKING GROOVES IN EACH END
EQUALLY SPACED AS SHOWN

120°
5
10
8
3
5

R1
1.85
5
90°
LOCKING GROOVE

R 0.7

38 GO
30 NOT GO

① GAUGING MEMBER (GO AND NOT GO)
②

30
2 X 45°
127
108
6
14
120°
Ø 21
Ø 21
120°
3 X 45°
M12 X 1.25
DRILL Ø 12 C'SINK
1 X 45°

6
90°
2
LOCKING PRONG

③ TRILOCK HANDLE

FIG. 27.7 DETAILS OF CYLINDER GAUGE

225

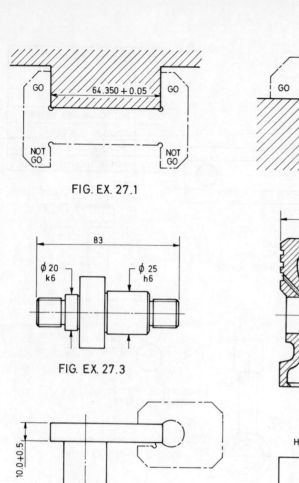

FIG. EX. 27.1

FIG. EX. 27.2

FIG. EX. 27.3

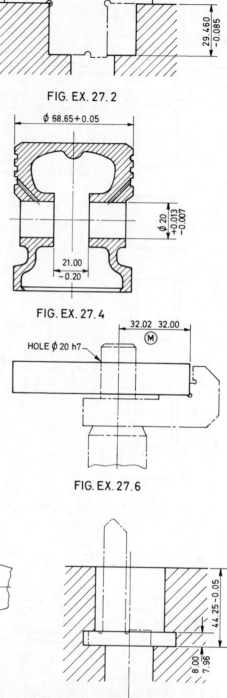

FIG. EX. 27.4

FIG. EX. 27.5

FIG. EX. 27.6

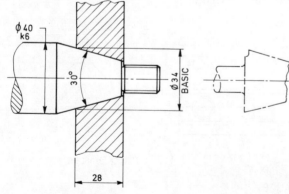

FIG. EX. 27.7

FIG. EX. 27.8

27. Gauges and gauge tolerances

Exercises for Chapter 27

1. A machined tongue is drawn in **Fig. Ex. 27.1**. Design a GO–NOT GO gauge on the lines of that suggested by the chain-dotted outline in the figure. (Note the difference in shape and size of the gauging member.)

2. Design a GO–NOT GO depth gauge to control the circular recess shown in **Fig. Ex. 27.2**. The chain-dotted outline suggests one approach to the design of the gauge.

3. **Fig. Ex. 27.3** shows a component machined from round bar. Design GO–NOT GO gap gauges to control the two diameters indicated on the drawing.

4. **Fig. Ex. 27.4** shows a section through the piston of an internal combustion engine. Design GO–NOT GO gauges to control the dimensions given on the drawing.

5. **Fig. Ex. 27.5** shows part only of a component which has a cam plate integral with it. The thickness of the cam is vital and it is required to design a controlling GO–NOT GO gap gauge. The chain-dotted outline suggests one solution to the geometry of the gauge.

6. **Fig. Ex. 27.6** shows, in dark outline, a rectangular plate in which is machined a hole of basic diameter 20 mm. The distance from the centre of this hole to one edge of the plate is important. Design a GO–NOT GO gauge to control this dimension. The chain-dotted outline suggests one combined gauge design.

7. **Fig. Ex. 27.7** shows a tapered feature on the end of a shaft which carries a pulley. Design GO–NOT GO gauges to control the tapered shaft and the tapered hole in the pulley. The chain-dotted outline shows one type of plug gauge design that could be used for the hole, the step being used to gauge the GO–NOT GO conditions.

8. **Fig. Ex. 27.8** shows part of a component containing a recess. Design GO–NOT GO gauges to control the depth of the recess from the top face and the recess width. The chain-dotted outline suggests are solution to the latter gauge.

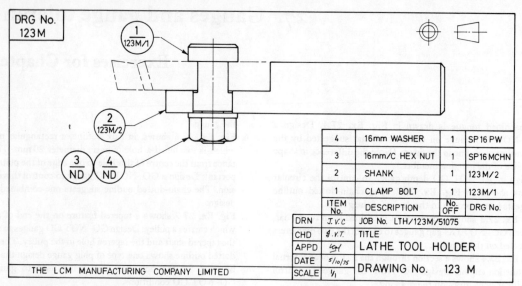

DRG No. 123M

	4	16mm WASHER	1	SP 16 PW
	3	16mm/C HEX NUT	1	SP 16 MCHN
	2	SHANK	1	123 M/2
	1	CLAMP BOLT	1	123 M/1
	ITEM No.	DESCRIPTION	No. OFF	DRG No.
DRN	J.V.C	JOB No. LTH/123M/51075		
CHD	J.V.T.	TITLE		
APPD	tøl	LATHE TOOL HOLDER		
DATE	5/10/75	DRAWING No. 123 M		
SCALE	1/1			

THE LCM MANUFACTURING COMPANY LIMITED

FIG. 28.1 AN ASSEMBLY DRAWING

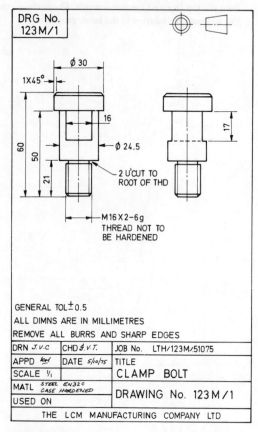

GENERAL TOL ± 0.5
ALL DIMNS ARE IN MILLIMETRES
REMOVE ALL BURRS AND SHARP EDGES

DRN	J.V.C	CHD J.V.T.	JOB No. LTH/123M/51075
APPD	tøl	DATE 5/10/75	TITLE
SCALE	1/1		CLAMP BOLT
MATL	STEEL EN 32 C CASE HARDENED		DRAWING No. 123 M/1
USED ON			

THE LCM MANUFACTURING COMPANY LTD

FIG. 28.2

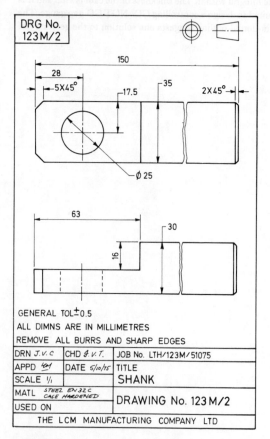

GENERAL TOL ± 0.5
ALL DIMNS ARE IN MILLIMETRES
REMOVE ALL BURRS AND SHARP EDGES

DRN	J.V.C	CHD J.V.T.	JOB No. LTH/123M/51075
APPD	tøl	DATE 5/10/75	TITLE
SCALE	1/1		SHANK
MATL	STEEL EN 32 C CASE HARDENED		DRAWING No. 123 M/2
USED ON			

THE LCM MANUFACTURING COMPANY LTD

FIG. 28.3

SINGLE-PART (DETAIL) DRAWINGS

228

28. Assembly drawings

Assembly drawings take two main forms: the complete item of equipment, often called the general arrangement, or part only of the equipment showing how certain components operate. The latter type of drawing is called a sub-assembly.

An assembly drawing is used to show how parts are positioned relative to one another in a design and how those parts are fixed in place. When a mechanism is involved the drawing will indicate the operations performed by the mechanism and how the mechanism itself works.

General arrangement and sub-assembly drawings are derived from ideas and preliminary drawings or sketches. From these main drawings all the individual component parts will be either drawn and dimensioned or listed if they are standard items such as nuts, bolts, washers, etc.

The detail drawings will, in addition to being fully dimensioned, give such information as the materials of manufacture, the finish of the article, e.g. painting, and all other relevant information required to make the component so that it does what the designer intended.

On the facing page can be seen assembly drawings of a simple lathe tool holder and its detailed component parts.

Fig. 28.1 is the assembly drawing. This is enclosed within a border which is usually a standard A size. Many firms buy standard drawing sheets with the border, title block and other relevant information printed on them.

In the top left-hand corner is the drawing number which, in the simple system adopted here, is a full number: 123M The parts drawings can now be numbered, 123M/1 and 123M/2. Such a system is necessary because the parts drawings will be issued separately to the workshops and nobody would know to which design the parts belonged unless they had some means of identification. The drawing numbers indicate that the parts belong to design number 123M.

In the right-hand corner of the drawing is to be seen the projection symbol. As this is usually printed on the drawing sheets, the information will be there even though, as in this case, only one view is drawn.

In the bottom right-hand corner is the drawing number, the title of the job, the job number, the signatures of those concerned with the drawing, the date, and the scale.

The vertical column, against which appears a number of signatures, uses abbreviations. Reading downwards from the top these mean: drawn, checked, and approved.

The job number has a code of identification which means 'lathe tool holder'; drawing number 123M; dated 5 October 1975.

At the bottom of the drawing is the name of the firm: The LCM Manufacturing Company Limited.

Above the title block in ascending order is a list of the items comprising the assembly. The manufactured items come first, followed by the standard parts. Each of these is fully identified and the standard parts have SP numbers (standard parts numbers). The code assists in the stores by identifying the parts as follows: SP for standard part; 16 for the millimetre size; PW for plain washer and MCHN for millimetre coarse hexagon nut.

The parts are identified on the assembly drawing, inside circles, by an item number and a drawing number for manufactured parts and by an item number and SP for standard items. This method of indication of parts is called *balloon referencing*.

Figs **28.2** and **28.3** show how each manufactured item is drawn on its own sheet and fully dimensioned. This enables each separate copy of the sheet to be glued to a board for issue to the workshops. These drawings are called single-part drawings.

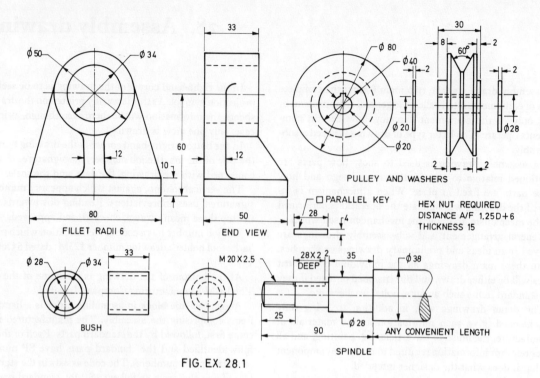

Φ 50   Φ 34

60

12

10

80

FILLET RADII 6

33

12

50

END VIEW

Φ 80   Φ40   2

Φ 20   Φ 20

PULLEY AND WASHERS

□ PARALLEL KEY

28

4

30

8   60°   2

Φ28

2   2

HEX NUT REQUIRED
DISTANCE A/F 1.25D+6
THICKNESS 15

Φ 28   Φ 34

33

BUSH

M 20 X 2.5

28X2
DEEP   2   35   Φ 38

25

90   Φ 28

ANY CONVENIENT LENGTH

SPINDLE

FIG. EX. 28.1

90

5

5   5

50

90°

10

30   10

Φ 50   Φ12

8

Φ 32   25

210

16   19

6

10

FRONT FACE   X

35

10

84

10

BACK CHEEK
PLATE 6 THICK
THROUGHOUT

HOLE 'A' Φ16

6

R54

M 10 X 1.5

10   R25

80   50

20

75

2 HOLES
Φ 10

18

Φ 32

FILLET RADII 5

30   50

50   20

190

80

15

NORMAL
HEX HD

29

Φ 16

M 10 X 1.5

25

12

22

19

Φ 83

Φ 127   Φ 38   Φ100

RUBBER TYRE
BONDED TO WHEEL

FIG. EX.
28.2

A

FIG. EX.
28.3

HOLE 'B' Φ 16

28. Assembly drawings

Exercises for Chapter 28

1. **Fig. Ex. 28.1** shows details of a bearing bracket and pulley.

   Complete the *end view* only, showing all parts assembled in their correct order.

   The items consist of a bracket body, a bush, a spindle, a pulley, two washers, and a nut. The pulley is held in position on the spindle by means of a sunken parallel key. Details of these parts, with the exception of the nut are given. *(CSE)*

2. **Fig. Ex. 28.2** shows details of a drilling jig.

   In first or third angle projection draw, full size, the following views of the drilling jig when all three parts are assembled together,

   (a) a front view in the direction of arrow *A*,

   (b) a plan,

   (c) the better end view.

   Show hidden detail, draw a title box, print the title, scale and projection used. *(CSE)*

3. **Fig. Ex. 28.3** shows parts of a heavy castor. The method of assembly is given below.

   (a) a *front elevation* of the assembled castor, viewed in the direction of arrow *X*,

   (b) a *sectional side elevation* taken on the vertical centre line,

   (c) a *plan*.

   Scale full size. Fully dimension the plan only.

   Devise and draw a simple means of oiling or greasing the bearing. Broken lines for hidden detail should not be shown, except any needed for clarifying the oiling or greasing arrangement.

   In a suitable block print the words HEAVY CASTOR, the scale, a list of parts, and the system of projection used.

   METHOD OF ASSEMBLY

   The wheel is placed between the *cheeks* of the *housing* so that hole *A* lines up with hole *B*.

   The *bolt* passes through *A* and *B* and screws into the tapped cheek of the housing.

   A *standard hexagonal nut* (not drawn in the figure) is tightened on the protruding threaded end of the bolt, locking the bolt to the tapped cheek of the housing. Any sizes not shown are left to the discretion of the candidate. *(CSE)*

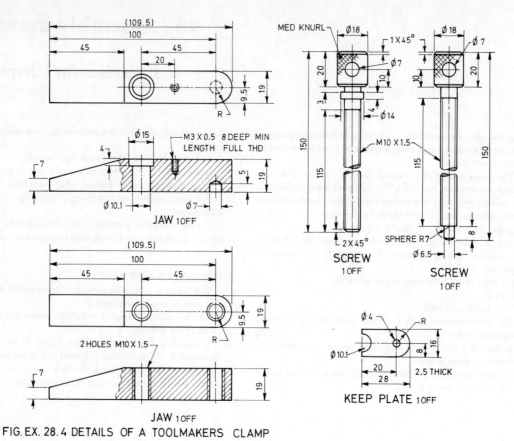

FIG. EX. 28.4 DETAILS OF A TOOLMAKERS CLAMP

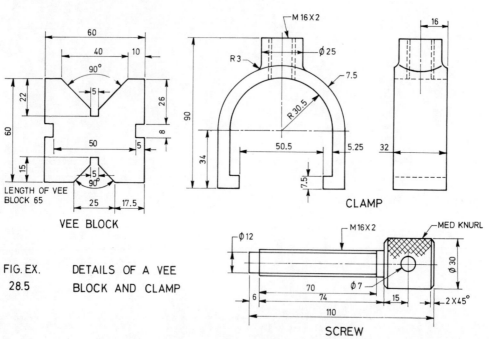

FIG. EX.
28.5

DETAILS OF A VEE
BLOCK AND CLAMP

28. Assembly drawings

Exercises for Chapter 28

4. **Fig. Ex. 28.4** shows details of a toolmaker's clamp.

Assemble the parts and draw, full size, two elevations in first angle orthographic projection. Draw a border and title block on the drawing and balloon reference all the parts.

Draw up a parts list.

5. **Fig. Ex. 28.5** shows details of a vee block and clamp.

Assemble the parts and draw, full size, three orthographic views in third angle projection. Draw a border and a title block and balloon reference all the parts.

Draw up a parts list.

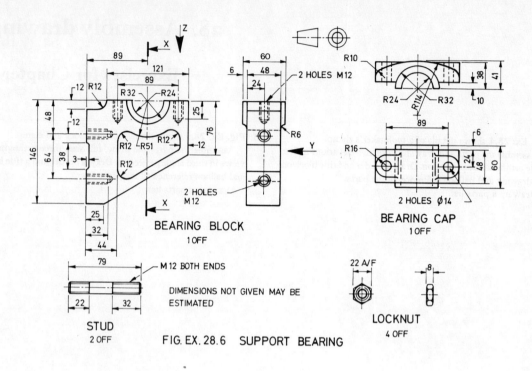

FIG. EX. 28.6 SUPPORT BEARING

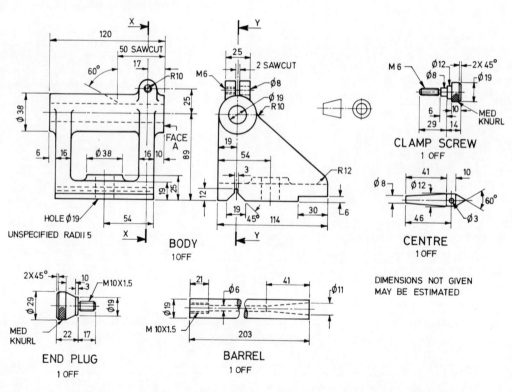

FIG. EX. 28.7 SUPPORT CENTRE

28. Assembly drawings

Exercises for Chapter 28

6. **Fig. Ex. 28.6** shows details in first angle projection of a support bearing.

   The cap is secured by means of studs, plain washers (not shown), and locking nuts.

   With the parts correctly assembled, draw, full size, the following views:

   (a) a front elevation looking in the direction of arrow Y. Stud, washer, and lock nuts are to be shown on the left-hand side of this view and a stud only on the right-hand side of this view,

   (b) a sectional end elevation taken on the bearing centre line and looking in the direction indicated by the arrows XX.

   (c) an outside plan projected from view (a), and looking in the direction indicated by the arrow Z.

   Hidden lines are to be shown in view (a) only.

   The following dimensions are to be indicated on the drawing:

   (i) the centre distance of cap fixing studs,

   (ii) the centre distance of wall fixing holes and

   (iii) the distance from the top fixing hole to the bearing centre.

   Either first or third angle may be used, but the three views must be in a consistent system of a projection.

   In a title block 152 mm long and 76 mm high insert: the title SUPPORT BEARING ASSEMBLY, in letters 8 mm high and the scale and system of the projection used, in letters 5 mm high. (*AEB*)

7. **Fig. Ex. 28.7** shows details in first angle projection of a support centre.

   With the parts correctly assembled and the *Barrel* projecting 50 mm from face A, draw full size, the following views:

   (a) a sectional front elevation, the section taken on the cutting plane YY and looking in the direction of the arrows,

   (b) a sectional end elevation, the section taken on the cutting plane XX and looking in the direction of the arrows,

   (c) an outside plan projected from view (a).

   The following dimensions are to be indicated on the drawing:

   (i) the overall length of the body,

   (ii) the vertical distance from the base to the centre of the barrel, and

   (iii) the vertical distance from the base to the clamping screw centre.

   Either first or third angle projection may be used, but the three views must be in a consistent system of projection.

   In a title block 152 mm long and 76 mm high insert: the title SUPPORT CENTRE ASSEMBLY in letters 8 mm high and the scale and system of projection used in letters 5 mm high. (*AEB*)

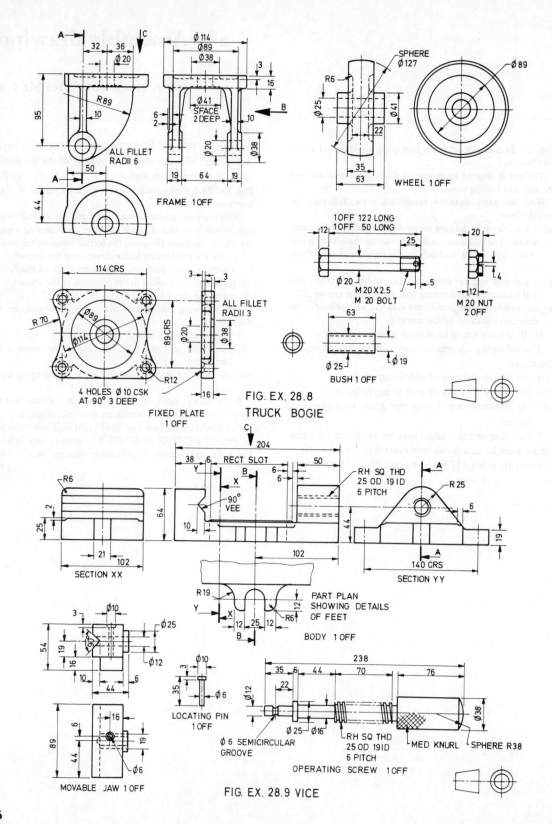

FRAME 1 OFF

WHEEL 1 OFF

1 OFF 122 LONG
1 OFF 50 LONG
M 20 X 2.5
M 20 BOLT

M 20 NUT
2 OFF

BUSH 1 OFF

FIXED PLATE
1 OFF

FIG. EX. 28.8
TRUCK BOGIE

ALL FILLET
RADII 6

ALL FILLET
RADII 3

SPHERE
Ø127

SFACE
2 DEEP

4 HOLES Ø 10 CSK
AT 90° 3 DEEP

SECTION XX

SECTION Y Y

RECT SLOT

90°
VEE

RH SQ THD
25 OD 19 ID
6 PITCH

R 25

PART PLAN
SHOWING DETAILS
OF FEET

BODY 1 OFF

MOVABLE JAW 1 OFF

LOCATING PIN
1 OFF

Ø 6 SEMICIRCULAR
GROOVE

RH SQ THD
25 OD 19 ID
6 PITCH

MED KNURL   SPHERE R38

OPERATING SCREW 1 OFF

FIG. EX. 28.9 VICE

28. Assembly drawings

Exercises for Chapter 28

8. **Fig. Ex. 28.8** shows details of a truck bogie. The fixed plate is secured to the truck by four 10 mm diameter countersunk screws (not to be shown) and carries the wheel and frame by means of a central bolt 19 mm diamter, 50 mm long.

With the parts correctly assembled and allowing a 2 mm clearance between the top of the frame and the underside of the plate draw, full size, the following views:

(a) a sectional front elevation looking in the direction of arrows *AA* and taken on the centre-line as indicated;

(b) an outside end elevation looking in the direction of arrow *B*, the longer side of the fixed plate being shown in this view;

(c) an outside plan projected from (b) above and looking in the direction of arrow *C*.

Hidden detail is to be shown in view (b) only.

The castle nusts to be shown in view (b) only.

Insert the following dimensions:

(i) the distance between the centres of the fixing screw holes in the fixed plate in both directions,

(ii) the distance of the centre of the wheel from the top of the frame,

(iii) the outside diameter of the wheel,

(iv) the internal diameter of the bush.

Add, in letters 10 mm high, the title TRUCK BOGIE, and in letters 6 mm high the scale and system of projection used.

First angle or third angle projection may be used but the three views must be in a consistent system of projection.   (*AEB*)

9. **Fig. Ex. 28.9** shows details of a simple vice.

With the parts correctly assembled and showing a gap of 6 mm between the jaws draw, full size, the following views:

(a) a sectional front elevation taken on the centre-line of the body and looking in the direction indicated by the arrows *AA*,

(b) a sectional end elevation taken on the centre-line through the feet and looking in the direction indicated by the arrows *BB*,

(c) an outside plan projected from (a) and looking in the direction indicated by arrow *C*.

The square-threaded screw is to be shown in the usual conventional method adopted for screw threads.

The locating pin prevents the screw from leaving the movable jaw when the jaw is being withdrawn to release the workpiece.

Hidden detail need not be shown.

Insert the following dimensions:

(i) the height of the centre of the screw above the base of the body,

(ii) the distance of the centre line of the feet from one end of the body,

(iii) the distance between the centres of the feet,

(iv) the thickness from the base of the body to the machined sliding face for the movable jaw,

(v) the overall width of the machined sliding face for the movable jaw.

In a rectangle 152 mm long and 76 mm high in one corner of the drawing insert, in letters 10 mm high, the title VICE and, in letters 6 mm high, the scale and system of projection used.

The three views must be in a consistent system of projection either first angle or third angle   (*AEB*)

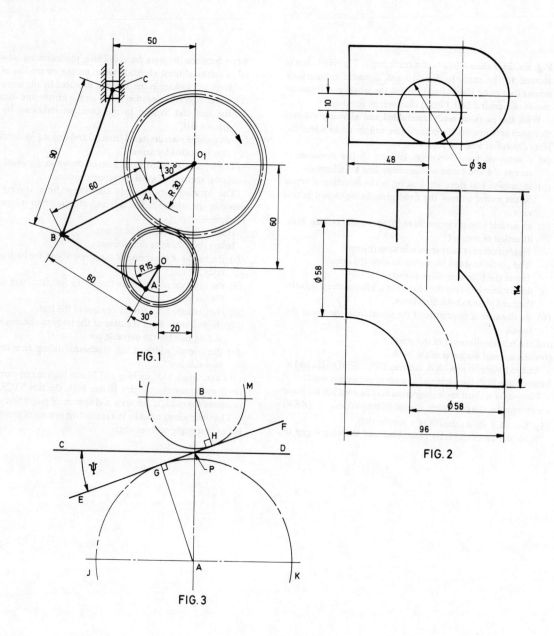

FIG.1

FIG. 2

FIG. 3

Miscellaneous exercises

1. (a) Draw the British Standard conventional representation for *three* of the following: (i) a compression spring; (ii) a screw thread assembly; (iii) holes on a circular pitch; (iv) a break in a solid shaft.

   (b) Show clearly, by drawing, the meaning of the following abbreviations: (i) $\mathbb{C}$; (ii) CSK; (iii) PCD; (iv) S'FACE. *(CGLI)*

2. Use neat sketches, where necessary, to show clearly how the following items should be indicated on engineering drawings, to conform to the recommendations of *BS 308, General principles of engineering drawing practice*:

   (a) Machined surfaces.

   (b) Abbrevations for the following words: (i) across flats; (ii) centre line; (iii) a screw thread 12 mm diameter and 1·25 mm pitch.

   (c) The conventional representation for; (i) holes on a circular pitch; (ii) a stud assembled in a blind hole. *(CGLI)*

3. Make a neat sketch or drawing of any type of self-supporting slotted clamping arrangement suitable for use for workholding on a machine table or on a fixture. Details of features such as the supporting spring, the heel-pin, or support, and the tightening nut should be clearly shown.

   Explain clearly the design features of the arrangement which would allow:

   (a) the clamp to adapt itself to small variations in work thickness, and

   (b) the clamping arrangement to take account of a larger variations in work thickness.

   Take as a guide a work thickness of 50 mm to 75 mm and a clamp length of about 150 mm. *(CGLI)*

4. Two shafts, each 50 mm diameter, are co-axial and one drives the other through a simple flanged coupling. The flanges are 200 mm diameter and 25 mm thick. They have a locating spigot and five fitted bolts 16 mm nominal diameter.

   (a) Using suitable sketches show how to dimension the bore, the spigot and the bolt-holes with reference to a suitable datum.

   (b) Show a suitable method of attaching a flange to a shaft to enable it to transmit the driving torque.

   (c) Explain briefly what is meant by a fitted bolt and why it is used in this application.

   (d) Show a suitable means of locking a fastener against vibration. *(CGLI)*

5. (a) Using sketches, show how a typical work feature requiring more than one operation, can be machined with the aid of a removable slip bush.

   (b) Make a neat sketch, in good proportion, of any type of removable slip bush assembly, showing how it is located and retained. The assembly shown should accommodate a maximum tool size of 30 mm diameter.

   (c) State the types of mating fits required in the removable slip bush assembly, and give tolerances for *one* of them taken from *BS 4500A*. *(CGLI)*

6. (a) Make sketches to show *two* of the following bearing arrangements: (i) a plain or shell type bearing with a thrust collar; (ii) a ball race which will take both thrust and radial load; (iii) a white-metal bearing.

   (b) In each case explain briefly the arrangements for lubrication and say what sort of lubricant would probably be used. *(CGLI)*

7. Draw or sketch neatly, in good proportion, any clamp or clamping device which uses in its action the principle of *either* (a) the toggle *or* (b) the cam.

   Indicate those parts of the clamp which would need to resist wear and state what metal would be suitable for them. *(CGLI)*

8. Show by means of suitable sketches or diagrams how the recommendations of *BS 308: 1972, General principles of engineering drawing practice* are correctly applied in the following case:

   (a) two methods of indicating a tolerance;

   (b) one method of dimensioning a hole with a counterbore;

   (c) the conventions and method of dimensioning for a blind tapped hole in section and in plan;

   (d) two ways of dimensioning a circle *(CGLI)*

9. Make a neat sketch in good proportion showing how *each* of the following items is commonly used in jigs or fixtures, and adding any explanation necessary to make the application clear:

   (a) a drill bush;

   (b) any quick release clamp such as a C-washer;

   (c) any common locating feature. *(CGLI)*

10. With the aid of sketches showing typical applications indicate clearly the difference between:

    (a) a bolt and a set-screw;

    (b) a feather key and a woodruff key;

    (c) a pinch bolt and a cotter-pin. *(CGLI)*

11. A differential stroke mechanism is shown in **Fig. 1**, in which two cranks OA and O_1A_1 are connected by two gears such that OA rotates at twice the angular speed of O_1A_1.

    (a) Reproduce the mechanism and plot the locus of the point B for one revolution of crank O_1A_1.

    (b) Determine the maximum stroke of slider C. *(CGLI)*

12. **Fig. 2** shows the plan and incomplete elevation of a curved duct surmounted by an off-set cylinder. Draw, full-size

    (a) the completed elevation,

    (b) a surface development of the cylinder. *(CGLI)*

13. **Fig. 3** illustrates the geometrical basis from which the action between meshing teeth of a pair of involute spur gears may be analysed. A and B are the respective centres of the wheel and pinion.

    (a) Reproduce the diagram when ψ, AP, and PB are 20°, 152 mm, and 76 mm respectively.

    (b) Construct two involute curves, one on base arc JGK and the other on LHM, making contact with each other at P. Limit the length of each curve to approximately 50 mm.

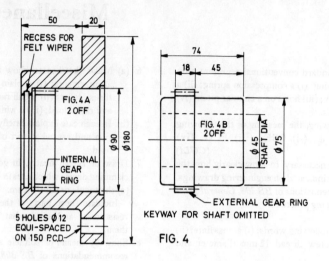

50
20
RECESS FOR FELT WIPER
FIG. 4A 2 OFF
Ø 90
Ø 180
INTERNAL GEAR RING
5 HOLES Ø 12 EQUI-SPACED ON 150 P.C.D.
74
18
45
FIG. 4B 2 OFF
Ø 45 SHAFT DIA
Ø 75
EXTERNAL GEAR RING
KEYWAY FOR SHAFT OMITTED

FIG. 4

76.10
76.00
44.45
44.40
Ø40
K
Ø20 h6
W

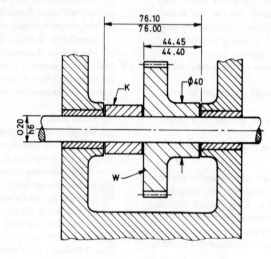

FIG. 5

(c) Assuming a portion of each involute to be the profile of a gear tooth, explain briefly: (i) the action that takes place along the line *EF* on rotation of the gears; (ii) the significance of the points *G* and *H*; (iii) the effect that a slight increase in centre distance *AB* would have on the angle ψ, and the length *GH*. *(CGLI)*

14. The two parts which make up one half of a gear coupling unit used for transmitting power between shafts subject to misalignment, are shown in **Figs. 4 (a)** and **(b)**.

    Draw, to scale, a cross-section showing the complete coupling fully assembled with shafts, keys, and one bolt in position.

    Balloon the parts and make a parts list. *(CGLI)*

15. In **Fig. 5a** wheel *W* and a spacer *K* are supported on a plain shaft between two bosses of a casting. The tolerances on the distance between the bosses and on the width of the wheel are shown.

    (a) Find the limits which must be placed on the width of the spacer in order to keep the axial clearance in the assembly between 0.25 mm and 0.38 mm.

    (b) Using *BS 4500* give the limits on the bore of the wheel for a push fit together with suitable limits for the bore of the spacer, stating the fit chosen for it.

    (c) Why are shaft-based tolerances used in this assembly? *(CGLI)*

16. The assembly shown in Fig. 5 has a gear wheel *W* on a shaft, which is to be driven by it.

    (a) Sketch or draw a suitable form of key and keyway for the wheel and shaft and explain how they would be assembled.

    (b) Sketch any form of fixing which could be used for the gear wheel instead of a key and state its advantages or disadvantages compared with keying. *(CGLI)*

17. Fig. 4 (a) shows the main details of one member of a gear coupling.

    Draw two views of this member as a working drawing, showing all dimensions and information needed for manufacture. The component is supplied as a steel forging and is to be machined all over. No details of gear teeth are required other than those shown. *(CGLI)*

Index

Abscissa, 43
Acme thread, 171
Acute angle, 9
Addendum, 195
Altitude, 11
Archimedean spiral, 41
Areas, 33
Assembly drawing, 229
Auxiliary plane, 49
  projection, 81
  dimensions, 145

Balloon referencing, 3
Base circle, 195
Bearings, 185
Bevel gears, 199
Bisectors, 5
Blanking, 213
Blanking and cupping, 217
Bolt, 169
Brazing, 175
Bronze welding, 175
Buttress thread, 165

Cabinet projection, 55
Cams, 187
Cavalier projection, 55
Chord, 20
Circle, 21
Circular pitch, 195
Circumference, 20
Clamps, 203
Concentric circle, 20
Construction of triangles, 11
Cotter, 177
Coupling, 179
Cycloid, 41

Datum, 147
Decagon, 17
Dedendum, 195
Developments, 101
Diameter, 20
Dimensioning, 145
Directrix
  of parabola, 41
  of hyperbola, 43
Drawing board, 1
Duodecagon, 17

Eccentric circle, 20
Ellipse, 25
Equilateral triangle, 9

Escribed circle, 23

First angle projection, 65
Fixtures, 201
Focus, 24
Follow-on press set, 215
Freehand sketching, 75
Functional dimensions, 145
Fusion welding, 175

Gauges, 221
Gears, 195
Geometrical tolerances, 161

Hatching, 2
Helices, 165
Helix, 43
Heptagon, 17
Hexagon, 17
Horizontal trace, 49
Hyperbola, 43

Inclined plane, 53
Intersections, 119
Involute, 39
Involute gears, 197
Isometric projection, 55
Isosceles triangle, 9

Jigs, 201

Keys, 177
Keyway, 177

Leader lines, 3
Lead, of thread, 165
Lettering, 3
Lines, 3
Locators, 201
Loci, 39

Machining symbols, 157
Major axis, 24
Major diameter, 165
Maximum material condition, 155
Milling fixture, 209
Minor axis, 24
Minor diameter, 165
Module, 195

Needle bearing, 185
Nonagon, 17
Non-functional dimensions, 145

Normal, 20, 24
Nuts, 167

Oblique plane, 53
Oblique projection, 55
Octagon, 17
Ordinates, 149
Orthographic projection, 65
  of a line, 51
  of a plane, 53

Parabola, 41
Parallelogram, 15
Pencils, 1
Pentagon, 17
Perpendicular, 5
Perpendicular planes, 53
Pictorial projection, 55
Pitch angle, 199
Pitch circle diameter, 150
Pitch cone, 199
Pitch diameter, 195
Pitch, of helix, 43
  of thread, 165
Plane, 5
Plummer block, 183
Pole point, 33
Polygons, 17
Positional tolerance, 163
Pressure angle, 195
Press tools, 213
Principal planes, 49
Projections
  auxiliary, 81
  cabinet, 55
  cavalier, 55
  first angle, 65
  isometric, 55
  of a line, 49
  of a plane, 53
  of a point, 49
  of solids, 93
  pictorial, 55
  radical, 33
  third angle, 67
Pythagoras, 11

Quadrant, 20

Radical projection, 33
Radius, 20
Rectangle, 15
Rectangular coordinate, 49

Removed section, 3
Resistance welding, 175
Revolved section, 3
Rhombus, 15
Right angle, 9
Rivets, 173
Roller bearing, 185
Rotation, 93

Scalene triangle, 9
Scale of chords, 9
Scales, 1
Screws, 167
Screw threads, 165
Sectioning, 2, 93, 127
  conventions, 132
Sector, 20
Segment, 20
Semicircle, 20
Setting block, 209
Shafts, 177
Similar figures, 33
Spot welding, 175
Spur gears, 197
Square, 15
Square thread, 165
Stud, 169
Stud welding, 175
Supplementary angle, 21
Surface roughness, 157

Tangent, to a circle, 20
  to an ellipse, 24
  to a parabola, 41
Third angle projection, 65
Thrust bearing, 185
Toleranced dimensions, 145
  geometrical, 159
  positional, 163
Traces, 49
Trammel, 24
Trapezium, 15
Trapezoid, 15

Undecagon, 17
Universal joint, 181

Vee thread, 165
Vertex, 11
Vertical trace, 49
Vertices, 21

Welding, 175